I0112538

LESSONS FROM THE FRONT

LESSONS FROM
HE FRONT

LESSONS FROM THE FRONT

A Rookie War Correspondent in Ukraine and Israel

Robert Sherman

BLOOMSBURY ACADEMIC

NEW YORK • LONDON • OXFORD • NEW DELHI • SYDNEY

BLOOMSBURY ACADEMIC
Bloomsbury Publishing Inc
1359 Broadway, New York, NY 10018, USA
50 Bedford Square, London, WC1B 3DP, UK
29 Earlsfort Terrace, Dublin 2, Ireland

BLOOMSBURY, BLOOMSBURY ACADEMIC and the Diana logo are trademarks of
Bloomsbury Publishing Plc

First published in the United States of America 2025

Copyright © Robert Sherman

Cover design: Chloe Batch
Cover image Photo of author by Will Budkins, NewsNation; Texture © iStock.com/-slav-

All rights reserved. No part of this publication may be reproduced or transmitted in any
form or by any means, electronic or mechanical, including photocopying, recording, or
any information storage or retrieval system, without prior permission in writing from
the publishers.

Bloomsbury Publishing Inc does not have any control over, or responsibility for, any third-
party websites referred to or in this book. All internet addresses given in this book were
correct at the time of going to press. The author and publisher regret any inconvenience
caused if addresses have changed or sites have ceased to exist, but can accept no responsibility for any such changes.

Library of Congress Cataloguing-in-Publication Data

Names: Sherman, Robert (Television journalist) author
Title: Lessons from the front: a rookie war correspondent reports from the
Israel and Ukraine conflict areas / Robert Sherman.
Description: New York: Bloomsbury Academic, 2025.
Identifiers: LCCN 2025022750 (print) | LCCN 2025022751 (ebook) |
ISBN 9798881807153 hardback | ISBN 9798881807160 epub |
ISBN 9798881867683 pdf
Subjects: LCSH: Sherman, Robert (Television journalist) | War
correspondents–United States–Biography | Russian Invasion of Ukraine,
2022–Press coverage | Israel-Hamas War, 2023—Press coverage | October 7
Hamas Attack, Israel, 2023–Press coverage | LCGFT: Autobiographies
Classification: LCC PN4874.S47165 A3 2025 (print) | LCC PN4874.S47165 (ebook)
LC record available at https://lccn.loc.gov/2025022750
LC ebook record available at https://lccn.loc.gov/2025022751

ISBN: HB: 9798881807153
ePub: 9798881807160
ePDF: 9798881867683

Typeset by Deanta Global Publishing Services, Chennai, India
Printed and bound in the United States of America

To find out more about our authors and books visit www.bloomsbury.com and
sign up for our newsletters.

To my parents, Kim and Bob Sherman, for always being
my biggest fans.
And to Cherie Grzech and Bartley Price—to whom I owe it all.

CONTENTS

Preface ix

PART I UKRAINE 1

1 Go East, Young Man 3

2 No Turning Back Now 11

3 Crossing into Conflict 19

4 Good Morning, Ukraine 31

5 Not Exactly the Blue Angels 37

6 The People 43

7 Glory to Ukraine, Glory to Heroes 55

8 To Catch a Spy 65

9 From Lviv with Love 79

10 The Most Innocent of All 87

11 Poland on the Brink 91

12 Home at Last 99

PART II THE MIDDLE EAST 107

13 Into the Fire 109

14 Tel Aviv Trembled 123

15 Clausewitz Couldn't Imagine 129

16 Seconds Count 135

17 When the Fog Clears 147

18 Heroes Shiver Too 153

19 Theseus in the Labyrinth 163

20 Imagine a World 171

21 The Ground You Stand on 179

22 Here Come the Houthis 187

23 Where Does the Truth Lie? 203

24 Cleveland Will Never Be the Same 213

Notes 219

PREFACE

I remember very clearly the first time I thought I was going to die.

Rap rap rap came the sound from my door as I was fast asleep. My eyes wobbled open, still blurry from the nap I had been taking.

"Sherman!" I heard a voice from the other side of the door. That's what pretty much everyone calls me, except for my parents. The voice sounded familiar, but I was in too much of a daze to fully comprehend it.

I now wake up in so many different hotel rooms and time zones that every now and then I forget where I am. *This is Gulf Shores, Alabama, right? Yeah, that makes sense.* Spring break. It was all coming back to me.

Suddenly, the door burst open, and it was one of my friends. "Sherman, come quick! The cops are here!"

"Why?" I responded sheepishly. And more importantly, *why are you calling me?*

Oh, that's right, I'm the "responsible" one of the group. My fraternity's president, which, at the time, seemed like one of the most important jobs in the world.

Well, time to see what trouble the idiots got themselves into this time. I rolled out of bed and waddled out to the hall where I could catch a glimpse through the window of the front yard. We had rented this place and had been here just a day.

Sure enough, there were Gulf Shore's finest. Maybe five or six police cars. A few officers stood at the front of their cruisers with their hands on their hips. Not good.

I turned around and walked toward the backyard where I saw the early onset of "Lord of the Flies syndrome" taking form as kids were grabbing beer cans and trying to hide them under tables. One person took a whole case of beer and tossed it over the fence.

There was another guy who drank a whole bottle of cough syrup to see if it would get him high. Turns out it just morphed him into a gremlin. He sat in the corner scratching his kidneys, giving a thousand-mile stare into the sun. *That's something we'll need to address later,* I thought.

I turned the corner to walk toward the front of the house. *What did we do wrong?* Stupid question. I know what we did wrong. We were loud and obnoxious.

Twenty-four hours earlier, we arrived in Gulf Shores and were blasting music as loud as we could. There were beer cans everywhere. It's hazy, but there's a strong possibility a chair went off a balcony somewhere in the fray.

As I made the slow walk toward the front of the house, I started counting the misdemeanors in my head. Half of those kids weren't twenty-one so there must have been a dozen counts of underage drinking. One guy drove a car full of beer across multiple state lines, beginning in Indiana. Pretty sure there's a law about that somewhere.

The fraternity leadership training started to come back to me. "If anybody dies, you're responsible," were the words I had brushed aside at the moment. I really began pulling hard for the gremlin out back to make it. Twenty-one-year-old Robert likely wouldn't do well in jail.

As I approached the officers, I saw one of the guys I was with trying to smooth things over. Probably the worst candidate for the job. One of his top skill sets was being able to bite the top of a beer can off with his mouth. It was his "party trick." Swear to God. You don't think you want to see it, but believe me, when it starts happening, you can't take your eyes off of it. It's like watching a small train wreck unfold.

Another one of my friends was also on the frontlines of the negotiations. He was one of the more cool, calm, and levelheaded people we had on that trip. That said, his nickname was "Wildcard" because he was one of the top five craziest people I've met in my life. I went to India with him and watched him pour lime juice in his eye while taking a shot of Tequila (yes, his eye). The locals loved it. His retinas did not.

When it came to talking to the police, he was one of the best we had. By now, you're probably realizing how shallow our bench was. As my dad would always say, "If your only horse is a camel, you've just got to saddle up and ride like hell." Yeehaw, cowboy.

Nevertheless, this was looking like the Hindenburg disaster all over again. The house was in disarray, we were clearly in trouble, and the human can opener was taking the lead on negotiations. All of a sudden, trying to impress those Tulane girls didn't seem like it was that important anymore.

I made my way up to the line of police cars, my blood pressure rising as the muscles in my upper back clenched. "Afternoon, officers," I said sheepishly.

The lead officer kept his hands on his hips and maintained a stern face with me without saying a word. I could tell the eyes behind his sunglasses were drilling holes in my forehead.

Finally, he broke his silence. "Look, it's been a long week. Just keep the noise down and don't make me come back."

"Yes, sir, officer, will do," I said in my best Midwestern polite voice. He gave the three of us one final stare, glanced at the house, and turned away to drive off.

A huge relief came over me. I almost felt lightheaded the way my blood pressure released like a safety valve.

Briskly walking back inside, I went to inspect the damage by the pool. Thank goodness the officers didn't come back here. There was a kiddie pool next to the real pool filled with what must have been thirty beers and a kid passed out. Another guy was crying, talking about how his college life was coming to an end and he would miss all of us. The gremlin was still in the corner frantically looking for relief from the nightmare trip he was on.

As long as that kid didn't die, I wasn't going to. My cause of death that day would have been at the hands of my mom, Kim Sherman, who would have surely made it a closed-casket funeral by the time I got home to Ohio. Thankfully, it never came to that.

So, that was the first time I thought I was going to die. The second time was probably when I opened the door to my hotel room in Ukraine and was staring down the barrel of a Ukrainian soldier's rifle. That was just four years later.

The third was probably when the Russian military fired missiles at Western Ukraine, and I heard the air raid sirens for the first time.

Then there was the time I got detained by some shadowy militants. My life flashed before my eyes there too.

The rocket barrage in Southern Israel I was caught in? Definitely said a couple of prayers there.

So, yeah, the last few years have looked a little different. But let me be the first to tell you: this is not how I saw my life going.

I mean, we all have our mid-life crises. And for my generation, a so-called quarter-life crisis (more on that later) is a seeming rite of passage for every twenty-something these days. Weeks start to fly by when you're a year or two into your first job out of college, and all of a sudden, you start to wonder if this whole "life" thing is working out properly.

It's a fair question to ask. Fulfillment is critical. But did it really have to come to this? Was all of this really necessary?

One of my best friends sent me a text out of the blue the other day that I think adequately sums this up: "Sherman, how the hell did you become a war reporter? What in tarnation?" (Yes, he actually used the word "tarnation." I didn't make that up.)

I guess I'll start from the beginning. I grew up in Cleveland, Ohio. I'm an only child, have two amazing parents, went to a nice high school, and then attended DePauw University (not DePaul!) in Indiana for four years. Most people who start on that path end up in law or business. My dream was always television.

At first, I thought my goal was to cover sports for a living. There was an afternoon when I found myself sitting in front of the television screen, pretending to commentate a college football game between Iowa and Northern Illinois. I was in love with the art of painting a picture for the listener, describing the uniforms, atmosphere, and the way a football play developed. At the time, I was certain that was going to be my lifelong pursuit.

For two summers, I lived in Kenosha, Wisconsin, and worked to build up the broadcasting side of a summer collegiate baseball team. They didn't have a radio affiliate, so I spent weeks setting up an online streaming platform so people could listen to our broadcasts.

During one of the most exciting games of the year, one of the players from Central Michigan hit a walk-off home run. "Back! Track! Wall! Gone!" I screamed into the microphone as he rounded first and began his victory trot. It was pandemonium in the press box, and the fans in the stands were loving it too. At the time, it was one of the most euphoric days of my broadcasting career.

My energy never came down until I glanced at the number of listeners tuning in. Thirteen. We had thirteen people listening to the game. In that moment, I asked myself "who really gives a damn about this?" Don't get me wrong, those were two of the best summers of my life. I learned a lot, and it was a great organization to work for, but I left Wisconsin feeling unfulfilled.

Then I thought local news would be my jam and that one day I would find myself sitting at the anchor desk in a major city. On an internship at a station in Houston, I tagged along with one of the company's top reporters who was assigned a story on a broken fire hydrant. That was it. There was a fire hydrant in Houston, and it was broken.

As I watched the highly talented reporter, who is still a friend to this day, do the absolute best he could with the story and show viewers how, indeed, the fire hydrant was broken, I sat there and said to myself, "This can't be it." I did end up starting my career in local news, which is where most begin their professional journeys, but I knew from the beginning that could not and would not be my endgame.

My first taste of national reporting came when I was given the opportunity to travel the country for Fox News. It was a role that changed my life and altered the course of my career. I was a small fish but was given big opportunities to be boots on the ground for some major stories.

"A one-man band," as we nickname it in the business. I would shoot and edit my own videos, then report for Fox affiliates across the country while setting the camera up by myself. And best of all, I started to find a sense of adventure. Every week, I would hop on planes and trains to keep up with politicians on campaign trails or be right in the thick of it for major moments.

Presidents? Met a few. A Pope? Still haven't washed my right hand. Hurricanes? Been caught in far too many. Wildfires? You bet. How about riots? If I were to describe the feeling of getting tear-gassed, would you believe me?

FIGURE 0.1 Meeting Pope Leo XIV days after the 2025 Papal Conclave (Photo by Vatican Media).

But there is nothing that compares to being twenty-five years old, young and dumb with little understanding of the world, and finding yourself en route to an active war zone.

How did that happen? I sort of volunteered in a half-baked way. I never *really* thought Vladimir Putin would invade Ukraine, so I threw my name in the hat to go. It seemed inconsequential at the moment.

And wouldn't you know? Two weeks later, one of the biggest wars of the twenty-first century broke out, and I was on a flight to Eastern Europe.

It's not like I had anything to lose. I had just started a new job with NewsNation, a startup cable network out of Chicago. It was a big break for me and an opportunity to work for Cherie Grzech, who I believe is the best mind in cable news to this day.

Despite the new beginning, there were a lot of holes in my life. I didn't really know where my career was heading, and my personal life was non-existent. Romantic prospects? Don't even get me started.

I was also stone-cold broke. People think everyone on TV is rich. Not I! It was becoming more and more difficult to watch the balance sheet kick out a red number every month and see all my friends zoom by me toward financial freedom.

And adding to all of that, yeah, I'll admit—I wasn't exactly as happy as I could have been. I started skipping the gym for months at a time. I wasn't eating very healthy. And all the while, I kept thinking back on the "glory days" of being my fraternity's president and spending spring break in Gulf Shores, Alabama.

That was just four years ago. What I wouldn't give to go back, I would repeatedly think to myself. Lesson learned there: never wish your life away.

Fast forward to February of 2022, and this shmuck (me) is standing shoulder to shoulder with Lester Holt and David Muir? It didn't make sense.

NBC had brought in the esteemed war correspondent, Richard Engel. CNN had the notorious, hard-hitting Clarissa Ward. Fox News enlisted the talents of the young but tested Trey Yingst.

And then there's me. A kid from Cleveland who nobody's ever heard of, who probably couldn't even tell you with confidence where Ukraine was on a map. A fish out of water. A guy in and over his head who had some growing up to do.

But let me tell you: the first time you hear a rocket explode, you start to get a little more mature. The first time you get a gun pulled on you and are accused of being a spy, things get more serious. And the first time you talk to a mother who walked 30 miles through the snow to save her child's life and escape an invasion, the world starts to come into perspective.

And I'm going to tell you right off the bat, I don't have any of this figured out. But believe me, just a few years ago, I most certainly thought I did. An "A" student who always drew praise from teachers and professors, I believed in my heart that I knew it all.

Boy, was I wrong, and it took me one day in Ukraine to realize I hardly knew a thing. Years later, I've seen more and feel like I know even less.

All of that to say, if you want to hear the perspective of a battle-hardened war correspondent who has been in the belly of the beast more times than they can count and now knows it all, I'm not your guy. This book is neither an expert's take on juxtaposing the wars in Ukraine and Israel to other conflicts, nor does it draw from any previous experiences.

This is, however, an account written by a then twenty-five-year-old journalist who found himself in his first war zone weeks after starting a new job. In this book, you'll see two of the twenty-first century's most pivotal moments play out through the eyes of a young, curious reporter who had to do some maturing along the way.

That reporter is me, Robert Sherman. I'm a correspondent for NewsNation who lives out of a suitcase and lays his head down in hotels in some of the most random places every night. But the day the war broke out in Ukraine and I was tasked to go is when my life hit its watershed moment.

To quote my dad once more, "A boy can't grow up in his own back yard." Well, this boy found himself thousands of miles away from the comfort of his West-side Cleveland neighborhood in the dead of Eastern Europe's harsh winter. I'm pretty sure my father *did not* have an active war zone in mind when he told me to get out there and see the world for myself.

Additionally, I'm quite confident my mother hoped the first one would be the end of it. And it was until the October 7 attack on Israel that rocked the globe.

Thankfully, NewsNation sent me to Ukraine with the best companion in the business: the intrepid Bartley Price. A journalist and producer with decades of experience, Bartley has found himself on the frontlines of every war you can think of over the last thirty years. Yet somehow, he managed to get in and out of Ukraine without strangling the rookie correspondent (me). As you'll read in this book, I had no clue what I was doing.

The following year in the Middle East, I still didn't know what I was doing. But all of a sudden, I had to take the reins and be the "expert" on global affairs alongside fellow wide-eyed journalist, Will Budkins. Quite a tall order for both of us.

These two wars changed my life and helped mold my perception of the world. Along the way, I picked up a stack of stories to tell—while some of them are funny or entertaining, others are so tragic they will weigh on my mind until I'm sitting in a nursing home rocking chair. Each one had a profound teaching impact on me.

So, to reiterate: this is not a book on how the geopolitical climate following the downfall of the Soviet Union led to Russia's invasion of Ukraine. This is not an analysis of decades of American policy in the Middle East to examine what went awry. I'm not qualified to write those books.

But before I sell myself too short, I'll say this: one thing that comes with a lack of prior experience is rawness. Think of it this way—the feeling of riding a roller coaster the first time isn't quite the same as the twentieth.

Well, what I can tell you as a journalist is that while years of experience add important context to one's reporting, sometimes lost along the way are those emotional details. The face of an orphan child—uncertain of the future as bombs fall on their city. The tremble in a mother's voice as she tries to explain to her daughter that daddy is gone, and there's no home to return to. When you've worked in journalism for a long enough time, sometimes you overlook those moments.

But when this is your first war zone, everything is new. Every blade cuts deeper. Every memory is seared eternally. Each story I'll be sharing with you in this book is one that is impossible for me to forget. The names, faces, and characters will stay with me for a lifetime.

That's what I intend to share with you: a collection of short stories and anecdotes that I hope will allow you, the reader, to see and feel what life was like in Ukraine and the Middle East during the onset of the wars there. I hope to briefly put you in the shoes of those who have lived and breathed this reality. The perceptions I'll share are based on what I saw, heard, and felt.

And as you read this book, there are many hopes I have.

First, I hope you read the words of the people living through these wars intently. They are taken from audio and video recordings I have held onto and are word for word. For many of the civilians we spoke with, it was their first and possibly only time speaking with a journalist. Their comments are largely filled with pain, anger, and fear.

Second, I hope you think about their experiences and imagine yourself in those positions. Every character in this book is real. Their stories are non-fiction. Names have been changed for the sake of protecting identities.

Lastly, I hope you take this book for what it is: a firsthand account. The perspective of a kid thrown into the deep end of the pool who had to do a bit of doggy paddling. I am not an expert, a veteran war correspondent, or some kind of action star. Just a kid with a notebook full of memories and stories.

I hope you enjoy the lessons I learned from them.

PART I

UKRAINE

1 GO EAST, YOUNG MAN

Feeling the rumble of the Texas highway system beneath our wheels, we rolled through the Rio Grande Valley of the Lone Star State. With every revolution of our vibrating tires, loose stones were dislodged and tossed into the wind.

We had just left the border town of Laredo that morning and had been kicking up dust for hours. Normally, long drives were a comfort zone for me. But by this point, the miles began to blend together while the days turned to mush.

The South Texas terrain sure didn't make it easier to concentrate. A quick glance out the window opened our eyes to an endless sea of beige sand and brush. You couldn't stare long as the reflection of the sun's rays could blind a hawk.

We were in the part of Texas where if you got lost, you might not make it home. The heat, even in the spring, could suck the water right out of your cells as the sun's rays pounded your neck and turned it lobster red. Not to mention the other kinds of critters that were out there lurking—just waiting for a poor sap with an exposed ankle to come trudging by. No, thank you.

I sat back and pressed my shoulder blades into the shotgun passenger seat, letting out a sigh as I tried to close my eyes. I was at the level of exhaustion where I was too tired to fall asleep. I wanted to. Believe me, all I wanted in that moment was a cozy bed and some mindless television to numb my mind into comatose.

Soon, I thought to myself. We were on the last leg of our journey and had booked a hotel on South Padre Island for that night. I could see the white sand and the Gulf of Mexico already.

South Padre seems to always conjure up mixed reactions from Texans. You either love it or hate it. For two weeks out of the year, it becomes a haven for college students and those wishing they were still in college to cut loose for spring break. Thankfully, we were missing that annual pilgrimage of degenerates by a few weeks.

Who was I kidding? As if I was somehow above such a display. Four years earlier I had been doing the exact same thing in Gulf Shores, Alabama, with my college buddies. A last hurrah with graduation around the corner and some of us taking jobs in different corners of the globe.

Those years had flown by so rapidly. Now, I was the decaying age of twenty-five. By Generation Z standards, I might as well have been dead and in the ground. You laugh. You think I'm exaggerating. But twenty-five is the hardest year of life for many young adults.

Four words that will strike fear into any twenty-something's soul: "The quarter-life crisis." That's right, fifty-somethings are wrong to assume they have a monopoly on misery.

Am I good enough? Am I smart enough? Are my best days already behind me? Is this really what the rest of my life will be? Those questions can haunt the most confident of young up-and-comers—or at least those who think that's what they are (another shower thought: Am I really on the way up?). One thing you'll find about me is that I love to get lost in my own thoughts. Fantasizing about the future. Reminiscing about the past. Letting my imagination run wild.

I looked over at the driver's seat. Manning the wheel was Bartley Price, our intrepid driver and field producer. His eyes were locked on the road intently with BBC radio murmuring softly in the background. We were driving a Chevy Suburban that had been re-outfitted into a satellite truck. Everywhere you looked was a gadget, gizmo, camera, or joystick that was far too expensive for me to even dare playing with. Anytime or any place we could pull the thing over and be ready to put whatever we saw on live television. That's what we had been doing for half of February 2022.

As such, the car was consumed with a cloud of mental exhaust. Two weeks earlier we had flown into San Diego, California, to tackle a special assignment where we'd drive the roughly 2,000 miles of US–Mexico border: telling stories of the people who call these communities home along the way.

"Assignment" is a loose term. Bartley and I volunteered.

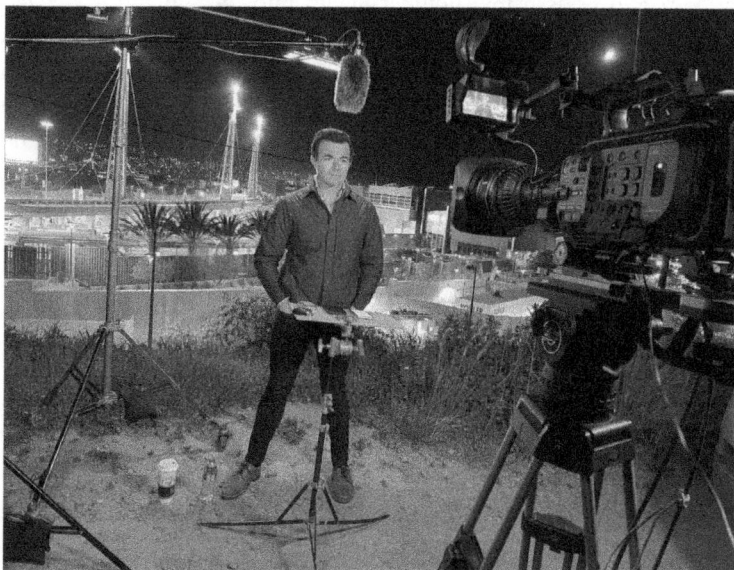

FIGURE 1.1 Reporting from the San Ysidro port of entry in Southern California, our first stop on a two-week-long border assignment. Photo by Bartley Price.

Or rather, my big mouth said, "wouldn't this be a great idea?" to which our bosses said, "yeah, go do it." Bartley got dragged into this by being in the wrong place at the wrong time. He still hasn't forgiven me.

At this juncture I still didn't know what to make of this guy. Tall and slender yet commanding with a New Zealand accent that could garner the attention of anyone in a room. A charming personality that could win over the dampest of souls—but a brutally realist view of the world. Add in the fact the man was a ruthless producer—hell or high water, the job was going to get done and it was going to get done right. At this point, I wasn't keen to find out if it was his bark or bite that was worse.

We started our jobs at NewsNation on the same day: January 17, 2022. In fact, it was that day I hatched this idea of touring the US–Mexico border for two weeks that he was ingloriously roped into.

Just a few weeks later, in the final days of February, there we were. Tired. Exhausted. Fed up with one another. Off to meet a farmer and put together a story about how his cows were getting some kind of disease from insects. It was a story pitched to us by a local down along the border on a slow news day, though we weren't very enthusiastic considering some of the stories we had reported on during that trip were, frankly, impossible to forget.

One of our first days of this border tour, we were in Yuma, Arizona, in the dead of night. We were standing right on the US–Mexico border where there just so happened to be a large section of unfinished wall. This one particular spot is colloquially called "the Yuma Gap" and was a favored illegal crossing point.

We were there only for a few minutes when we heard the scuffing of stones. Then, it was the sound of groans and a yelp. Deep, breathless pants that grew louder and louder. All of a sudden, out of the Arizona night emerged a family of three. A man, a woman, and a young boy—no more than five years old. Each clad in dark clothing. They made a beeline right for us—probably drawn to the headlights of our cars.

The family of three came right up to us. The man leading them dropped their bags at our feet and looked us straight in the eyes. He tried to speak but words didn't come out on the first attempt. They didn't need to. One look into his eyes told me all I needed to know: these people were knocking on death's door.

"Water. Agua!" he croaked. I turned around and sprinted back to our truck—fearing if I didn't run fast enough the man would keel over right then and there. Likely not true, but one thing you'll find with me is my mind has a habit of latching onto the worst-case scenario.

I retrieved two large bottles of water and handed them to the family. They quickly snatched the bottles out of my hand, cracked them open, and started guzzling the whole thing. A few moments later, after ensuring their child had enough, the man looked back up at me and wiped his lips. "Gracias por la agua," he said with a smile. Even my fifth-grade level of Spanish knew that meant "thank you for the water."

They told us they were hoping to speak with the US authorities as they were seeking asylum in the United States, but I never got the opportunity to dive further into this. Before I could even find a way to mutter out "why?" in Spanish, a border patrol agent drove by.

The family's faces lit up with ear-to-ear grins as they eagerly allowed themselves to be taken into Border Patrol custody and driven away. Just like that, they were gone. To this day, I don't know what happened to that family, but your perception of the world changes when you meet someone on their most desperate day.

That wasn't the only story that stuck with me. Also in Arizona, while in that same area, another family had crossed into the United States. This one was five people with a man, a woman, and three young children.

They came upon an irrigation canal that they had to cross. The water wasn't deep, but it was fairly swift. The man picked up one of his little girls and kissed her on the cheek, then tried to descend slowly into the narrow, concrete canal.

Just then, he slipped and fell onto his back. His daughter landed right on top of him, breaking her fall. But a split second later, the current pulled her away. She started screaming at the top of her lungs as she drifted farther and farther downstream from her dad.

The man quickly stood up as water rushed out of his shirt and pants. He trudged after her and grabbed on by her wrist. After holding her against the current for a few moments he hoisted her up into his arms. The little girl continued to bawl, but her tears slowly subsided as the man bobbed her up and down slowly.

Tears dry and nose stuffy, she let her father carry her out of the canal. The rest of the family was already on the other side. They embraced, held each other for a few moments, then started walking into a farmer's field until they were out of sight. This all happened over the span of a few minutes, but as I sat there in helpless horror, the seconds felt like hours.

Our travel was not exclusive to the American side of the border. We also spent one day in Ciudad Juarez, Mexico—which I didn't realize at the time was one of the top-five most dangerous cities in the world.

The locals will tell you things like "it's just like Chicago or St. Louis, you just have to stay in the right part of town." When our driver took us across the bridge and said "you guys should probably put your heads down," so nobody could see us in the backseat of the car, I knew we weren't in Kansas anymore.

Our driver took us right to a shelter in Ciudad Juarez that was housing migrants attempting to *legally* enter the United States. Some had been waiting for over a year.

The outside of this shelter was white stone, which was cracking from years of neglect. We stepped foot inside this shelter and I was immediately taken aback by how many people were there. Entire families were sharing one single twin bed in a dormitory with twenty bunks. The pastor who ran the shelter came out to greet us. He was a big fellow with a charcoal grey mustache and short hair. He wore a blue sweater vest and black slacks—I couldn't believe he was wearing this in the Mexican heat.

He extended a hand to greet us and gave a deep sigh. Our driver, who doubled as our translator, explained they were always struggling with resources and just didn't have the ability to keep up with demand.

He allowed us to walk around and it didn't take long until a man wearing a red t-shirt and a baseball cap came right up to us. "American?" he asked.

"Yes," I responded.

The man did not know any more English so turned to our driver and started talking. He was becoming hysterical and giving hand gestures toward his heart and his head. As tears started to roll down his cheeks, he then turned to me. Without saying a word, I knew what he was trying to communicate. *Can you help us?*

Our translator butted in. "This man is wanted by the cartels. He refused to do business with them. As a result, they burned his home and are now looking for him," he said. The man's heart sank as he stared down at the ground, and my faith in humanity dropped as well. I didn't even know what to say to the man. All I could do was squeak out a soft "I'm so sorry," as he put his hand over his heart then into my hand and held it there while staring into my eyes. I knew what that meant: he wanted his story told (of course, in a manner that would protect his identity and safety). One of many reminders I've had that covering a crisis from a broad view is one thing, but it's the on-the-ground accounts from everyday people that make it stick with you. He departed after that exchange and we crossed back into the United States a short while later. Once stateside, I vowed to never take what I have for granted again.

No disrespect to the farmer we were driving to see, but cows and Lyme disease couldn't really hold a candle to what we had seen in the previous few days.

The car fell silent, except for the woman on the BBC. Bartley loved listening to the station. His hand instinctively went for the dial to turn it up. The journalist was talking about how Russia was bolstering its forces and appeared to be gearing up to invade Ukraine. It was the story the whole world was talking about but nobody was believing. Especially Bartley.

"It's not going to happen," Bartley said, keeping his eyes on the road. The dismissiveness of his tone came with an air of firmness as if he'd talked to Russian President Vladimir Putin himself that day.

To be fair, you'll be hard pressed to find someone who has reported on wars as extensively as Bartley Price. Every conflict you could think of over the previous three decades, he'd been there on the frontlines working with some of the finest journalists in the world. Much of his adult life was spent bringing the images of war into people's living rooms every night.

"No way Putin's going in," he repeated. The certainty was unshakable in his voice.

"I don't know, man," piped up little old me, twenty-five-years-old with absolutely no concept of war outside the confines of movies and video games. I'm ashamed to admit that on that day, if you asked me to name the capital of Ukraine I would have probably blurted out something like "Ukraine City." Calling my understanding of the situation "an inch deep" would have been generous.

That said, I was not oblivious to the world. I was just five years old when 9/11 happened and my parents picked me up from school early out of fear more attacks would come. My whole family spent the next few years huddled around television screens glued to reporting on the war in Afghanistan and, later, the war in Iraq. I remember watching correspondents like John McWethy and Geraldo Rivera reporting live from across the globe in cities and countries I couldn't spell. I was awestruck by their line of work, but never felt it was for me. Politics? Sure. Sports? Sounds pleasant. War zones? Pass.

Still, the potential outbreak of war between Russia and Ukraine was impossible to ignore. Every network had pundits on their airwaves opining if Russia would invade or not, why or why not, and how quickly would they win. The consensus? If Russia invades, Ukraine's capital of Kyiv will fall within seventy-two hours. A week at best.

What I didn't tell Bartley is that shortly after volunteering for this two-week long project along the border, I had also volunteered to go to Ukraine if the war did in fact break out. That didn't seem likely, however, as NewsNation was just getting off the ground.

"Probably for the best I sit this one out anyways," said Bartley. He was in Ukraine less than a decade earlier when Russia annexed the Crimean Peninsula. Another producer I worked with in the Middle East years later once said "every bullet has an address, and you don't need to run toward all of them." It seemed like that's where Bartley's head was at.

I had already come to peace with the fact that I wouldn't be going. Frankly, I don't even know why I had volunteered. The fear of God was put into me a few days later when I had floated the idea again to one of our network anchors, who had also spent some time in conflict zones. I laid out my whole plan of how we would get into Ukraine, drive east toward the Russian line and report from there. After I had fired off a message or two, he picked up the phone and called me. "I read your message and said 'He's going to get him and everyone he knows killed.'" His words hit me like a load of bricks. When my colleague said that to me, I didn't want to go to Ukraine anymore. Missiles and tanks seem cool and fun until you consider the fact that they're weapons of war meant to end lives. You, the savvy reader, are at this point surely thinking "this guy is absolutely tone deaf. Talking about how cool and fun tanks and bombs are as if the horrors of war are not real?" Indeed, you are correct. A fair critique. Twenty-five-years-old, young, dumb, and naïve. Don't worry, that all changes.

In short, I wasn't so high on this anymore. Being in Texas covering the border seemed much more safe and secure. Shortly after those thoughts trickled through my head, headlines started to flash across my phone. All signs were pointing to a Russian attack *that night*. I showed the headlines to Bartley.

"He's not going to do it," Bartley insisted. "It doesn't make sense. What is there to gain from attacking Ukraine?" Couldn't tell you. But it sure seemed inevitable. I felt the vibration in my right pocket, which belonged to my work cell phone. I pulled it out as the screen illuminated.

"Incoming Call: Cherie Grzech," it said in bold letters across the front.

I stand firmly by this assertion: there is no leader in television news more brilliant than Cherie Grzech. She and I used to work together at another network a few months prior. "Together" is a stretch. She was the boss; I was sitting on one of the bottom-most rungs.

But even from my view in the basement, I could see the way she commanded a news operation. Every decision made was with absolute certainty. Every strategy highly communicated from the top down. She loved managing, and in turn everyone loved being managed by her. She left that network to help lead the newsroom here at NewsNation. A few months later, I was at a crossroads with what to do in my career. I had no idea at the time what NewsNation was or what it was purporting to be. The fact that Cherie joined the network led me to believe it was worth exploring. In the end, she convinced me to come aboard and work for her again. Knowing what I now know, I owe my whole career to Cherie Grzech and every opportunity that has come my way.

So, when Cherie calls, you answer.

"Good afternoon, General," I said into the phone with a smile.

"Hey there," she said in a warm but assertive tone. "I hope you're enjoying your drive through Texas."

"Can't complain," I said with a smile, looking over at Bartley. "I'm shocked Bartley hasn't killed me yet," I joked.

"Not for a lack of trying!" Bartley interjected. I can't even begin to articulate how much it bothered me he was so perfectly witty.

Cherie chuckled on the other end of the line. "Well listen, I'm gonna get right to the point," Cherie said. "In light of what's happening, the network doesn't have much interest in what you two are doing right now."

Fair enough, I thought to myself. Russia and Ukraine are on the brink of war, who cares about cattle?

"So, we were wondering if you'd have interest in going to Europe for the war?"

"Yes!" The word just spilled out of me. I couldn't hold it in. Not a moment taken to consider what I was even saying. I was not expecting this in the slightest. I had thought it had already been established that NewsNation would not be sending anyone, and I understood why. We were the small but mighty network. Scrappy and smart, but candidly without the international footprint the other networks have.

But sometimes, the moment calls upon you to step up and rise to the occasion. I guess that's what was happening.

"Bartley?" Cherie asked to see if he was interested.

Bartley paused. "Yeah, all right, fine," the more level-headed person in the car finally said.

"All right, sounds good. We'll be in touch but I guess we'll see you in Europe," Cherie said then hung up the phone.

I looked over at Bartley. A grin was starting to form on his face as he nodded his head. "Cool," he finally said.

Cool indeed, I thought, as I began telling everyone I knew, including my folks that I was going to be on a plane overseas that week. Bartley wheeled the beast of a vehicle around and started heading north to the airport. That night, the Russians made good on their threats and invaded Ukraine. The gravity of the situation didn't hit me until the ticket went through showing we had secured passage to Poland—the first leg of the journey.

What the hell are you getting yourself into, Robert? Never been in a war zone. Never set foot in eastern Europe. No idea what to do, where to go. As the old saying goes, "I didn't even know what I didn't know."

Nothing like baptism by fire, I suppose.

2 NO TURNING BACK NOW

The comatose slumber I surprisingly found on board the 787 Dreamliner was quickly vanquished once the rubber pounded pavement. I woke up with a jolt as we touched down in Warsaw, Poland. My eyes barely open, I looked across the aisle as Bartley stirred from his snooze. He cracked a smile at me.

"You ready?" He asked.

"I think so," I responded. *And if not, no time like the present to get ready,* I thought.

Our plane pulled into the gate, and I collected my backpack from under the seat in front of me. It wasn't an overly full flight, as international travel hadn't quite rebounded since Covid-19. Even so, we made the slow walk cluttered by other passengers to customs.

As we trudged down the hall, I saw two signs: "citizens" and "foreigners." Without thinking, I started to make a left toward citizens.

"Sherman!" Bartley barked. "This way," he said, pointing toward "foreigners."

Oops. I forgot I'm considered a foreigner when not in the United States. It had been about five years since I'd put my passport to use. Hardly an "international man" by any measure.

I slid behind Bartley as he turned and shook his head with an incredulous grin. He may as well have said what he was thinking out loud: "you stupid child." He wouldn't have been wrong. The customs line moved quickly, and in a few minutes, I was face to face with a Polish official. Orange jacket, no hair, and spectacles, he asked the classic "Are you here in Poland for business or pleasure?"

"Business," I sheepishly replied.

"What's your line of work?" he asked. I told him journalism, to which he queried, "Where will you be going?"

"Ukraine," I said. He glanced up, gazing over his spectacles as if to ask, "Are you sure about that?" He then gave a sigh and shook his head a little in disbelief. Maybe it was just my paranoia, but it felt like a small message from the universe saying, "You can still turn around and go home." With that, I heard the loud snapping sound of the man stamping my passport. Booklet in hand, I was gone. *Onward.*

After collecting our bags, we stepped outside into the freezing Polish cold—a kind of cold that penetrates and stings your very soul. Every breath seemingly burns in this kind of climate, forcing you to decide if breathing is even really worth it. This would only get worse throughout the trip.

A small clunker of a car pulled up. It was an old, dark green sedan from the 90s at best. I had flashbacks to the movie "Vacation" with Chevy Chase as the boxy-looking "family truckster" jammed full of gear with bags strapped to the roof came to a halt right in front of us.

No way this is us, I thought to myself. *Yes way.* Out of the car sprang two men in their mid-20s. We'll call them Aaron and Larry.

"Is one of you Bartley?" one asked in a whiny Eastern European accent.

"That would be me!" Bartley replied in his chipper voice. Everyone greeted one another and shook hands.

This was the formation of our team in Europe, and I'll be frank: not what I expected. Aaron wore a beanie cap that covered his brown, curly hair which had a tendency to flop over his eyes. Thick-rimmed glasses sat atop his nose, and an unbuttoned flannel covered a white t-shirt. He would be our "fixer"—effectively, the guy who makes things happen. Fluent in roughly half a dozen languages, his job was to help get us around Europe, show us where to go, who to talk to, and what to avoid.

At least, that's what the job description calls for. Judging by his appearance, I thought I'd have a better shot at getting a critical analysis of Shakespeare's *Merchant of Venice.*

Larry was just over six feet tall with short, dirty blonde hair. Despite the cold, all he had on was a t-shirt and skinny jeans. His lanky arms popped out of the sleeves where his goosebumps were clearly visible amid the frigid temperatures, yet never once did the thought of putting on a sweater seem to cross his mind. He would be our first of many cameramen throughout the trip. I say first of many, but I wish he was our only since, in hindsight, he proved to be our best.

Aaron and Larry ushered us toward the car, explaining they had made some room for us in the backseat. *Our chariot awaits,* I thought to myself. We threw our bags in the trunk, slammed the doors shut, and were off.

I stared out the window as the hulking cathedrals of Warsaw towered over us. One of the most beautiful cities I have ever seen, yet not a common destination I hear most Americans put atop their lists. We would spend more time in Warsaw later in the trip, but I was so impressed by the city's architecture as spires appeared to penetrate the heavens above and buildings of yellow, red and green brick dazzled in vibrant color. My first city outside the United States in years served as a key reminder that it's a wide world ripe for exploring.

Rubber on asphalt, we rolled on until the city started to melt away in the rearview mirror—being replaced by sweeping, serene Polish farmland. It was quaint and beautiful despite the thin layer of frost on the ground. It reminded me a lot of states like Iowa back home. The crops sat atop rolling hills broken by windmills and barns in the distance. Occasionally you'd see cows and goats mulling about outside. As a Midwesterner, I loved it. For whatever reason, driving through the countryside inspired a warming nostalgia for home in Ohio. Aaron seemed less impressed. "Poland is the Scranton of Europe," he quipped. I've been to Scranton. I like Scranton. But I don't know how I'll ever be able to see Poland any other way since hearing that comparison.

Larry remained pretty quiet the whole ride. He was behind the wheel giggling at a few of the cracks Aaron made, but seemed content remaining focused on the road. Aaron had this sense of curiosity about him. I'm not certain he had met Americans before, but he couldn't get enough of asking us about where we were from, what it was like living in the United States and more.

Finally, I had to turn it back on him. "Where are you from, Aaron?"

"I am from Ukraine originally but now study in Poland," he explained. "I study languages and literature." *Nailed it.*

"How did you become a fixer?" I couldn't help but ask. It's not a field people get into back in the US, though to be fair you wouldn't really need one in America.

Aaron giggled. "Well, I was studying in Poland and am proficient in English, Polish, Russian, and Ukrainian, and it seemed like a way to get out of the classroom and make some extra money, so I started doing this about a year ago," he explained. "Now that there's a war going on, we're very busy."

Supply and demand in wartime. What a concept.

"Don't mind me if I open my laptop and work on a paper for my poetry class," he laughed. Unbelievable. This guy is working on Russian prose as all hell breaks loose. "I'll be with you guys when we go into Ukraine," he said confidently.

I then turned to Larry. "What about you, Larry?"

He laughed. "My girlfriend would kill me if I went into Ukraine," he said with a beaming smile. "I will go to the border but that is all. They're bringing in someone to cross the border with you all." Larry might have been the smartest in the group for that.

This wouldn't be the whole team. Our security detail would be joining us later that night as we got closer to the border. Our plan was to make it to the Polish-Ukrainian line by nightfall and spend a night or two in Poland before crossing over.

Maybe an hour before reaching the border, we stopped off at a restaurant. It was essentially a farmhouse in rural Poland with big glass windows. The hostess greeted us with a warm smile, but not as warm as the heater unit which thawed us out. She wore a white button down shirt and black apron. "Right this way," she said, leading us to a wood table in the corner. The restaurant was small. Maybe twelve tables in total.

We sat down and quickly realized there was only one other group here. Six or seven people were sitting two tables over from us drinking wine and finishing off plates of dinner.

As our group started chit-chatting and pulling out our laptops to get a little bit of work done, I heard someone say "You aren't from around here."

We all looked up and one of the women at the other table was looking at us with a big smile. Her dark hair was braided and tied into a ponytail and she wore a black winter coat. I could tell she was from somewhere in northern Africa based upon her accent.

"That obvious, huh?" Bartley chirped back.

The woman laughed. "It's ok, we aren't either," she chided back.

"Africa, I presume?" Barley queried.

"Indeed. Nigeria." She answered. "I can tell he's American, but you're not," she said first pointing at me, the clear Yankee of the group.

"Maybe I'm from Boston!" Bartley joked.

Her smile flattened. "You're not. Australia or New Zealand?"

"New Zealand originally. Now Connecticut," Bartley said. "We're on our way to Ukraine. We're journalists here for the war."

The woman sighed. "How unfortunate," she said, briefly pausing. "We are fleeing Kyiv right now. We are medical students there," she said motioning to her group.

"I'm so sorry," Bartley replied, never breaking eye contact with the woman.

She shrugged. "What can you do? This is the world we live in. I hope you stay safe," she said.

"You as well," I chimed in. She smiled, and turned back to her group. Never once did I consider that the first victims of the war we were going to cover would be medical students from Africa. They weren't Ukrainian, but war neither cares nor neatly unfolds: everyone bears the burden.

That was just the beginning of it that night.

* * *

Sorted and ready to roll out from the rental home we were staying at not far from the Ukrainian border, we made our way downstairs and set foot outside. Immediately, the rush of cold air smacked me in the face and made me want to turn around. It felt like a thousand needles fresh out of the oven stabbing my face prick by prick. I quickly made a dart for Larry's car and slid into the backseat. One by one, Bartley, Larry and Aaron did as well. Larry started the engine, which I was thankful kicked on so the heat would blast, and we were off and rolling.

Russia had invaded Ukraine maybe 48 hours earlier so the situation was very fluid. At this time, millions of Ukrainians were packing up their homes and trying to flee the country at all costs. It didn't matter if they had a plan or not, prime objective number one was "get out." While Ukraine shares a border with multiple countries, Poland would be the main place Ukrainians would go.

Belarus was effectively aligned with Russia, so Ukrainians weren't going there. Slovakia, Romania, and Moldova would get some refugees but not nearly as many, and Hungary was less interested in taking people in at all. My travels to Hungary years later would make me realize there are still unresolved tensions between Hungary and Ukraine following the end of the Second World War, but that's an entirely different book in and of itself. We started getting closer and closer to the border and you could just feel the energy in the air shifting. Earlier in the day we were remarking about how quaint and quiet eastern Poland was. But now, we were seeing ambulances, fire trucks, and Police cars zooming down the highways.

We arrived in the small Polish down of Medyka where flashing emergency lights painted the nighttime, forested landscape in red and blue. Screams of children echoed, shouts of women pierced the air. I couldn't see any of the pandemonium for myself in that moment, but I knew it was just down the road. It became clear to me we were no longer talking about Ukraine, some foreign country thousands of miles away: we had arrived at the border.

As if it were a scene straight out of a film, a woman appeared; stumbling out of the abyss-like haze with a pair of children clinging to her heavy winter coat. With their hands raised to shield their sensitive eyes from the lights, they trudged forward: their faces ghostly white and dreary from exhaust. Men clad in orange stood in the middle of the road, urging them to hurry toward them. They were Polish medics who apparently were not permitted to enter the border crossing or get too close, so stood at the edge of Polish soil. The family of three continued trudging forward slowly before collapsing in the arms of the medics—embracing strangers like relatives separated for years and using those orange jackets as shoulders to sob into. Tears of relief for safety, or tears of despair for country? Impossible to know.

Our fixer, Aaron, jogged toward them while we stayed back. He reached the family, who now stood hunched over with hands on knees. You couldn't hear what they were saying, but the way the woman looked him in the eyes, you knew her story was a tragic one. Aaron nodded along as she passionately professed to him. They hugged. He gave her a final nod then walked back to us, head down.

"They walked thirty miles to the border and stood in line for two days," he told us in a hushed tone. The family was from Kharkiv, a city in Eastern Ukraine near Russia that already was being torn to pieces by bombings. Everything they owned was gone. While the woman's story was heartbreaking, it was hardly unique as we would find. In the shadow of the crossing was a makeshift refugee camp. The unmistakable sound of a newborn baby crying led us to a family, wrapped in gold colored thermal blankets. The mother trying everything to calm her child down to no avail.

We slowly approached them with Aaron taking the lead as the only Ukrainian speaker. The woman turned to him and, to my surprise, flashed a warm smile at us while tending to her child. Through Aaron's translation, she told us her name was Yulia and ditched her car in Ukraine—forced to trudge through the snow while carrying her child.

"Spiritually, we are not afraid anymore," she said to us. "We left everything behind. The whole house. We just took our clothes." Then she paused and looked down, unable to make eye contact. She took a beat, met our gaze and continued. "My brother was drafted into the military four days ago." She had no idea where he was or if he was even still alive. This would become a theme for us in our travels. Every able-bodied man was being pressed into military service by order of Ukrainian President Volodymyr Zelenskyy. Husbands, brothers and sons had rifles thrust into their hands and then were whisked away. What else could a nation do staring down the barrel of invasion?

We kept wandering around the camp. Off to the side was a small group of people huddled around a fire burning in an open barrel. There stood a man with a brown beard and a beanie cap gazing straight into the flames. He was in his 20s, and I couldn't help but notice a small smile stretched across his face. Aaron approached him from the side, and the man turned to him—smile still intact. The man explained he was from Ukraine but had been living in Poland for months, which explained how a young Ukrainian man had made it out. He was smiling because his family was leaving Ukraine and coming to him today.

"And then I'm going back," he said, looking straight into our eyes. "Once they're safe, I'm going back." We thought he was joking at first, but the gaze he held told us quite the contrary. He explained he was well aware of the draft taking place

FIGURE 2.1 A live report from the refugee camp in Medyka, Poland, as the first displaced Ukrainians fled their homeland in search of safety. Photo by Bartley Price.

in his homeland and couldn't stay in Poland while others were taking up arms and preparing to serve. The man didn't strike me as a fighter. He was thin and lanky and by no means built like a Marine. But nevertheless, he was determined to return home and fight. In the coming days, it would be reported that thousands of Ukrainians would do the same from across the globe.

Nearby, we found a woman in her thirties. She had three children tucked under her arms and clutched them dearly as she stared off into the scene in front of her. She was seemingly in a state of shock and unable to process what was unfolding in the world around her.

Aaron tried to get her attention and speak with her. She briefly acknowledged him but avoided making eye contact. I could see Aaron kept politely trying to engage with her, but she kept shaking her head. Her face was pale, and all she could do was stare off into the abyss while holding her children more and more tightly. On his final attempt, she turned to him and gave him her full attention. Aaron motioned us over. As we approached, she immediately started talking.

"My mother, she stayed in Kyiv. There is a shelling right now," she said through Aaron's translation. Her voice was trembling. "Our house was hit. Now, they sit in the basement," she explained. She then grabbed my arm firmly. I was taken aback as she now stared directly into my eyes—a deep red color from the tears. "Tell Putin to stop this madness," she said, this time without a single waver in her voice. Her words reminded me that the despair at that camp wasn't caused by some unforeseen force of nature. Decisions were made by real-life human beings to wage war, and they were well aware of the widespread suffering such a conflict would cause.

If you were to walk around that refugee camp, you'd see the same things and hear the same stories over and over again. And just as that woman and her daughter strolled out of the Polish night, there would moments later be another. And another. The stories of heartbreak, just like the people, kept coming.

We stayed a few more hours before driving back to our cabin. I didn't say a word the whole ride. All I could think of was that woman and her three children. "Tell Putin to stop this madness." Those words rattled around my head over and over. I was really struggling with the idea that this was all manmade pandemonium. I didn't understand it. And for that matter, I quickly realized I didn't understand war properly.

And there was only one way I was going to. We had to go into Ukraine.

3 CROSSING INTO CONFLICT

Every now and then, you see things that you will never be able to unsee.

It was just after 7:00 o'clock in the morning in Eastern Poland, and we had just spent the entire night at the Polish–Ukrainian border. The college kids call these "all-nighters."

It's ironic to me that I pulled only one of them in college to study for an economics exam. But in television news? I'm at well over a dozen. About half of them have been from covering hurricanes that made landfall overnight. In those cases, you'd never be able to sleep even if you tried, as the howling winds of mother nature will cause the adrenaline to course through your veins, keeping you wide awake.

This one particular all-nighter was miserable on every front. We had spent two days now reporting from the Polish border, and due to the time change, live programming ended at precisely 6:00 a.m. local time. Now it was seven, and sleep wasn't an option as the first rays of sunlight could be spotted streaking out of the horizon. The day was starting, and we needed every hour possible.

We were set to cross from Poland into Ukraine. The border crossing did not open until 8:00 o'clock, and in order for us to make it in by nightfall and for our evening programming, we needed to leave right at eight to go through the port of entry and into Ukraine. It would take us all day to get to Ivano-Frankivsk, which is where we would be staying.

So there we were, pulling all-nighters, with one more hour yet to go until the port of entry opened. What made things worse was the weather. I had to constantly recalibrate my mind as the temperature was written in Celsius on the car thermometer. My elementary school science teacher taught us the equation to convert Celsius to Fahrenheit years ago, but as my mind began to melt due to fatigue, I gave up on putting my arithmetic skills to use. All that's important here is 0 degrees Celsius is the "freezing point" of water—the same as 32 degrees Fahrenheit. The morning of our crossing it was −15. Brutal.

It's one thing to be cold. It's another thing to be exhausted. Both simultaneously are abject misery. You're so delusional from the lack of sleep that you don't realize how your fingers are screaming in pain to find warmth until it's too late. You try to wipe the tears from your eyes brought on by the dagger-like winds only just to feel the sting of more wind again. The salt left behind from your watery eyes then burns away at your cheek until you have no choice but to rub your eyes again. The cycle repeats.

The only thing, and I mean the only thing, getting me through that was a lone McDonald's two blocks away that I would walk back and forth with coffee in hand. I owe my fortitude that day to those heavenly golden arches. After maybe my seventh or seventeenth (hard to count) visit to America's finest, I trudged back to our group. At this point, both of my feet had fallen asleep, and I was just counting down the minutes until 8:00 o'clock. I finally arrived back at Aaron and Larry's car.

When I had left, all of the parking spaces next to us were empty. But now, parked next to us was a blue minivan which must have seen twenty years of middle school soccer games. At first, I thought nothing of it. What I didn't realize at the time was that this car was our team's and would be my home on wheels for the next month. Something else I learned that day: *typically*, when you go into a war zone, you're supposed to have an official indication on the side of your vehicle informing the military that you're press. Why? So they don't blow you to Kingdom Come, of course.

They're not always perfectly effective, as every now and then an over-eager sniper will use a press vehicle for target practice. It's not supposed to happen, but it has happened many times throughout years of war zone journalism. It didn't matter if those indicators were effective, ineffective, or somewhat effective: we didn't have them. I'm not sure if it was an oversight by the crew we hired or if they couldn't get their hands on them in time, but either way, we needed to improvise. So, someone on the team decided to, quite literally, take white duct tape and lay strips on the side of the car to spell out the word "PRESS." You can't make it up.

What's more, the car was ours under a "you break it, you buy it" pretense. None of the rental companies were giving out vehicles to anyone heading to Ukraine (gee, I wonder why?), so the company we had employed to iron out logistics, which also assigned us Aaron and Larry, provided this minivan. If the Russian air force turned the thing into Swiss cheese, we were on the hook for it. Not something I really wanted to think about.

I opened up the back seat and lifted myself into the passenger side. Bartley was on the opposite end, and Aaron found himself in-between us. There wasn't a seat there, however, so he would have to sit on a bag in the middle aisle. Up front were two men who I had not yet met or seen before. We'll call them Pat and Brian. Pat was our new cameraman replacing Larry. He was heavyset with a bald head and a clean-shaven face. His nose had a big bump in the center of it causing the front to droop down.

Brian, on the other hand, had a chiseled and defined jawline. I have no idea what color his hair was because he always wore this black beanie cap, but I can only assume it was a pale blonde color to match his eyebrows. Bartley told me Brian was retired from Polish intelligence. Either he was in Poland's equivalent of the CIA or the Secret Service. I can't quite recall what I was told, but he apparently did have a lengthy resume of experience.

Larry wasn't kidding when he said the border would be as far as he would go. He stopped by the back of our car and we rolled down the window. "Good luck my friends!" he said with a big, innocent smile. Pat turned the key in the ignition, fired up the minivan, and just like that we were off. The car made a slow roll to the port of entry which was just a couple hundred feet away from where we were parked. Every revolution of the wheels caused another individual hair on the back of my neck to prickle up.

The sun was now above the horizon and it was easy to see the entire border crossing. Eight o'clock had finally arrived so the facility was up and running. This was when we caught our first glimpse of the Ukrainian border guards who were clad in a tan-like camouflage that covered their bodies head to toe. The only thing that stood out was the Ukrainian flag slapped onto their sleeves as the blue and gold popped off their uniforms.

We pulled up to the crossing and Pat threw the van into park. A group of the guards then came forward with automatic weapons strapped to their shoulders. I couldn't help but notice that while the crossing seemed to have a hum of activity, we were the only car there at the time. I didn't think anything of it, and chalked it up to us being the first in line on our way to Ukraine.

One of the guards approached the driver-side window. As Pat rolled it down, the soldier barked something in Ukrainian. Pat turned around and looked back at Aaron. I quickly realized that Aaron was the only one who knew Ukrainian—neither Pat nor Brian could speak the language, though they were both pretty fluent in English. Aaron explained that the guard wanted to see all of our passports. One by one we retrieved our booklets from underneath our heavy winter coats and gave them to Aaron. As it so happened, I was the only American in our group. Aaron, Pat and Brian were all Polish citizens and Bartley is originally from New Zealand.

Aaron handed the stack of booklets to the Ukrainian soldier. He took hold of them and began shuffling through them one by one until he stumbled upon one that was blue with gold print: mine. He opened mine first, took one glance at it, then looked at me and smiled.

"Ah, American! New York City, yes?"

"Yeah," I replied with a chuckle, thinking it was probably not in my best interest to try and explain where Cleveland, Ohio is on a map. The guard nodded his head smiling, then flipped through each of the other booklets. Seeming satisfied, he then said something to Aaron, who he now understood was the only Ukrainian speaker in our car. Apparently for good measure, he wanted to check the trunk of the van to see what all we had in the back. We all piled out of the car, strolled to the back and helped him prop up the liftgate.

You could hear the guard's throat drop into his stomach as he let out a kind of exclamation that I can only imagine would be roughly translated to "oh, geez."

The back of our van was now absolutely jam packed with suitcases, camera equipment, snack bars and other miscellaneous supplies. It looked like a jigsaw puzzle the way every odd shape fit in to form a wall. If you were looking for space to fit a pair of flip flops, I promise you we didn't have it. The guard was clearly petrified by the task that laid before him. He slowly approached the mountain of gear and put his hand on one suitcase. After giving a timid, brief tug he abruptly let go, evidently performing some internal analysis which suggested if he moved one item in this trunk, he'd be causing an avalanche.

He just stood there for another 10 or 15 seconds before muttering something in Ukrainian to Aaron, which must have been "you guys are fine." If we had a bomb, a dead man, and six kilos of cocaine hidden under that mountain of gear we would've been home free. With a look of defeat plastered on his face, the guard shut the trunk and sent us on our way. We climbed back into the van and continued on to the next station in the crossing which was all the way at the end of the compound. We could finally see Ukrainian soil and were no more than 100 feet from the exit.

That's when we saw a line of Ukrainians waiting patiently to get out of the country come into view. One by one they were queued up preparing to present their documents to the guards. I couldn't see the end of the line as it stretched around the bend. But what I could see clearly were their faces. Even from a distance, it was evident how worn out and exhausted these people were. Their eyes were cast downward at their feet with their shoulders hunched forward. One woman was clutching her son who was standing in front of her. She held him tightly and brushed his hair. A man held a small dog in his arms while petting its neck. Each person had the same, empty look in their eyes. It was as if their souls had left their bodies and all that was left was a freezing, tired shell void of consciousness.

As our car came to a halt, another guard came forward to collect our documents once more. This was the guy responsible for stamping our passports. He retreated into a small wooden shack the size of a toll booth.

Suddenly, we heard a commotion. People were screaming and shouting. The yells were coming from the direction of the line. We all sat in the car craning our heads urgently. Then, we saw it. A Ukrainian man, who must have been in his 40s with a thin beard, was trying to push through. The guards were holding him back. He kept screaming and fighting, though I couldn't possibly tell you what he said. Some of the women behind him in line had their hands clasped over their mouths, frightened by the outbreak of pandemonium. The man was caught in between two guards who weren't letting him through, despite his struggle.

That's when another guard stepped forward and smacked him right in the stomach with his clenched fist. A fourth guard rushed in from behind and leaped on top of the man's back. Like a camel being brought down the man slowly dropped to his knees, then the ground. Eventually, the man was lifted back to his feet after calming down and the guards led him away out of the port of entry. The soldier who was stamping our passports emerged from the shed and strolled up to the driver-side window of our car passports in hand. Before giving them to Pat, who was driving, the guard took a brief stare at the commotion. He then handed the documents over. A brief smile cracked across his face as he made a quick remark in Ukrainian to Aaron. Nodding his head, Aaron quipped a question back. The guard answered, slapped the side of our car and motioned us along.

As we pulled out, Aaron explained "the man's papers were no good so they wouldn't let him enter Poland. He tried to run." The guard's lack of expression said enough. This was a painfully ordinary occurrence. The new normal.

Picking up speed, our blue minivan barreled through the open gate onto a two-lane road. One lane was ours while the other was occupied by the line of people trying to escape the country. Nose to bumper in the lane opposite us as horns blared, the minivan hit the bend which is when it all became clear. Multiple people in the car even let out a gasp when they fully comprehended what they saw.

This line of cars stretched on for miles, well out of our line of vision. It was seemingly endless. What we were seeing looked like an apocalyptic world. Some Ukrainians were ditching their cars on the side of the road and walking the rest of the way. Others were running out of gas in line as they had been there for over twenty-four hours.

These Ukrainians would just abandon their cars, frantically gather the items they could carry, and hurry to the border. It became a wasteland of automobiles. Many clearly believed they were saying goodbye to their homeland forever, and a car was a small price to pay.

"This is unbelievable," Bartley exclaimed. On the other side of the cars, you could see mothers leading their children along as they trudged through the snow. A man had an older woman over his shoulder as he tried to push forward. People were doing anything and everything they could to get out of the country.

We continued on for several more miles. The line just kept going. We finally stopped off to get out and see it up close. The second we opened the door the rumble of old motors and people shouting filled our eardrums. A man rolled down his window and yelled something angrily at us. I had no idea what he was saying. Aaron threw up his arms and shouted back at him. The two went on for a few moments before the man waved his arms as if to say "enough."

"He says we are going the wrong way and should turn around," Aaron said.

Going the wrong way? What the hell is he talking about? And then, I made the single biggest mistake I had made the entire day: I turned around.

FIGURE 3.1 The line of cars carrying fleeing Ukrainians stretching over a dozen miles from the Polish border into war-torn Ukraine. Photo by Robert Sherman.

We were standing most of the way up a rolling hill so I could see a bit more into the distance toward the Polish–Ukrainian border. What I quickly realized is that there were thousands upon thousands of cars trying to get out of Ukraine. But we were the only, and I mean the *only* car, that decided to drive *into* the country.

We never passed a car heading the same direction as us in the port of entry. We never came across one on the road, and there wasn't a single one in sight.

That was the scariest part, and the doubt began to eat away at my mind. The people at the end of the line would wait days to get to Poland: the place we voluntarily left less than an hour prior. I couldn't help but think we had made a grave mistake coming here that day.

But there was only one direction we could go: forward.

* * *

The port of entry in the rearview mirror, we were now picking up speed rolling down the highway. Revolution by revolution, the blue minivan carried us deeper into war-torn Ukraine.

A low mist clung just above the tundra weaving its way in between hills and valleys. Every now and then you'd pass by a home. Some had boarded up windows and appeared to be empty, despite being fairly new homes that had been upkept. I can only assume some of the homeowners made the choice to skip town and bolt for the border. It's so eerie to see whole towns that you know *should* have people bustling about deathly quiet and seemingly devoid of life.

We stopped off at a gas station shortly after crossing the border. Before going deeper into Ukraine, there was a bit of an issue to deal with. One thing that a reporting team *must* have when entering a war zone is enough bulletproof vests for everyone. Even though we were in Western Ukraine where the on-the-ground fighting wasn't taking place, we still needed them.

It's like a life jacket in a boat. What are the odds you need them on the water that particular day? Low, but you have to be prepared. That's why it's the law.

This may come as a shock to you, but getting your hands on legitimate, combat-ready body armor is not easy. If only you could pick them up at a sporting goods store in whatever color you wanted. But alas, this required a bit more diligence and planning.

As it so happened, there were only four vests left in all of Europe. Just four. All in the Netherlands. We ordered them and luckily they arrived right before we rolled into Ukraine. These things showed up and I was taken aback by how massive they were. It feels like gravity is pulling you into mother earth and if you're not careful, you'll sink right into the soil. These were the highest grade vests, meaning they could stop a hefty bullet right in its tracks. They also came with helmets which, again, looked impressively fortified.

Bartley took one look at them, however, and threw up his arms in disbelief. "They're the wrong color!"

I thought he was joking. He most certainly was not. Bartley pulled over Brian who delivered the vests and pointed at the fabric. "These are camo. Journalists are to *never* wear camo. They're supposed to be blue."

Now I understood. If we were in the middle of the fray, the camouflage would make it appear we were soldiers—thus making us targets and not protected by the rules of engagement. In short, you're not supposed to shoot at journalists—though those rules aren't always followed.

A royal blue color is out of place on a battlefield giving off a more clear indication that the people wearing the vests are not service members. Again, I'm thankful Bartley was there because this is a detail I would have never considered.

Bartley was visibly furious with Brian, who put his hands up and said, "Okay, okay, relax, I'll fix it." Brian ran off to the gas station and returned with a can of blue spray paint and began painting the vests. *Unreal. This is what we're doing?* Bartley and I just gave each other a look of disbelief.

Give Brian credit, though: the vests turned out all right. They were definitely blue, not camo, and didn't look half bad. Not aesthetically perfect, but they would get the job done.

I guess we're finally ready to go, I thought. We got back in our car and started driving. After not seeing a car traveling in our direction for dozens of miles, we finally caught some traffic on the highway. I lifted my head above Brian's seat in front of me to try and see what was going on. Off in the distance maybe fifteen cars ahead you could see a few men walking around in orange and neon yellow vests.

Amid my American naivete, I assumed at the time there was construction going on. Not quite.

A general rule of thumb when in warzones: in many cases, normalcy is nonexistent and things are rarely what they seem. What my myopic eyes assumed were shovels and jackhammers clearly became rifles as our car approached. We had reached the first of many checkpoints we would encounter.

This was a four-way intersection and just like a Police officer would direct traffic after a sporting event, they were waving through one car at a time.

But it wasn't that simple. Once your car pulled up, the checkpoint guards would demand to see your passport and credentials and ask where you were going. Sometimes the questioning was forceful, other times it was fairly pleasant.

I would strongly advise against practicing your "unlawful search" legal argument in these situations, however, as there was no nonsense less than a week into the war. In cases like these, you were a threat unless proven otherwise.

It's important to note that the people manning these checkpoints were usually *not* soldiers with the Ukrainian military. In fact we found in many cases, they were just local militias or even everyday citizens of their respective towns. One guard we came across wore a long black jacket, black bowling cap and carried a long rifle. He looked as though he was easily seventy years of age, maybe older.

In the distance we could see one car pull up to a guard. A man in his 40's clad in a reflector vest leaned into the driver-side window. Something was clearly wrong because he started shouting at the driver, banging the side of the car. Finally, the driver produced a set of documents. The guard gave it a quick skim, tossed it back into the car, and waved them on through. As I said, absolutely no nonsense.

"This is where tensions sometime flare," warned Bartley, who I had to keep remembering had seen all of this before in dozens of countries including the Middle East and Balkans.

"Why do they even have these checkpoints?" I quietly asked, unable to take my eyes off the men combing through cars ahead.

"They're looking for Russian spies and saboteurs," Bartley replied looking straight ahead without making eye contact.

I'm thankful he wasn't looking because I'm ashamed to admit I cracked a bit of a smile. It seemed cool. Like straight out of a James Bond film. *How wild would it be to see them yank a spy right out of one of these cars?* I thought to myself. Remember this moment for later on.

Finally, our car rolled up to the front of the checkpoint and came to a halt. A tall and heavy set man wearing a green hunting jacket and an orange vest approached our car and asked to see our identification. Aaron told him in Ukrainian we were on our way to Ivano-Frankivsk. The man looked at our passports one by one the motioned over another man to take a look at something. He was holding open one of the passport booklets and I could see that it was mine.

"American?" the second guard said, peering in the back of our car. I was sitting in the back seat on the passenger side, giving a sheepish wave. The man then asked Aaron a question in Ukrainian, to which Aaron tried to explain something earnestly and honestly. It almost seemed like he was getting anxious. The guards then held out his hand and wiggled his fingers, as if motioning for us to provide him something else. "He wants to see our Press credentials," Aaron explained.

I started to understand. Journalists often times come under added scrutiny in situations like this as they want to make sure we are who we say we are. After all, it wouldn't be the first time a saboteur pretended to be a reporter to sneak through enemy territory.

"Standby," said Bartley. He pulled out a stack of documents that he had been holding onto and handed them off to the soldier. The guards glanced at our credentials and gave a quick nod, seeming to be satisfied. They handed them back to us then sent us along.

We would have to get used to this because every 20 miles or so we would come upon another checkpoint and go through the same ritual over and over again. Most of these interactions were straight forward and smooth. Other times, a guard would badger us a bit more than usual for our foreign passports. It is what it is. We made it through the checkpoint and were back on the road again. Aaron had set up arrangements for us to stay in "housing" that his father owned and managed in Ivano-Frankivsk. It was a nice gesture.

We got off the highway and pulled off into the driveway. The second we laid eyes on this place everyone was letting out an internal, "oh boy, here we go." If I said to you "think of a Soviet-era dormitory," the first image that pops into your head would be pretty close. This complex was setup with two buildings on either side. In the middle was a rusty old playground with overgrown grass. If your kid played on this thing they'd likely need a tetanus shot.

The road leading up to it hadn't been maintained in years. It looked like a gravel driveway, but it wasn't. It was battered, cracked, broken down asphalt that crumpled under the weight of our tires. The two buildings were old, gray, and boxy—as if the architect had the life sucked out of him before beginning construction. Some windows had bars over their frame. Others were broken and were covered by cardboard. The rusty roof steeply slanted down in a way we could see all the missing plates up top.

We hopped out of the minivan and everyone had the exact same anxious stare on their faces as they glanced around the complex. The front door to one of the dorms swung open and a big man wearing a leather cap came out. He said something in Ukrainian and held his arms out wide with a big smile to welcome us. It was Aaron's dad. Aaron walked right up to him and embraced him. His father then shook our hands, keeping that big smile plastered across his face. He then led us inside to show us around. We stepped through the rickety door frame, careful not to skim the edges for fear of accidentally cutting our hands on some loose metal. We were standing in the front foyer which I can only describe using the word "damp." It just felt murky. A slight hint of mold could be smelled. The building clearly hadn't been fixed up in decades.

Aaron's father led us through the lobby area into a narrow hallway which had tattered floors and some exposed ceiling. It was so hard to see anything inside as there was no natural light entering and the halls had not been outfitted with much any lighting hardware. We were shown to our room which must have been 8 feet by 8 feet with three beds jammed inside of it. Those would be ours. Next up was the bathroom which was par for the course: missing tiles on the floors, shattered mirrors, and of course three showerheads in the open without doors or dividers privacy.

"We're all about to get *real* comfortable with one another," Bartley said in a sarcastic tone. This was a less than ideal spot but frankly, it's all that was available. Most hotels were shut down and the ones that were open had no vacancy. Despite a little bit of initial shock factor, I was fully prepared to stay there. Then, right on cue, Aaron swung the door open and came back into the room. "Guys, I found something better." He had been working behind the scenes to rent a vacant apartment for a couple of days. Apparently it had hot water, a kitchen, and plenty of space for everyone.

It didn't look like they would have availability, but in the eleventh hour, he secured it.

"Brilliant," said Bartley. We hadn't even unpacked the car so were ready to head out no more than twenty minutes after arriving.

To my surprise, Aaron's father did not even bat an eye. He seemed to clearly understand our reservations and only offered his dorms up in case we couldn't find anything else. Before leaving, I looked back at these dormitories. It hit me that this is how a lot of people lived in Ukraine, before the war even broke out. I thought of all the amenities we take for granted in the United States.

Aaron's father was a good man. I would later learn that the dormitories were a bit of a passion project for him as he wanted to give housing to the poor and in need. With the millions ultimately displaced by the war, he ended up offering shelter to dozens of refugees with nowhere to go.

I felt guilty we found other housing for this reason. We could afford it. We had the money. But millions of Ukrainians had absolutely nothing.

Our team hopped into the blue minivan, ready to head off to our accommodations. Pat got into the driver's seat, started the engine, shifted into reverse then *WHAM*. He slammed the thing right into a tree.

"Dude! Are you kidding me, Pat?!" shouted Bartley.

"Sorry," Pat replied, ears drooping like a disobedient puppy.

We got out to inspect the damage. The right taillight was smashed and a dent was punched into the bumper. The tree Pat backed the car into was a towering oak that must have had a trunk diameter of three feet.

Put simply, it was a big tree. Granted, the back of the minivan was jammed full of gear so the rearview mirror was worthless. But even so, I don't know how this guy could have possibly missed seeing a tree this big. Little did we know that busted taillight would get us into a lot of problems down the road.

"I'm not paying for that, you are," Bartley said, scolding Pat.

"Ok ok, that's fine," Pat replied defensively, putting up his arms.

We got back into the car and drove into downtown Ivano-Frankivsk, which was very beautiful to see. An old-fashioned European city where not a single building was over ten stories tall. You could feel the rumble underneath us as the road turned from pavement to cobblestone. At the heart of the city was a tower where the Ukrainian flag proudly waved over it. We pulled down a back alley into a secluded apartment complex that overlooked the city. Night was beginning to fall, and we had to file reports in the next few hours, so time was working against us.

What made things more difficult is that in an hour, a curfew would go into effect. Nobody except the authorities were allowed on the streets and lights were expected to be out. The reason we were given is that light would give enemy aircraft a target to drop their bombs. That was incentive enough for us to comply.

We climbed the stone staircases into this apartment complex that reminded me of a California stucco-style home. We reached the second floor and opened the dark wooden door. It had a den, a living room, a kitchen, and two beds. Plenty of space for everyone. Aaron, Pat and Brian had their own room downstairs.

"Fine," said Bartley in a chipper tone. My sentiments exactly. It was by no means the Ritz, but compared to the dorms it may as well have been the French Riviera. Sometimes, just the necessities will do.

Showtime was coming up so we would have to do our live reports from inside the apartment. We closed the blinds and set up the tripod in the living room—making sure no light could escape for fear the Police would come.

I was standing there in my socks holding the microphone and reporting on what we had seen that day—telling the stories of our time crossing the border, going through the checkpoints. My goal was to give the viewers a sense of what the feeling was like on the ground here. It didn't dawn on me at the time but that report from inside that apartment without shoes on was my first from a war zone. Not exactly how I envisioned it, but it is what it is.

After we wrapped for the night, Bartley ordered us all to bed immediately as we would try and get going early the next day. I climbed into my cot and put my head on the pillow.

Before falling asleep, I checked my work emails one more time. I skimmed through the list of notes that had been sent back by producers in Chicago on what were the latest developments in the war. My eyes locked on one email that had a subject line saying "Congrats" and clicked on it. The email was from a woman

FIGURE 3.2 Our reporting location in Ivano-Frankivsk that first night in Ukraine had to take place inside our apartment unit due to a strict curfew imposed by the local government. Photo by Bartley Price.

on our assignment desk. It was a short note which read, "Congratulations. You're officially a war correspondent."

I flicked my phone off upon reading that. *No I'm not,* I thought to myself. I've been here all of one day. *I'm certainly no Richard Engel or Clarissa Ward.* Even so, I finally closed my eyes as I lay back. My mind was still racing from everything that had happened that day. But what mattered most to me was that I hadn't royally screwed anything up. We got into Ukraine, made it to Ivano-Frankivsk, and I [so far] had not said anything stupid in any of my reports.

Maybe I'm starting to get the hang of this already? I thought to myself.

If reality were a person, they would have laughed. *You wish, young man.*

4 GOOD MORNING, UKRAINE

Complete silence.

That's my choice for the two most beautiful words in the English language. The way the consonants effortlessly collide and the syllables seamlessly slither from one to the next.

The meaning of those two words is worthy of admiration. I've found this degree of silence is a rarity. Noise always finds a way to survive, so it seems.

I'm probably alone in this thought, however. Henry James once famously gave the title to "summer afternoon." Believe me when I say *no one* wants to talk about a summer afternoon amid an Eastern European winter.

I will say this: the scientists are on to something when they recommend sleeping in the cold for an optimal slumber. Combine that with a tinge of exhaust, and you have the perfect potion for a REM cycle circus.

As my eyes slowly forced their way open, I could hardly remember where I was. In that moment, I was lost in the silence. Engulfed in the darkness brought on by the blinds. A sliver of sunlight was attempting to sneak its way through a crease in the curtains over in the corner, but that was all.

I sat up in bed as the life slowly returned to my body. It was our first morning in Ivano-Frankivsk—a city I hadn't even heard of days before. It finally started to hit me that we were in Ukraine. Such an effort had been made in the previous few days to get to this place. Flying out of Texas, driving across Poland, navigating the Ukrainian checkpoints. Now, we were finally here.

Up to that point, it did not feel like we were in some exotic, foreign land. People would hear the word "Ukraine" and associate the dangers with being there as similar to that of an American in Iran. Not even close. Despite building it up in my mind that this would be an incessantly scary, dangerous situation, so far it felt more like a European extravaganza. I'd soon learn to not get too comfortable.

My eyes were finally starting to de-blur as my body came back to life. Swinging my legs to the side of the bed, I let my bare feet touch the tile floors. A burning sensation of bitter cold ran up my legs and to my spine before tingling the hairs atop my head. Upon composing myself, I stood up and walked toward the blinded window. I quickly peered over at Bartley, who was asleep on the other side of the room. Still out cold. He deserved every bit of sleep.

A question I always get asked is "What does your producer do?" It's hard to accurately articulate their value and effort, but here's my best attempt: everything behind the scenes with the exception of writing (though some lazy reporters *will* make their producers write) and reporting on-air.

Bartley was an expert at nailing down logistics and making things happen. Concerns that I would have never even thought of were addressed before I even needed to weigh in. He anticipated trouble ahead of time and found ways to navigate around it. If I didn't have him, I would have been up a river without a paddle.

I turned my attention forward again toward the window. Gripping the edge of the curtain, I allowed my fingers to come within a few inches of the glass—feeling the chill emanating from outside. Peering through the opening, I saw Ivano-Frankivsk in all its morning glory, a pretty European city with its cobblestone roads and scenic fountains (albeit, shut off during the winter cold months). Gray clouds blanketed the sky, which hardly gave the sun a fighting chance.

Even so, there was just enough light that I could make out a few Ukrainians milling about, making their runs to the grocery store, and walking their dogs. One little girl carrying a pink backpack appeared to be on her way to school. It sure didn't look like a war zone.

At that point, it didn't really matter. With the windows shutting us off from the outside world, I closed my eyes and relished what we had in that moment: *complete silence.*

But just like that, it was gone.

FIGURE 4.1 The view of Ivano-Frankivsk, Ukraine, from our apartment rental on our first morning. Photo by Robert Sherman.

Knock. Knock. Knock.

Jarring. Forceful. Neither bashful nor timid in the slightest. Knuckles hammering into the wooden door of our unit.

That got Bartley up in a hurry. We both threw on sweatshirts and waddled over to the door, trying to minimize our impact on the freezing floors.

I assumed it was Pat, Brian, and Aaron coming to have a morning meeting about security or make meal plans. There wasn't a meal Pat was going to miss, and Brian, while annoying at times, was highly intent on maximizing security and minimizing risk at all waking hours.

Thinking it was nobody important, I didn't even bother to throw shoes on. I just had socks, pajamas, and a sweatshirt covering me. Bartley reached the door first and grabbed the deadbolt, sliding it to the unlocked position. Then, he took hold of the handle and gave it a slow turn as he pulled the door inward slightly.

The door hadn't even opened six inches when a shoulder slid its way through the doorway. The trunk of the figure forced the door all the way open. The details came slow at the time as I was still in a lull from just waking up.

First, I noticed the man's face. I did not recognize him. He was young. Mid 20s with dirty blonde hair. Blue eyes. Next, I noticed his shirt. It was beige in color and matched his pants and boots. *How odd,* I thought to myself. Lastly, I noticed the rifle in his hand. He held it low, pointed at the ground, but wielded it firmly as if he were able to clear paths with it. I wasn't scared in that moment. Frankly, I was just confused as to what was happening, too tired to fully comprehend.

I started to put all the pieces of information together, then took a look at the broad picture: a Ukrainian soldier had entered our apartment unit. He wasn't alone. Two more were right behind him and followed his lead in. One pointed his gun behind the door to see if there were any surprises. Another made a beeline right for the bedroom and began squatting down to check underneath the mattresses.

I heard the meek voice of Aaron from the hallway outside the unit. "Uh, Bartley, these men want to talk to you," he said, lacking conviction. *Some help you were, Aaron* I thought.

The three soldiers started making the rounds in the unit, checking cupboards and drawers. The refrigerator for good measure. Closets. One stayed close to us, keeping Bartley and me in his line of vision.

The soldiers seemed satisfied that there wasn't anybody else unaccounted for. It was the truth, after all. Then the lead soldier, who was near us, pointed straight down at the floor. We interpreted that as "stay here."

He walked outside the unit, returning moments later with Aaron, Pat, and Brian in tow. There was also one other Ukrainian security guard at the time assigned to us, but I never knew his name. He didn't speak English.

With all six of us in that apartment unit together, the soldier started pointing from one person to the next, barking something in Ukrainian. Everybody filed in shoulder to shoulder like a hockey line, staring straight ahead. I followed suit.

The lead solder said something else softly but firmly in Ukrainian to the whole group. Aaron looked over at Bartley and me, then spoke up. "He wants to see your documents."

Fair enough. I thought. I motioned over to my bag, trying to tell him that's where my passport was. The soldier seemed to understand and nodded, but watched intently as I retrieved my passport wallet from my backpack and returned to the lineup.

Just a simple misunderstanding, they'll be gone soon, I thought. One soldier stood at the door, rifle in hand with a scanning stare sprayed across his face. A second soldier was at the far side of the lineup. The leader of the group, seeing everyone had assumed their positions, began at the far end of the line and grabbed Brian's passport. I was the last one in the row all the way on the near side.

It seemed pretty routine. The soldier glanced at the passport, looked Brian up and down, muttered a couple of quick questions, and then it was on to the next person. Apparently, he spoke Polish well enough as well. One by one, he went down the line.

Then, the soldier came to me. He took the passport from my hand and opened it to the main page with my photo and information. This time, he scanned the document intently. Without moving his head, he rolled his eyes up and stared directly into my soul.

"CIA, huh?" He said tersely.

The whole room was stone silent.

What? Caught off guard was an understatement. *CIA? What is he talking about?*

I did the only thing a nervous person could do in that situation. I smiled. Gave a chuckle. My eyes darted toward my colleagues who gave a slight laugh as well—nervously—before I shifted my gaze back to the soldier.

I was hoping to see him smiling. He was *not*. Just holding a death stare, refusing to break his gaze.

"CIA." This time he said it authoritatively, stabbing his gloved finger into my passport. It wasn't a question. More like a statement. As if he'd cracked the case. I stood there, mouth slightly open. Words couldn't come to me. I was petrified.

Then I understood. *He thinks I work for the CIA. He thinks I'm a spy. What an utterly ridiculous accusation,* I thought to myself. I wasn't exactly built like Daniel Craig so I'm not sure how I got lumped in with those who have a career in espionage.

I thought back to the previous day about the checkpoints. How cool spy-hunting seemed at the time. Now, not so much. More on the side of terrifying.

I felt the muscles in my upper back tighten. I wanted to speak. I so badly wanted to tell these soldiers they had it all wrong and that I was just a journalist working in Ukraine. I opened my mouth but no words could croak out. The air rushed out of my lungs and nothing came back in. All that I could do was stare into this soldier's eyes as his gaze drilled through me. Every muscle in my body was locked into place.

The exchange lasted moments, but it felt like hours. My mind flooded with every horrific scenario I could think of.

I'm going to prison. This is it. I'll never see my family again. Am I going to be a prisoner of war? Will they torture me? Surely the State Department will sort this out. But will they? Will anyone care about me? Will President Biden have to get involved? I didn't do anything wrong! How do I convince them I'm innocent? I don't know anything. Will they think I'm lying? Surely they'll think I'm a liar. They already think I'm a spy.

I met the soldier's stare again, hoping he would take pity on me. Here I am, just 25-years-old. How did I get in this situation? A journalist in his first war zone biting off more than he could chew.

Then, the soldier raised his gloved right hand to which I thought for a moment he was going to smack me across the face. Instead, he brought it down and slapped me on the shoulder. I was caught off guard again and jolted. He smiled and started cracking up. "I'm just messing with you," he said with a beaming grin in perfect English. Everyone now started laughing. Even my own teammates, who moments ago had looks on their faces of genuine worry, were now belly laughing. Everyone was howling. Except me, of course. I couldn't see my reflection, but my face must have been as bright red as a tomato I was so embarrassed.

"Ok," I said with a nervous wheeze. I tried to fake a smile but they knew they got me good. The air finally returned to my lungs in relief. The soldier closed my passport and slapped it back into my hand, then chirped something to Aaron in Ukrainian which I took to mean, "you're free to go."

All three of the soldiers were chuckling and shaking their heads. My own insecurities kicked in. *They must think I'm so stupid,* I thought to myself. The three walked straight for the door, gave a quick wave, then shut it behind them. Just like that, they were gone. Out the door as quickly as they burst in.

Bartley came up and gave me a slight pat on the back as if to say "take it easy, kid." He had a big smile on his face, still unable to get over my utter humiliation. "That was not funny," I muttered to myself. Who am I kidding? It was hilarious. At least, as I write this now, it most certainly is. Looking back on it, I'm in disbelief those soldiers were able to maintain such a sense of humor given the uncertainty in their country and the threats they were facing.

I walked back over to my bed and sat back down. Still wearing my pajamas and sweatshirt, I just kept staring at the floor by myself. Brian, Aaron, and Pat went back to their rooms. Bartley had already put the whole situation behind him and had cracked open his laptop to get started on the day. Finally, I let it go. "I guess it *was* kind of funny," I said to myself with a smirk tucked under my chin.

Oh, well. Who says you can't have a little innocent fun in a war zone? Especially at the American's expense.

I guess it is true: all is fair in love and war.

5 NOT EXACTLY THE BLUE ANGELS

I grew up on the west side of Cleveland, Ohio. My neighborhood had that quintessential Midwestern suburban feel. Daybreak was met with the smell of green grass caked in dew, while the sounds of lawnmowers and leaf blowers rumbled around nearby yards. I loved my Cleveland upbringing and I cherish the memories made in that city.

The outsiders can call it "the mistake by the lake" all they want. They may even toss in a playful jab about the Cuyahoga River catching on fire. It doesn't matter to me. Cleveland's home. And it always will be.

One of my favorite memories is the air show, which would come to town once a year. I think my dad only bought tickets and took me to the actual event once, but he really didn't need to. The planes would thunder over Lake Erie, which was right across the street from us, and zoom by our home. Sometimes the windows would rattle as those jet engines roared.

That's where I developed my initial love of aviation, which I still have to this day. First, it would be the Second World War era fighters that would pass by—their green paint and lone white star glistening amid the blue Ohio skies.

Then would come the stealth bombers and the modern fighter jets, which would show just how much the world of war has changed. That's when I first learned about the speed of sound. It amazed me that as those jets approached, they were silent. But once they passed by you, the blast of their jets could finally be heard. The science of acoustics left me in awe.

The marquee event, however, was always the Blue Angels. Oh, how those blue and gold birds of prey would take flight and hold formation overhead, then break off performing tricks of all kinds. My dad and I would lay out in our backyard watching them spin, dive, and leave patterns in the sky with their contrails. It was mesmerizing for a six-year-old boy to see firsthand.

And yes, I won't leave out the Thunderbirds. What powerful machines they were as well. The air show would alternate each year—one year, the Blue Angels would be the headline. The next it would be the Thunderbirds. No disrespect to the latter, but the Blue Angels were the act that got me excited every time.

We always carry pieces of our childhood through life. It's inevitable, however, that our bubble of innocence gets popped.

With the dust settling from the visit made by the Ukrainian soldiers, the team was getting ready to roll out from our apartment in Ivano-Frankivsk. The game plan was to make our way into the city and meet the people of Ukraine firsthand.

Who was still in Ukraine? How were the people coping with the war? What were the everyday people doing amid the fighting? Very rudimentary story content, but considering the invasion began less than a week ago, it was still important to take the pulse.

Everything was a bit of a learning curve for me. I didn't even know what to bring aside from the heaviest coat I owned, which was a black puffer jacket I had picked up before the trip. *Passport? Check. Laptop? Check.* I sat there on the bed perplexed, staring into my mostly empty backpack. It sounds silly, but I was still a little rattled by the Ukrainian soldiers. I shouldn't have been. It wasn't a big deal—in fact I'm sure every battle-hardened war correspondent would tell you that interaction should have been the *least* of my concerns.

The best career advice anybody gives you in this business is when you're a young reporter, you have to do everything with confidence. Never been in a hurricane before? Act like you know what you're doing. Never covered a presidential campaign before? Carry yourself like it's your one-millionth. If the audience or a fellow journalist senses the slightest bit of uncertainty in your voice, forget it. Your credibility is shot.

FIGURE 5.1 A live report from downtown Ivano-Frankivsk, Ukraine. Photo by Bartley Price.

I'm not a fan of the phrase "fake it until you make it" because I don't think journalists should "fake" anything, but the spirit of that sentence stands: go forth with confidence and poise in everything you do. Like many twenty-somethings, I was much better at giving advice than taking it. These words of wisdom escaped me in the moment. We were a long way from Northeast Ohio, that was for sure, and everything around us was new and foreign.

Bartley sat across the room on his own bed, filling his bag with parcel after parcel. He'd done all this before and had a meticulous system in place. I needed to act like I had as well. Part of that is just a safety concern. There's enough that can go wrong in a war zone that you can't afford to not have your own house in order. Imagine your own carelessness or lack of experience causing someone to get hurt? Beyond unacceptable.

There were moments when I wanted to ask Bartley what to do or which items to bring but kept them to myself. Such simple questions would have slowed him down. Another piece of advice I was given at an early age? "Just figure it out." Put those critical thinking skills to the test and piece the answer together yourself. The world won't always hand you a blueprint.

I sat back up and stared blankly out the window. Snow had started to fall. None was sticking to the ground but flurries fluttered to the ground intermittently. It was rather beautiful. Those moments sound little, but they really stay with you. It's as if mother nature is trying to inject some sense of normalcy into the situation. Looking upon the cobblestone roads, you'd never know the people walking outside were living through the most terrifying ordeal of their lives.

The beauty of snowfall in an old Eastern European city amplifies that conundrum. How could war ever come to a scene so serene? Even more, how could mankind knowingly bring it here? Thoughts like those infiltrated my mind daily. The snap back to reality was instant. A soft but shrill sound started to come from outside. It grew louder and louder. It took a moment for it to all register, but after realizing what it was, I went stiff.

Sirens were blaring across Ivano-Frankivsk.

I remember being in the middle of a tornado in Vance, Alabama when the sirens blared and hundreds of people flocked from their nearby homes to the storm shelter—packing the space built for a few dozen people. I can vividly recall seeing the terror on those people's faces. Some dearly clutched their family pets as if it would be their last embrace. Others clenched their hands in prayer so tightly their white knuckles looked like they were about to burst.

That sound, if you're lucky enough to have never heard it, will bring overwhelming fear to the strongest-willed of people. It pierces the air, unabashedly penetrates your eardrums and rattles around inside your skull.

Of course, that's in the context of a tornado. This had the makings of an air raid.

I stood up immediately, but my feet couldn't move. They may as well have been cemented to the floor as I was petrified in place. I could see people outside hustling to get off the streets, but I was frozen in place. Bartley's instincts took over. He stood up immediately. "Get down!" he shouted, making a dive for the door to get into the adjacent hallway and away from the windows. My instincts, on the other hand, were lethargic at best. I just stood there. Bartley's order might as well have been shouted in Mandarin as his words simply didn't resonate.

Even worse, my naïve curiosity got the best of me. I leaned over toward the window, craning my head toward the sky to see what was happening. Even the most foolish of people know this is exactly what you should *not* be doing in this situation. I could hear a hushed rumble. Like thunder after lighting many miles away. It grew louder and louder. There they were. A few black specs bounding out of the sun which grew larger and larger by the moment. It was a wing of fighters rushing right toward us.

"Get down!" Bartley shouted again. I, to this day, don't know why I couldn't heed his command. My eyes were glued to the sky.

The fighters were now right in front of us in all of their glory. No green paint or white stars. No blue bodies with gold trim. They were a dull grey.

The thunder grew a bit louder, yet still muted by the distance. Then the planes passed right by us overhead. A deafening lion roar blew me back as the jet engines finally were on top of us. The windows shook and the floors vibrated as if Earth was shifting underneath us. It was just like my first time seeing modern jets at the Cleveland air show. That delayed howl as the speed of light bested the speed of sound in an all-out sprint. The only difference? This wasn't an air show. It was the real deal.

But just like that, the fighters were gone. Here and there, in and out in an instant. If you blinked you would have missed seeing them. The rumbling stopped. The ferocious growl of the jets simmered in the distance.

They were Ukrainian jets, not Russian. There were no missiles, no payload, no explosions. Just the unmistakable rumble of their engines.

My mind stopped racing and my senses returned. I hustled over to Bartley who was outside the door in the hallway. He was sitting on the floor, back against the wall. I pressed my shoulders against the plaster opposite him and slid down to the ground. Bartley shook his head and gave me an incredulous look. The same look a mother gives her son after he does something so outlandishly stupid that the English language won't suffice for reprimand.

"What the Hell was that, Sherman?" he finally said, almost laughing as if he couldn't believe how dumb or deaf I was. I didn't say anything back, as I hoped my somber body language would communicate it. *I know, I know. I'm an idiot.*

We sat there quietly for what must have been ten minutes. Not a single word was exchanged. The sirens continued blaring outside. I can still hear them to this day. Once they penetrate your ear drums, your mind will never be able to shake them.

Suddenly, the sirens shut off. Everything was still. Absolutely still. Quiet had returned to Western Ukraine. One thing I learned about sirens that day is they blare whenever there is a threat in the area. The exact target could be where you're standing or 50 miles away, but in the moment it is impossible to know precisely, so everyone has to take cover. Either way, it's enough to put chills into your bloodstream.

Bartley lifted himself up off the floor, which I took as my cue to do the same. As I tried to re-enter our room, he stood in the doorway to confront me.

"When I say get down, you get down," he said firmly. His eyes drilling into mine. "Got it?"

"Yes sir," I replied meekly. He was right and I knew it. On this day, we were lucky the jets overhead were Ukrainian. Tomorrow, they could be Russian and a fly-by would be the least of our worries. I tell everyone back home those first days in Ukraine were such a learning curve. Every instinct and semblance of curiosity had to be quashed. As you can tell, I wasn't doing a very good job of that so far. But here, you saw the consummate example between a veteran war producer and a 25-year-old kid. The veteran hears jets overhead, and thinks "take cover." I hear jets overhead and think "oh, boy! Planes!"

Deep down, I knew I needed to be better. Making a mistake like that again in a situation that wasn't a drill could have put Bartley in danger. He never said that. But I got the message from him. *Get your head in the game,* I internally scolded myself.

"All right. I'll be back in three and a half minutes," Bartley said in a chipper tone, having delivered his teaching moment. This was his way of telling me he was going to have a cigarette.

"Sounds good," I replied. Stepping back into the bedroom I tiptoed back over to the window.

There I stood, watching the world come back to life. The sirens had melted away moments earlier, but I could hardly notice. They would become part of the day-to-day norm in Ukraine. The people clearly felt the same way. Some residents had already returned to the streets. It was incredible. Business as usual. Almost like these same people weren't fearing hellfire was about to rain down fifteen minutes prior.

My eyes turned back to the skies. Flurries of snow were still coming down. It looked like a crisp, January afternoon in Cleveland.

But one thing was for certain: the Blue Angels were most definitely not in town that day.

6 THE PEOPLE

The eyes of the world were on Kyiv, Kharkiv, and Mariupol as Russia continued to grind out its assault on Ukraine. Nobody was talking about Ivano-Frankivsk, and I'm not certain I saw another American journalist while I was there.

We had the whole city to ourselves, and the decision to be here was Bartley's alone. Be it wartime or peace-time, Ivano-Frankivsk is not a place in Ukraine that garners much attention. We took a short drive to the downtown area and found ourselves in the central forum of the city.

In the middle of the square was a beautiful tower with the blue and yellow Ukrainian flag proudly flying in the wind. Coffee shops and restaurants lined the exterior of the forum, which, surprisingly, bustled with life.

Some Ukrainians were sitting at tables inside, reading newspapers, others were enjoying friendly conversations with old pals. Teenagers strolled by with their backpacks stuffed full of notebooks, chattering and laughing about some inside joke they all shared. It all seemed shockingly normal.

There's no shortage of history in these cities. The average American is likely unaware of the fact that cities like Kyiv, for example, are well over a thousand years old. Ivano-Frankivsk's timeline does not go back that far, but it still has a recognized birthdate of 1662, meaning it predates American Independence.[1] The stone roadways, churches, and gold decorations adorning some of these Ukrainian buildings really put you in a different world.

But the fact that remained hardest for me to grasp is that we were standing in such a historic place that only gained its independence in 1991. The United States' short existence is defined by casting aside British rule to gain its sovereignty, but Ukraine's much longer history has mostly consisted of being part of another nation's empire. I used to have an instructor in high school who would say, "There's not always a winner in war, but there is most certainly always a loser." How true.

All that to say there are plenty of people in Ukraine who distinctly recall the Soviet days and have since spent decades living in an independent state. It's a unique position to be in. The reason I was most excited to be in Ivano-Frankivsk is because nobody around the world had heard the perspectives of the people here. They had heard from the pundits, the so-called "experts," the people in Kyiv. But nobody had heard from any of these everyday folks about the war effort, the toll on civilians, what they made of the politics behind it, and the like. So, we wanted to change that. In television, this is called the infamous "man on the street interview," where you ask questions to the people who pass you by. You never know what you're going to get.

Aaron flagged someone down. A man in his 30s with a dark beard and a slender build. He was dressed in all black with a heavy wool coat shielding him from the cold. Aaron fired off a couple of quick questions to see if he'd be interested in talking to us. I then saw Aaron's face turn into a big smile when the man answered. "This man has a Phd. And is very well informed on the war," Aaron said excitedly, as if he had just struck gold on his first swing.

"Perfect," I replied. The man extended a leather-gloved hand, which I eagerly shook as Bartley set up the camera. Bartley gave a nod as if to say he was ready.

I asked the man how the war was impacting him and what it was like living in Ukraine amid this conflict. Aaron translated the question into Ukrainian. The man leaned back, giving a "where do I even begin" kind of gesture, and started speaking passionately, using emphatic hand gestures and allowing his body to flail loosely. He spoke for what seemed like a whole minute.

I turned to Aaron for the translation. His face wasn't so gleeful anymore. Instead, he became reserved. Almost nervous. "He said, 'the war makes me angry, and I hope to enlist so I can kill as many of those Russian f**gots as possible,'" Aaron croaked out. "All I want to do is kill Russians and send those gay boys home."

I sat there stunned. *This will never make it on television,* I thought to myself. Bartley said the quiet part out loud. "Tell him to stop f**king swearing!" he snapped at Aaron. The irony of that order was as thick as molasses.

FIGURE 6.1 Flakes of snow falling to the ground in the center of Ivano-Frankivsk. Photo by Robert Sherman.

Aaron nodded his head in agreement and then turned back to the man, explaining what Bartley had said. The man looked at us, shrugged his shoulders, and walked away. So much for that. Our first interview on the ground in Ukraine and there was absolutely nothing usable in it. It did articulate a feeling people had there, which was anger at the situation and at Russia. We just needed our next interviewee to be a bit more tactful in their language.

On to the next one, I guess. Aaron flagged down another man who appeared to be a bit older, maybe in his late 30s or early 40s. Thick dark beard, olive green beanie cap, and winter jacket.

Aaron appeared to be a little shell-shocked after the last guy, so he came into this conversation more cautiously. He exchanged remarks with our second interviewee, then told us, "This man used to live in Russia. He has a lot to say about Russian President Vladimir Putin." Good to go. We'll call him Gary. He said he was from a southern part of Russia and asked to first say what he had to say in Russian, then translate.

Gary just started talking, hardly taking a breath. His hand gestures were measured. Despite the fact I had no idea what he was saying, I could tell he was picking his words carefully as if this was his chance to say something he had spent a lot of time contemplating. His Russian monologue lasted nearly three whole minutes. Then he stopped and Bartley cut in. "Okay, now you need to tell Robert what you said."

Gary smiled. "I said Russia has committed crimes around the world. Syria. Georgia. This time Ukraine." He continued on, "I want people to know what's happened here. Russia has attacked. This is not a war. Russia has attacked Ukraine. This is all Putin's ambition. He is a little crazy man."

Gary finished his statement and gave a nod, signaling he had said his peace. It was interesting to hear a Russian speak so candidly about his home country and Putin. The day before, I had watched clips online of Moscow citizens, when asked about the war, running from the camera fearing they would be prosecuted if they spoke out.

But Gary was no longer in Russia. He had called Ukraine home the last few years and finally felt free to express himself. I thanked him and shook his hand, then he departed.

During our interview, I couldn't help but notice an older gentleman idling nearby. He was watching us intently while smoking a cigarette. He wore a navy blue coat, had gray hair and a gray mustache. When he saw our interview with Gary wrap up, he approached Aaron—recognizing immediately that he was the Ukrainian speaker in the group.

He got close to Aaron and asked him a question. The two exchanged words, then the man came over to me. He cordially but firmly grabbed my arm and looked me in the eyes, saying something in Ukrainian with passionate emphasis. Then he turned and pointed at the top of the tower in the center of the square where the Ukrainian flag was flying.

He kept speaking, then prodded his bony finger into my sternum. He knew I hadn't a clue what he was saying, but I got the gist of it. Aaron then tepidly butted in and gave a rough translation. "This man says he was here the day the Soviet Union flag came down and the flag of Ukraine was raised for the first time."

I looked back up at the flag trying to picture what that day was like here. Independence achieved. Sovereignty secured. Aaron then wrapped up his statement. "He said Ukraine will never go back." I nodded at the man signaling I understood. He gave me a friendly pat on the back then left. Something I didn't even consider to that moment was the amount of national pride people had in Ukraine despite the country gaining its independence just a few decades prior. Or perhaps, that's exactly why people had so much of it.

We continued on with these man on the street interviews for the next hour and gleaned a bevy of perspectives. Largely, the Ukrainians we spoke with were united. One man told us he was strongly against the election of the President Volodymyr Zelenskyy but was unabashedly behind him now in the face of conflict. Another woman told us the war distressed her, but didn't want the Ukrainian military to stop fighting until all the occupied lands, including Crimea, were back under Ukraine's control.

Our work wasn't done as Aaron had planned to take us to a food pantry to meet volunteers sending supplies to the frontline. We pulled up to a church that was being used as a storage facility. Standing outside were five or six armed guards with full assault rifles. It looked like the entry way to a high security bank, but instead of precious jewels and gold bars inside it was canned goods.

We walked through the grouping of soldiers which parted at the entry way and allowed us inside. The warmth of the building pushing a numbness into our faces as the blood returned to circulation. The roof of the church was painted with beautiful murals as stained glass windows lined the edges. I could only glance at their splendor for a moment as the scene inside was filled with hurried activity.

The floor was quite literally a maze of boxes. Some piled ten feet high. There were paths carved out on the floor you could narrowly walk through. They led to the center of the church where the pews had been removed. On the floor was a smattering of all kinds of supplies. Canned goods. Boxed cereal. Candy bars. Toiletries. Diapers. All lumped in a large pile. A group of workers, mostly young women, was feverishly sifting through the pile. Taking each piece and jamming it into a brown cardboard box. One by one, the boxes would be sealed and added to the maze-like walls.

A man came forward and shook Aaron's hand. He was tall with a dark beard and gray beanie cap. Aaron smiled back, greeted him in Ukrainian while clasping his forearm. By the way he carried himself, I could tell he was in charge of the

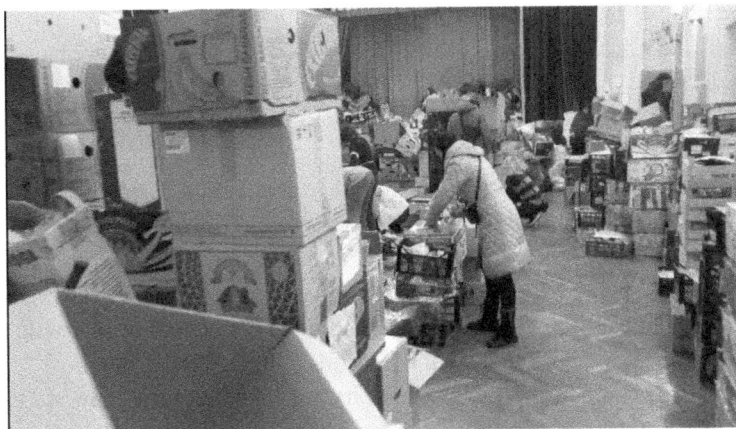

FIGURE 6.2 Volunteers working to pack food supplies that will be delivered to those in need living on the frontlines of the war with Russia. Photo by Robert Sherman.

operations. He turned to Aaron and started pointing around the room while speaking in Ukrainian.

"These are all Ukrainian volunteers trying to get supplies to the east," explained Aaron. At the time, some cities such as Mariupol were seeing their supply chains cut off, so this group was trying to find a way to get them food and other necessities.

We started walking around. It was difficult to hear anything as the sound of dozens of duct tape rolls squealing echoed throughout the chapel. One young woman, hunched over a box, looked up and smiled at us. Aaron crouched down next to her and asked her something in Ukrainian, which she answered in her native language.

"She says her heart breaks for her people, and she's doing anything she can to help. She is still in school," said Aaron. Just days into the war, there was truly an "all hands on deck" mindset. Those that could fight signed up or were drafted. Those that could not fight either fled or stayed behind to help. No job or task was too small.

We kept walking around when one woman caught my eye. She was older, probably in her 60s but craning her back as she shoveled supplies into a box. She appeared somewhat frail but minded her own business as she kept on working. She had on this big white furry hat with a matching scarf and gloves, while her jacket was light blue and stylish. Most dressed for comfort, but she had an air of old-school sophistication about her.

Aaron approached the woman and said something in Ukrainian, but I was able to make out the words "American journalist" as he appeared to explain who we were. The woman remained hunched over but cocked her head—making eye contact with Aaron through her peripherals.

"American?" She asked.

"Yes," said Aaron, motioning toward us. The woman turned her gaze toward us. She had a sour look on her face.

"Gah," she said, waving her hand dismissively toward us. *Maybe the word "American" doesn't always work.*

But now I was too curious to not persist. This was one of the first Ukrainians we met who did not seem excited to see an American journalist. I pressed Aaron to ask her what her deal was. Using his timid tact, he appeared to politely inquire with her as to why she wasn't thrilled by our presence. The woman stood up, turning her back to us. She said something in Ukrainian under her breath, but I could make out the word "American" again with a vile sting hanging off her tongue.

Aaron kept badgering her. Finally, she had enough and turned toward us. She raised her voice, flinging her arms around emphatically. Then she pointed her white-gloved finger at me, firing harsh Ukrainian words my way. She finished her speech, nodded her head, then went back to packing her box.

Aaron came close to my ear to explain. "She said that the West left. The whole world left Ukraine," Aaron meekly stated. "She said this war should not have happened. In her opinion, the United States and the whole world deserve contempt."

I stood their shocked, but got the message. We nodded our heads respectfully and walked off to leave her be. But that woman's words stuck with me. Another bubble was popped. For the first time, I stopped looking at this as purely a war taking place in a faraway world. *Maybe there's more to it than that? Maybe the United States has played a role in all of this coming to a head? Perhaps the world is more intertwined than I had considered?*

I don't have answers to any of those questions, and I will not opine. I'll leave that to the pundits. But the thoughts did begin to cross my mind. It's easy to come into a foreign land and prescribe the "good guy/bad guy" moniker to people (a favored set of terms for Americans), but it's obviously never that simple. Good and bad are purely subjective things based upon one's own experiences. And in that moment, I really had no idea where the actual lines were drawn.

We stepped out into the Ukrainian night. A low-hanging silvery haze engulfed the street, hiding the tops of buildings from our line of vision.

How apropos considering today's lesson: the world isn't colored in black and white—it's shaded in gray.

*   *   *

There is one interview we conducted in Ukraine that stood above all the others. It wasn't with a celebrity or a key head of state, nobody whose name you would recognize. Yet still, this is the one I always think about.

Aaron had gotten a call the night before from his father. Apparently his dad, who owned that series of dormitories around Ukraine, had been taking in more and more Ukrainian refugees. He said one had agreed to do an interview with us. That was all we knew.

As it so happened, our interview would be taking place at the same dormitory we almost stayed in. I was reminded once again of the contrast. *We* got to pick and choose where we stayed. Refugees who were desperate to survive did not.

Our car pulled into the dormitory parking lot. Staring back at us was that same dull, grey façade and gloomy windows. The rusty playground was empty out front. No children swinging on the swing or climbing on the jungle gym, and the yard was desolate as if happiness and joy had left this place a long time ago.

As I said before it was the consummate Soviet-era living complex. Nothing had been updated in decades so the aesthetic was unwelcoming. But the building still stood and the roof didn't leak (as far as we could tell) so it was good enough for the desperate people here.

Aaron's dad came out and greeted us. He stood atop the short steps out front as he beckoned for us to come inside and led us upstairs. One lone, hazy window allowed for a bit of sunlight to seep through. Even so, the inside was gloomy. The lights above were either extremely dim or not working. Corners of hallways disappeared in the darkness. Each step led to a loud scuffing sound as much of the tile on the floors had broken away. Left behind was a dark, soot-like substance that had mixed in with dirt from the outside.

We made it to the top of the second floor landing. Light beamed through one open door. Aaron's father walked right up to the doorframe and gave it a little knock as he peered inside. We could hear a woman's voice on the other side. Aaron's father turned back to us and motioned us inside. The room was small, similar in size to a college dorm. There was one bed on the far side of the room, a desk next to it, and a small coffee table was in the center. One single window allowed the sunlight to sneak through.

Sitting on the edge of the bed was a blonde haired woman I'd estimate to be in her 30's. She wore a turtleneck sweater and jeans. By her legs was a little girl playing with her toys and giggling. She had a turquoise sweater and dirty blonde hair tied into a lone braid.

The woman's face was engulfed in this sense of dread and dejection. She looked exhausted. Sometimes you just know someone has a story to tell without them even saying a single word.

"Her name is Olivia. Her daughter is Mary. They just escaped Kherson and arrived here the other day," explained Aaron. My heart sank. Kherson had just been captured by Russian forces a day or two earlier. Located by the Black Sea and on the Dnieper River, it's a highly strategic city that connects the Crimean Peninsula to the mainland.

"She's still comfortable talking with us?" asked Bartley to Aaron, who turned and asked the same question to Olivia. She nodded her head. "Yes. I speak English if that's okay."

That was a welcome surprise. We finally had an on-the-ground interview with an articulate English speaker.

As Bartley set up the camera which took a few minutes, not once did Olivia look up. I could see the way her feet fidgeted and her hands trembled she was nervous, but not for the interview. This was the simplest part of her life at the moment.

Olivia sat on the edge of the bed as Mary climbed up next to her. The little girl was fiddling around with another one of her toys and looking toward her mom to see what was happening. She was such pure innocence.

Olivia looked up as we were about to begin. This was the first time I could see her eyes clearly. They were filled with sorrow. No tears welling in the ducts, just dry pain. I looked down at the floor to gather my thoughts. It was hard for me to maintain eye contact with Olivia. She was far braver than I.

Finally, I raised my head and began with the first question that popped into my head.

"Your home of Kherson is a city that has been constantly under attack the last few days. Do you know what's happened to your home. Is your home okay?"

Olivia's voice cracked as she began to answer. "Our home is still okay but the stories we've heard from our relatives and from our close friends are terrible and awful. I can't even say."

She briefly paused. I looked over at Mary who had now put her hands over her ears. At first I thought she was just being playful. I quickly realized Olivia had recounted these events before, and this was no game.

"The young girls are raped. Buildings are destroyed. Just any building. It's not the army it is not the military buildings, it is just buildings where people live. Where ordinary people live. And we cannot call our relatives because we are calling and we are speaking and our calls are interrupted and that's awful because we don't know what is happening now. Why is it interrupting? Probably some bomb is falling there and so it's just horrible."

I couldn't imagine trying to call home and not knowing what was happening. Or worse, knowing quite possibly the phone call you're sharing with a friend could conceivably be the last time you hear their voice.

"Can you believe that war has just entered your community?" I asked.

"No. No. I can't believe it," Olivia said. Her voice trembled, causing her to stumble over her words. "Sometimes we wake up and it seem it's a horrible dream. I can't imagine it."

Olivia then explained her sister lived in a Russian city not far from Kherson. "I couldn't believe that she would be my *enemy*. And so this is just a horrible dream for us. For every one of us. Because a lot of Ukrainians have relatives in Russia."

This is a thought I had never considered. Growing up in Ohio, I've known people my whole life from Canada or have family just across the Great Lakes. Could an American really look at the Canadian people as an enemy if the two went to war? Considering the relationship between the northern United States and Canada and all the cultural similarities we share, I personally would struggle to do so. That was the dynamic at play for many Ukrainians, especially those who lived in Olivia's region.

I looked back at Mary. She was now back on the floor playing with her mother's shoe laces. Returning my gaze to Olivia, I asked, "How hard is it for you, a mother, to have your six year old daughter witness war?"

"It's very hard because I think and most other mothers think that children shouldn't see the war. And they shouldn't understand what indeed happens," Olivia said, glancing down at her daughter before continuing. "And so, we try to smile. To be happy and to be cheerful with them and it's very hard to make such emotions that you haven't in your soul."

I am not a parent, so cannot begin to empathize with the responsibilities that come with parenting. But further, I cannot fathom trying to fight through the tumult of horrific emotions to put on a good face for their child's sake.

"How do you explain this to her?" I asked.

"We try," Olivia said with a big sigh, as if to suggest there's no good answer to that. "We say they are orcs. That orcs are here."

Orcs, the mythical, goblin-like creatures seen in fantasy films, the characterization really took me by surprise. There was no good answer to that question, so saying mythical creatures have arrived at your city and you have to run is about as well as you can explain it to a young child. Children look to their parents to have all the answers. Sometimes, a fib is the best one can muster.

"Mary asks when are we going back," explained Olivia. "And we try to say that everything will be ok and we'll go back soon."

"How hard is it knowing your city, at this moment, is not a Ukrainian city . . . but is under Russian control?" I asked while flubbing through my own words. I tried to think of how I would attempt to stomach waking up and learning my hometown was no longer an American city. A tough swallow as a hypothetical. A stark reality for Olivia.

"We hold that this is still a Ukrainian city," Olivia said firmly. "People are resisting now. And people still believe they are Ukrainians. They don't want to be a Russian city. They don't want this in any way. It is not our reality. We are Ukrainians. We have been Ukrainians for over twenty years."

Olivia's hand motions began to get more rapid as she searched for the most powerful English words she could find. She started to become fervently emotional.

"There was a time we were a part of the Soviet Union, but we don't remember this. We are Ukrainians now. We want to live here. We like Ukraine. Especially Kherson. It is near the Black Sea coast. We were always happy. And all the Ukrainians came there to the seaside."

Olivia's emotions intensified again. She became incredulous to the words she was saying. As she articulated them, they did not make sense to her.

"And not only Ukrainians, but Russians and real Russians came to our seaside and we were all together. They swam there. They ate there. We were all together. There was no discrimination for them. It's just imagination that something was bad for them. No time it was bad. They always had equal rights with us. They came when they wanted, they did what they wanted and anything they liked."

At the time, a key piece of Russian wartime messaging was that the attacks on Ukrainian territory were not an "invasion" but an attempt at "liberation." They contended the people in these Ukrainian cities wanted to be annexed by Russia.

What I can tell you as a matter of fact is that there were people in those cities that sympathized with Russia and there were others who were loyal to Ukraine. Like any war of words, the truth is somewhere in the middle.

I continued on with my line of questioning to follow up on this point. "Those people who you swam with, broke bread with, shared a community with . . . those people are now supposed to be your sworn enemies. And this is all out of your control. This is all politics. How does that make you feel that this is where the world has gone?"

Olivia gave another deep sigh. This was a question she had clearly pondered many times. "I have my sister and cousins who live in Russia. A lot of Ukrainians have their relatives in Russia and it's just so unbelievable that we are enemies now. We have different blood but all use Instagram and TikTok and social networks, and there is no difference between Russians and Ukrainians. We are just the same. It was never such a problem."

I had a college professor who would constantly hammer this point home. Throughout the history of the world, groups that are on paper so similar with few differences have gone to war over those small breaks in uniformity. Pick a topic. Religion. Politics. Economics. Even small differences in opinion on these subject matters have led to grave conflicts throughout the history of the world.

"There are a lot of Americans and Canadians and British and French who are thousands of miles away but watching everything that happens here in Ukraine. What would you like them to know?" I asked.

"We are afraid of everything," Olivia answered without hesitation. "We are afraid of sleep. We just sit in silence because we are just permanently nervous." I heard her voice quiver on these words as she gave thought to the future. "We are waiting for the worst. We hope that somebody in the world can do something with this awful personality. You know who I'm speaking about."

And there it was. The first time Olivia brought up Russian President Vladimir Putin. She danced around the subject, and may as well have explicitly said "he who shall not be named." She looked down at the ground and rubbed her forehead anxiously.

"I don't know the methods of stopping this. But we are asking for help. Every Ukrainian right now is asking for help. Every child and every mother," Olivia continued. She paused again, picking her words carefully.

"And we are afraid for our husbands," she said, looking straight into my soul. "They are not soldiers. They are just ordinary people. We would like them to be with us and we would be safe with your support." Olivia stopped again, giving a moaning whimper. She appeared to be on the verge of tears. "I am very afraid for my husband," she said at last. "I feel safe when we are all together."

"And where is your husband?" I asked.

"My husband is in Kherson," Olivia replied dejectedly. "He's staying with our parents. There are a lot of relatives there."

I now knew why Olivia was so consumed by anxiety. Yes, she was worried for her home and her country. But most of all, her husband who had stayed behind to protect the extended family. Olivia said that included her grandmother who was unable to walk.

Unfortunately, family separation was very common for Ukrainians in the first few days of the war. Fighting-age men were being drafted and barred from leaving the country as many women and children fled. Even those who stayed behind were likely not together as a single family unit due to the fighting and needs of the Ukrainian military.

Mary put her hands over her ears again, not wanting to hear her mother continue on with her recount. My heart broke when I saw that. She did it so playfully, bobbing her head around and sticking her tongue out. I wanted to believe she didn't know what was happening, but that was very clearly not the case.

"As someone who has now witnessed war firsthand and seen the horrors that come with it, do you still have hope? Do you still believe in humankind?" I asked earnestly.

Olivia gave another deep sight. "I do believe in humankind but at this point I do not believe in humankind from Russia." A strong statement.

"I do not believe their leader has even a little humanity in his soul," she said, choking on the words while refusing to say his name. "These things that they do to our people, they're just so violent. They're just so terrible." Her English began to fail her as her emotions intensified.

"Nobody can even imagine to do these things. To your neighboring country." Olivia then lost it and started to shouting. "To people you know. Who speak the same language you speak! It's not people from the other world, that people who are similar to us as we are similar to them. We speak the same language!" Olivia wiped a tear away from her eye. The first one that broke through during the conversation. "I just can't put this in my head."

"If you had the opportunity to meet the Russian President, what would you say to him?" I asked.

Olivia put her head down and raised a finger to her forehead. "I don't know that's such a question," she mumbled, pausing again to gather her thoughts. "I'm a kind person, but I don't want to see him or tell him anything. It seems to me this personality is not worthy to be among people."

She started hastily looking around the room as she tried to compose herself.

"I don't know where this aggression has come from," she sputtered out. "To ordinary people, we haven't done anything bad to him. We don't deserve that."

Olivia shrugged her shoulders and stared blankly ahead. She was done trying to understand the reasoning behind the war. She gave up.

I looked over at Bartley. He gave a nod as if to say we'd asked enough questions. I agreed. This was already a difficult enough conversation for Olivia to endure that we didn't need to press anymore. Mary sat on the bed and stared at her mother with those big eyes of hers as Olivia put her arm around her. Through it all, at least they had each other.

We thanked Olivia for her time. She nodded and thanked us in return for being there to tell her story. We stood up and walked out of the dorm room. Olivia didn't move. She just kept staring blankly forward: digesting thoughts that the strongest of minds would have difficulty stomaching.

We walked back downstairs and my legs felt heavier after that conversation. Every *thump thump* down the steps felt more limp and weighted.

Throughout our time covering the war in Ukraine, we met countless people. Young, old, rich, poor, strong, weak. Some with harrowing tales of survival exemplifying the will to live. To this day, there is nobody I think back on more than Olivia and Mary. My biggest regret is I never asked for their contact information. It seemed out of place and intrusive at the time, and maybe it was.

But even so, I can't help but wonder about what happened to them. Did they make it home to Kherson? Did Olivia ever reunite with her husband? What does the future hold for little Mary? How can she possibly grow through her childhood with her innocence so forcibly ripped from her?

These are questions I will likely never be able to answer. I can only hope and pray they are safe. The fact they might not be tells me all I need to know about war: what a horrific, costly waste of mankind's energy.

7 GLORY TO UKRAINE, GLORY TO HEROES

Breathe. Take it all in. Be more present.

Over the last few years, my life has been constantly in flux. It's not a matter of if but when the phone will ring and an assignment desk manager on the other end of the line will shout, "There's breaking news in Fond Du Lac, Wisconsin! Get on a plane now!"

And I will not mislead you: I do enjoy the hustle. It keeps my mind occupied and challenges me to see, learn, and do more. But sometimes, the lifestyle of jet-setting across the country, living out of suitcases, and opening up rental car throttles to make it to developing stories on time spoils the most beautiful moments in life.

My poor parents have been victimized by this for years. Far too many times they've watched me run out the door, breaking off holidays and vacations to get to assignments. In the last year alone, I have walked out of weddings, ditched reunions, and stood up from family meals to catch flights due to breaking news. I'm grateful to have such understanding friends and loved ones.

I have tried to make it a goal of mine to unplug more, to smell the flowers, hear the birds, and not always be thinking about what's next, but to focus on the here and now. One of my favorite quotes comes from Albert Einstein, who said, "I never think of the future. It comes soon enough." I'm not there yet, but it's something to aspire to.

I would come to quickly realize that doesn't really work in an active conflict zone. You always have to be alert because the situation can change rapidly, especially during the time we were there. By this point, Russia had invaded Ukraine maybe five or six days ago. The first few days of a war are often the most dangerous because the battle lines are not drawn, meaning everything is in play.

For example, the Russian forces just made a move on Chernobyl, which struck fear into every nation in the Western world. The nuclear accident had happened there just over thirty-five years ago, and nobody wanted to even speculate as to what Russia was going to do with it. As it so happened, Russia would actually withdraw from the Chernobyl area about a month later when they gave up on their offensive in Kyiv. Nevertheless, those first few days of the war were extremely uncertain.

On one particular afternoon in Ukraine, we decided to take our lunch break in the central square of Ivano-Frankivsk. A quaint little restaurant with walnut picnic tables for seating claimed to serve "American fare." I'm not one to shy away from experimenting with the local cuisine, but every now and then, you need a sandwich and French fries. This was one of those occasions.

The whole group sat around the table, surprisingly filled with energy. The layout of the table allowed everyone to get close enough to listen and chime in on the conversation. Bartley is the first person I've worked with in news who *insists* on sit-down meals every assignment. Most people in the business will settle for the quick five-minute snack to save time and get through the day, but Bartley never will. He believes it's important for team chemistry and morale, which I'll begrudgingly admit he's right about.

Aaron, Brian, Pat, Bartley, me, and one of our rotating Ukrainian security guards were all huddled around. This was the first real chance we had to get to know one another. Aaron admitted he was just a kid in university who thought being a fixer would be a fun side job as he studied foreign languages and pursued his higher degree. I guess he thought gallivanting around a war zone was a good break from reading poetry. Pat was a man of simple interests. He loved basketball, and his dream was to go visit Chicago to watch the Bulls play. He never explained why that was his team, but he loved them nonetheless. Brian was an incessantly paranoid sort, always scanning every room he walked into and constantly issuing warnings to the group about dangers to be on the lookout for. But even he was kicked back and relaxed. That lunch was the first moment since entering Ukraine we were all able to catch our breath.

Unfortunately, the reprieve was short-lived. The warm sandwiches had just been plated and arrived at our table when we heard it. That sound that makes your spine crawl. That sound that strikes at your very core. That piercing wail which slices through your eardrum and dribbles around your cranium. The sirens were blaring again. But this time, we weren't in an apartment unit where we could barricade ourselves. We were in a restaurant adjacent to the center square. Right out in the open: just about the worst place we could be at that very moment.

"Time to go," said Bartley with a sharp snap. The whole team stood up in uniform like a commencement procession and slung their bags over their shoulders. Looking back, I can't help but think about the nonsensical things that crossed my mind in that moment. *Shouldn't we pay for our meal first?* The wait staff was too busy frantically throwing their aprons on the ground and heading for the door to care about securing their ten-dollar tip. When the sirens go off, it's fight-or-flight mode.

With a hastened pace, we galloped to the door and swung it open, battered by the Ukrainian afternoon cold. We were about a twenty-minute drive from our apartment unit, meaning that was out of the question. We would have to find a bunker nearby that would allow us to wait out the attack underground.

Bartley was all over it, thankfully. He told us the nearest shelter was inside City Hall, which happened to be right across the square. The problem? That was the only one downtown. Right as Bartley began directing us to the shelter, streams of people came pouring out of the nearby buildings, every which way, making a break for that same bunker.

We made our way closer to City Hall, which was now engulfed in a mob of people. A big man wearing all black except for an orange reflective vest started waving his arms, motioning for everyone to get back while shouting something in Ukrainian.

"This shelter is full, we can't get in," piped up Aaron. I could have sworn when he said that, the sirens grew louder and more ominous. Now, we had a very serious problem. The whole team was standing in the middle of the town square in Ivano-Frankivsk with no shelter to be found.

"We need to get off the streets," said Bartley, glancing at the map on his phone. "There's a school just down the road." *Good idea. They'd never hit a school,* I thought. Little did we know that just a few days later, the Russians would bomb a maternity hospital in Mariupol, which would make international headlines. It felt like nothing was off-limits at that time.

Nevertheless, the school seemed like the best option at the moment so we set off. Walking down the tight, cobblestone streets of Ivano-Frankivsk, the sirens echoed off the buildings, distorting the sound into a spooky, horror movie wail. It's as if we were haunted by the ghost of war's past. We kept a quick pace, following the GPS on our phones, with the sirens serving as a constant reminder that we didn't have a moment to waste. Then we came to an intersection and saw an underground parking garage.

"Here," pointed Bartley. This seemed like an even better idea. We stepped down the concrete ramp into the garage. Light could only enter through this one passageway, so everything the sun couldn't touch was pitch black and damp. Now I know how the cockroaches always survive a nuclear Armageddon.

We weren't the only ones with this idea. A young man and woman with backpacks strapped over their shoulders stood there sheepishly waiting for it to all be over. If they were at all nervous, they certainly knew how to conceal it. The man had dark hair and a pair of glasses with a brown-colored turtleneck under a gray coat. The woman was wearing a black, light winter jacket with long brown hair parted in the middle.

"This happens every day," the young man said with a bit of a grin while shaking his head.

"Aren't you at all scared?" I couldn't help but ask.

He shrugged. "Not really. You just get used to it," he responded.

I noticed the man was carrying what appeared to be a pair of textbooks under his arm, giving a clear indication they were students.

"Are classes still going on?" I asked.

He laughed. "Oh yeah. I have a test this week." I thought back to my days of school in Ohio where even a blizzard wouldn't cause my school to shut down. I guess it's the same stubbornness here, only trade the threat of snow-induced traffic accidents for the threat of missiles.

"Unless we're being bombed at that moment, I'm still going to class," he said with a laugh.

"I guess the biggest problem we're getting used to is the alarms, because we hear them every day," the woman chimed in. "It's not something that happens randomly or spontaneously. We're already used to searching for bomb shelters, we're already used to hiding ourselves underground, uniting together and going with the crowd together to the shelters. And this is horrible we are getting used to this type of life."

That last line from the woman stood out to me. When I tell this story about running to bomb shelters back home in the United States, most people tremble and have a difficult time imagining themselves in such a situation. One Ukrainian joked to me that everyone in the country knows where their nearest grocery store, laundromat, and bomb shelter is. Ever since Russia annexed the Crimean Peninsula in 2014, these safeguards have become a part of everyday life.

The couple explained that they were originally from Kyiv but were studying in Ivano-Frankivsk. Like us, they too were sitting in a coffee shop a few minutes earlier before the sirens broke out.

"We're sitting in a café, you know, just trying to work, pretend nothing's happening," the man said. "You try to do that, but at some point you just get used to it, and then you just wander out when you hear the sirens and go to the nearest shelter."

The sirens were hardly their biggest frustration. They told us what bothered them the most was being so far away from Kyiv and their families. The woman said she was trying to help the war effort by offering food and rides to Ukrainian soldiers.

"But still my parents, they're just asking, persuading us not to move anywhere. Just stay here because it's more or less safe. And I don't like it," the woman said. "But all I can do is just agree and do what I can just here."

Finally, after what seemed like half an hour, the sirens stopped. The echoes pattered to a halt. Everything was still. We decided to give it a few more minutes before moving. No explosions, no fires, no screams or terror. It was like nothing had happened at all.

We were fine during that episode, but a few towns over, an airport was bombed. The Russians were making it a priority to knock out any and all military infrastructure in Western Ukraine as they encircled and hoped to choke off Kyiv.

I looked at Bartley to see if it was safe. He nodded. One foot in front of the other, we emerged from the parking garage like timid little mice poking our heads into the open. The sunlight added at least fifteen degrees of warmth to our chilled bodies. We climbed up the ramp and back onto the cobblestone street. A shop owner across the way opened his door and flipped a sign around written in Ukrainian. Using my liberal arts education and context clues, I presumed he shifted his sign from "closed" to "open."

Window barricades slowly came down, revealing the glare of the sun hitting glass beneath. Doors swung open, and out came residents with brooms in hand, sweeping off their doorsteps and porches. Children hurried by without a parent in sight, playing a game that looked like "tag, you're it." It was bizarre to see normalcy try to resume instantaneously, like the flip of a switch. One moment, people were terrified and running for cover. The next, people were back at restaurants and work. That was evident on our walk back from that garage.

When we reached the heart of the city, the restaurant we had eaten at before was already open again. Setting foot inside that little café, we recognized all the same faces. Servers were back making their rounds, and patrons who were there when we left had returned to their spots. To my surprise, when I looked at the table we were sitting at, our food was still there. The coffee was cold and the sandwiches, with bites out of them, sat lonely on their plates. We slid back into our seats, pulled out our laptops, and got back to work.

Keyboards pattering and silverware scraping, we picked up right where we left off, as did everybody else in that city. Life goes on.

*　*　*

Throughout our time in Ukraine, Bartley and I would spend many hours underground in the bunkers around Ivano-Frankivsk. That episode in the restaurant would hardly be our last run-in with the sirens. In fact, it quite literally became a part of our day-to-day life.

After the fiasco where we couldn't get into the air raid shelter at City Hall, our team became much more diligent about plotting out our safety plan. There were multiple shelters by the hotel we were staying in, which we ultimately became very familiar with.

The Ukrainians were no-nonsense about public safety. Every night, as soon as the sun tucked its beaming rays beneath the horizon, it was a strict "lights out" policy citywide. I made the mistake one time of keeping a nightlight on to peck away at my computer and get ahead on some work for the next day.

Sure enough, the sun went down, and the phone in my room rang.

"Hello?" I meekly said into the speaker. On the other end of the line was a woman speaking Ukrainian. Well, actually, more like screaming. I had no idea what she was saying, but I could tell she was not happy with me.

"I'm sorry, I don't understand," I said into the phone.

"Gah!" said the woman back. I could hear the handset jostling as it changed hands.

"Hello sir?" A new woman's voice on the other end of the line, pleasant and kind, and speaking in fluent English. "You must turn out your light. The Ukrainian military says they see your lamp on and it could be a target for Russian bombings."

Oops.

"Got it, I'll take care of that," I responded, hanging up the phone before switching off the lamp and letting in the darkness. *Don't have to tell me twice*, I thought to myself.

This is how it was every night: strict curfew, nobody on the streets, no lights of any kind. I cannot tell you with certainty what the consequences were for breaking these rules, but I was not at all interested in finding out.

Despite the dark and quietness of downtown Ivano-Frankivsk, sleep was hard to come by. Almost every night, a loud "beep" sound would come over the hotel's intercom, similar to the bell you may have heard in high school. That blaring blast would jolt me awake, and then woman's voice would come on the intercom. First, giving instructions in Ukrainian, then in English. Something to the effect of "Attention, this area is under evacuation. Please make your way to the nearest shelter." The stillness of a quiet, Ukrainian night was formally disturbed by the threat of bombings.

Moments after the announcement came over the intercom, the entire hotel seemingly came alive. People were shouting. Children were crying. Doors opening and slamming. I rolled out of bed, quickly threw on my tennis shoes and a coat, then made my way to the staircase. I opened the heavy metal doors and was hit by the cacophony of shoes pounding landings. Dozens, if not hundreds, of people were trudging down the steps. Some had lifeless-looking faces as they were caught in their nightgowns and potentially fatigued from dealing with this threat incessantly. Others were more frantic, scooping their children into their arms and carrying them downstairs to safety.

I followed the column all the way to the ground floor. That's where I found Bartley and the rest of the team. We had planned to meet here in case this happened. To no one's surprise, it did. We all exchanged silent, zombie-like glances. I could tell everyone was exhausted. The column was filing out of the staircase landing on the ground floor through an external emergency exit door that led to the freezing cold Ukrainian night. The entrance to the shelter was across the street, so we fell in line and followed the other guests. There was a single light emanating through a doorway, which is where we were heading.

As we approached, I could see two men standing at the entryway, both of them Ukrainian soldiers. Tall and imposing, they were dressed in full uniforms and flak jackets with rifles pointed at the ground. We passed by them and nodded our heads, but they neither responded nor showed any acknowledgment through body language. Their eyes were fixed forward, gazing intently at the crowd that was coming in.

As we stepped through the opening, a second door came into view a few feet ahead. We entered and found ourselves inside the chapel of a church. I did not expect the shelter to be inside a religious site, but in hindsight, it made sense: places of worship are supposed to be protected by international law unless they are used for military purposes.

We navigated our way in between the rows of pews as two more soldiers stood at the next passageway near the altar, motioning us through. They were raising their voices at us as their hand gestures intensified. One can only assume they were telling us to "hurry up!"

Through the next door we went, which quickly became a set of stairs. The walls were no longer plaster but stone. The staircase was steep, lit by a lone LED lamp below. Step by step, we descended deeper and deeper into the underworld. Pretty soon, the stone walls took on the imagery of a mine shaft with wooden beams framing the support system. I couldn't believe how long the staircase was, as it seemed to go on forever.

Finally, our feet made contact with the ground, which were now concrete-poured floors. Another soldier ushered us through so we could make way for the next group of folks attempting to take shelter. The area was dimly lit and had a damp, murky feeling. I can't tell you how far down we were, but it felt like at least a hundred feet. Whatever the exact distance was, we were down there with no telling when we'd resurface. There was one final door to pass through. Inside was a big atrium filled with rickety, wooden bleachers. Nearly each seat was occupied. Some families were huddled up on the floor in front. Bartley and I looked at each other, then found a spot in one of the first rows. We both sat down and gazed ahead.

Another beeping sound, just like the one that roused us from our slumber, belted out over a speaker system. "Please keep quiet and turn off your cell phones," came a woman's voice from the speakers, offering up the command both in English and Ukrainian. We came to realize that the shuttering of phones was not like trying to be respectful in a movie theater. The Ukrainian government did not want anyone's devices to give away the position of the shelter. No photos, no videos, no phone calls, no WIFI.

Bartley and I sat there silently on those stone-cold bleachers as we heard the rumble of jets overhead. There was no way to know if they were Ukrainian or Russian. The uncertainty hung over that city like a black cloud.

And beneath the surface, the situation wasn't much better in that bunker. Looking around, the despair was palpable. I saw young children playing board games while their parents held them tightly, turning their gazes toward the ceiling.

An elderly couple sitting next to us had their hands clasped together. They never made eye contact with one another. They just stared upward.

It took me a while to realize it, but just about everybody in that shelter was staring at the ceiling. It was as if they were longing to see the surface world— or worse, fearing they would *never* see a sunrise or star-lit sky again. That might seem hyperbolic, but when seconds turn to minutes, and minutes turn to hours underground, your mind inevitably races. There were occasions where we spent the whole night in bunkers. That's an experience that really makes you appreciate the sun and the wind.

Looking around that shelter, there were some who tried their very best to make do. I saw what appeared to be a couple of students hunched over and reading textbooks sprawled across their knee caps. A woman not too far from us was trying to knit what appeared to be some kind of scarf. In the same way a stock broker living in Connecticut tries to pass the time during the commute every day to and from Manhattan, folks in Ukraine tried to best capitalize on the downtime they had in those shelters.

The only connection anyone down there had to the outside world was one single screen playing Ukrainian state television all night long. I must have sat there watching it for at least an hour, not having the faintest clue what the reporters or anchors were saying. When you're completely cut off from the outside world, you'll do anything to try and reconnect.

After a few hours, we heard another loud "beep" sound as the intercom crackled to life once again.

"Attention!" the voice said. This was a male voice I had never heard before. We all became alert, waiting to see what the news was. "All clear! Glory to Ukraine. Glory to heroes."

All at once, everyone inside the shelter stood up and began making their way to the exits. Bartley and I looked at each other, having not said a word all night. *Good to go, I guess.*

We followed the shuffling of feet through the narrow corridors back to the stairs from which we came. The climb was much more comforting than the descent as you knew you were returning to the surface. Even those with the strongest fortitude would feel at least slightly claustrophobic down in those bunkers.

Step by step, we climbed. One foot hoisting the trunk of our bodies higher. Eventually, we returned to the same chapel we had been in before. There was now a door leading directly to the outside open in front of us. An orange hue was emanating from outside, blasting light through the opening as the blanket of darkness melted away.

It was the rays of the sun poking out from behind the distant horizon that brought color to that dark, dreary dawn. I have never in my life been more thankful to see it after spending hours underground. But after a few moments, I realized that we had also lost an entire night of sleep. And by "we," I mean everyone in that city. Gone, just like that.

When I made it back to my hotel room, I fell face down on the bed with a loud thump and shut my eyes as tightly as I could. Tried all I did, I was inexplicably unable to slip into sleep. It was too bright outside for the curtains to hold in the dark. Adding in the slight bit of adrenaline still seeping through my veins from the sirens and the wake-up alarms, and my body was just refusing to cooperate.

This cycle would repeat itself almost every day we stayed in Ivano-Frankivsk. Those blasting alarms that woke us up every night became my enemy. Those long walks in the cold back to the shelter started to feel longer and more draining. Those waits in the darkness of the shelter seemed to grow more pessimistic as prospects of returning to the surface seemed to wilt away. But what stuck with me the most is that male, monotonous, almost robotic-like voice that let us know everything was going to be all right.

Glory to Ukraine; Glory to Heroes.

When I heard those words, I knew that despite my mind's best attempts at crushing my spirits or my body's desperate ache for sleep, the sun would indeed rise again.

8   TO CATCH A SPY

"Weren't you scared?"

That's a question I get asked a lot about being in Ukraine. The honest answer is no, not really. That is not because of some steel-like courage coursing through my veins but more so because the threats and dangers we were facing never really sunk in.

The first time I heard the sirens blare, yeah I got a little nervous. I had no idea what was going to happen, but the fact I didn't have a close brush with death then and that missile fell elsewhere made it all seem like I was removed from the possibility of harm. Until danger comes knocking and it hits close to you, it doesn't feel real. But if I had to point to one moment in Ukraine where I felt the proverbial rattling of my cage, it was this one.

It was around 7:00 o'clock in the evening local time, and our team was sitting in a restaurant in downtown Ivano-Frankivsk. Half of our workday was done so we were mindlessly scarfing down sandwiches and sodas without much of a care in the world. We were getting comfortable in Ukraine. In fact, we were so comfortable that Bartley and I felt fine grabbing dinner without Aaron, our language connoisseur and the only one in our group fluent in Ukrainian. He was off spending time with his father, whom until that week he hadn't seen in years, so it was just me, Bartley, Pat, and Brian.

What's the worst that can happen? How hard will it be to explain to the wait staff what kind of dumplings we'd like with our meal? we thought.

What's more, today was Saturday. Tomorrow would be Sunday and our first "day off" in weeks to recharge, which included the US–Mexico border assignment. Bartley was already making lunch reservations and planning out our day of rest in war-torn Ukraine. That was where our minds were at. Not on the present.

The waitress came over and poured us another round of coffee. She was sweet. She always greeted us with a smile and giggled as she tried her hardest to squeeze out the few words of English she knew to accommodate us. Inevitably, she'd always have to call over her colleague who could understand the language. I give her credit for trying.

The door to the restaurant opened with the jingle of bells to alert the staff that someone had arrived. But judging by the way our waitress' throat sank into her stomach, something was off. It felt like time stopped for a moment and the oxygen was sucked right out of that small café. The waitress stopped pouring the coffee and just stared at the door. She was frozen stiff. Her face went flush and her arm, coffee pot in hand, was cemented in the air. I didn't turn around to look at the door and just stared at her face to delay the inevitable of and knowing what it was. Bartley, meanwhile, was so busy editing video he didn't even look up from his computer.

I slowly turned my head. In had walked eight men dressed in all black. They were big guys with broad shoulders, and their combat boots made a loud *thumping* sound with every step they took. The second they walked in, the café went silent, and everyone was looking at them. I didn't know who they were or what they were doing, but this clearly wasn't good.

And worst of all: they made eye contact with us and came right over to our table. They didn't waste any time and surrounded us, each of the eight spreading out at equal distance around our small group.

Bartley finally looked up from his computer. "Oh," he muttered under his breath with a hint of nervousness. Now I really knew to be worried. The leader of the group started barking at us in Ukrainian. Without Aaron, we had no idea what his words meant. He started flailing his left hand around, pointing at the table. We all just stared at him. Then he reached his right hand under his coat and held it there. I've seen enough Hollywood films to know what that meant. He had a gun and was making a veiled threat to draw it on us right there in that café.

One of his partners did the same. The second Ukrainian pointed at Bartley's laptop, then at the center of the table. Bartley slowly closed his laptop and placed it right where the man pointed. I followed suit. The leader started jostling his gun underneath his coat, then used his other hand to point at our phones.

"Are you kidding me?" Bartley muttered in disbelief. We did what he said. One phone on top of another. A third Ukrainian came in and scooped them up, putting them into a black backpack. *Are we getting robbed?* I thought. *No, this doesn't seem like a robbery. This definitely seems worse.*

The leader again jostled with his gun under his coat, this time upward as if to say "stand up." We guessed right. Slowly rising, our hands were stretched slightly out to the sides like in one of those old Western movies in an attempt to signify we weren't armed. He waved his arm, telling us to follow him, and so we did. "It's going to be all right, just stay calm," Bartley said with a whisper. I was, frankly, more composed than I thought I would be in that moment. But the hairs on the back of my neck started to stand up as I slowly followed these men out of the restaurant.

Do you know that feeling you get when you know everybody is staring at you? The way you just know dozens of pupils are piercing holes in your back and laser-focused on your every move? I made the mistake of turning to confirm my suspicions. Everyone in this café was looking at us, and not the way one gawks at a zoo animal. It was the way you stare at a convicted murderer or animal abuser. Some of the men had their arms folded in sternness. Others had this look of spitting anger on their faces. *What the hell did we do?* I wanted to blurt out.

We slowly made the perp walk toward the door. The sweet waitress, in her best English of the night, piped up and said, "I hope you'll be okay." *I sure as hell hope so too, I thought to myself.* I was desperately looking for some kind of sign to let me know everything would be okay. Sadly, at every turn, I was less and less sure of that. We stepped out into the bitter Ukrainian night. The wind had picked up, burning our faces with that all-too-familiar frigid air. The lead Ukrainian led us across the street and then right by where our blue minivan was parked, then pointed firmly at the ground like telling a dog to "stay." We complied.

There was a bench a couple of paces behind us, but I didn't even think about sitting down. It seemed like a great way to get us all killed. My only focus was compliance and getting out of this situation. We all lined up shoulder to shoulder again and stood facing forward. It was me, Bartley, Pat and Brian. The leader came over and held out his hand, saying something in Ukrainian. We just looked at him. He said it again, this time with much more vinegar in his voice. This guy had our laptops, our phones, and our dignity. The only other thing we had was our passports, so we handed them over. Turns out, we guessed right and that was what he wanted.

We stood there, without moving an inch, for what seemed like an hour. It was clear that the men in black were waiting for someone or something. They scuffled around with hands in pockets, occasionally flipping through our passports, but that was it. The fact that none of them had the ability to communicate in English felt reassuring, for whatever reason. As if the language barrier made these hulking men human all of a sudden.

Finally, someone else arrived who seemed to take the lead. All of the other men acknowledged this new guy with nods of respect and appeared to pull him aside to brief him on the situation. He was a tall, lanky fellow, probably 6'3", with tightly cut dirty blonde hair, wearing skinny black jeans, a black winter coat, and a black hat. He had a jawline that could slice a diamond. He walked directly over to the men who were huddled up, listening intently as the situation was explained to him. He nodded his head, saying a word here or there. Then, he slowly strolled over to us with his hands behind his back. I felt like I had seen German officers in old Second World War movies perfect this same stride.

Then he stood face to face with me. "You are American, yes?"

"Yes," I quickly replied. He told me his name. We'll call him Jack. "And these men are with you, yes?" he queried, motioning to the rest of the team. I responded affirmatively again.

The way Jack spoke, he sounded like the spitting image of a Bond villain. He had an Eastern European accent mixed with a flair for suspense and drama. His sentences flowed off his tongue and had an almost musical cadence. His voice would crescendo, and his pitch would rise at the end of each statement. Jack then gave a brief look behind him to the eight men in black, then turned back to look at us.

"These men here have reason to believe you are spies," he said with a curt flavor. My heart sank. *Not again.* "Since you are in Ukraine, and there is a war going on, we must investigate," he declared, then paused for dramatic effect while raising an eyebrow. "Espionage is a very serious crime, you know?" There was a slight sinister smile at the end of that last sentence that made me take a big gulp of my tongue.

Keeping his hands behind his back, he did an about-face and walked back to the huddled-up men. He stretched out his hands, and they handed him a stack containing our passports. He turned around, slowly, and came right back to us, sifting through the pile until producing my blue, American passport. He flipped it open to my photo page—glancing back and forth from me to the booklet.

"What is your business in Ukraine?" Jack asked me, staring down at the booklet.

"We're journalists covering the war," I replied.

"Funny," he replied tersely before lifting his gaze. Now I could see the beady pupils in his eyes that honed in on me. "What a coincidence that just this morning we arrested six Russian spies with American press credentials."

That's it. We're toast. Guilty until proven innocent strikes again. Jack turned around again and walked back to his pals, pointing at my passport then flipping through all of the pages. My press credentials were still tucked away in the pages, so he examined them briefly. Now all of a sudden, I started to worry that the fact Bartley hastily made and printed these things out himself right before we left would be used as evidence at our executions.

Just a few days earlier, I thought nothing in the world would be cooler than seeing a spy hunter in action breaking up an espionage ring. The day those Ukrainian soldiers burst into our apartment, it lost its luster. But now that this spy-hunting extraordinaire was on the case, I really thought we had a problem and never wanted to hear the word "spy" ever again.

But were these guys even spy hunters? Who the hell were they? Nobody flashed a badge, nobody introduced themselves as law enforcement. They were certainly conducting this meticulous investigation like the CIA or MI6 would in movies but—there was something off. I couldn't put my finger on it.

Jack strolled back over and handed me the pile of passports. *Judgment Day. What's happening?*

"Your story checks out," he said with a hint of disappointment. "You are free to go."

I took the booklets from his outstretched hand, completely surprised. *That's it?*

"Sorry for the misunderstanding," he said, shrugging his shoulders with a coy smile indicating he clearly was *not* sorry.

"What was the problem?" I couldn't help but blurt out.

Jack was taken aback by the question. "Oh, you don't know?" I shook my head, still with a hint of nerves. "You are all over Ukrainian Reddit."

Huh? Reddit, for those unaware, is a community board on the internet where anyone with a phone or laptop can share something and get the public's opinion. I stood there speechless, utterly confused by the words that had just trickled off his tongue. Jack sighed and pulled out his cell phone. He slid next to me to show me what was on his device. What I was staring at was a photo of our car, the blue minivan that was parked right next to us.

"People all over town called us saying your car appeared suspicious," he explained. He opened the comment section, which was in Ukrainian, and gave us some rough translations.

"This person thought it was odd your car had Polish license plates and 'Press' written in tape on the side, so asked what others thought." Jack explained. He pointed to the next comment and the one below it. "This person said a journalist would never drive a minivan. This next person agreed and said journalists don't drive cars with broken taillights."

Bartley gave Pat a glare for that one. He stood there looking embarrassed.

Jack continued on. "Everyone agreed that you were likely spies, so they called us and we came," Jack said, cracking a smile that was anything but inviting. "But, I guess you're not," he added with a giggle.

Geez, man, this is no laughing matter for us.

Jack then put his phone away in his breast pocket and pointed at our car's taillight. I had forgotten it was parked maybe three parking spaces away from us. "You might want to get that taken care of," he joked. I looked at Bartley, who nodded, which I took to mean *as soon as possible.*

With a swift turn, he began walking away. Then, he halted, turned back around, and returned.

"By the way, what kind of stories are you reporting on while in Ukraine?" he asked. *Oh boy, more questions. I thought we were done with this.*

I told him we were doing a bit of everything and focusing on the day-to-day developments of the war. He smiled again, this time his eyes lighting up like a shark coming across a wayward seal. "Give me your contact information. I have a story for you."

Hoping for this interaction to be over, I gave him my phone number.

"Perfect. I'll see you tomorrow morning," he said, and walked off. We all sat there silent as the dead while Jack and his merry band departed. Not a single word was said for what seemed like a whole minute.

With the coast clear, Bartley broke the ice. "Well, I guess we're not off tomorrow anymore."

What the hell did we just agree to?

*   *   *

How did I end up here?

That's a question I have found myself asking throughout my career. I've hunkered down in storm shelters jam-packed full of people. I've slept in hotel rooms on the Gulf Coast as Category Four hurricanes made landfall. I've sat in courtrooms listening to testimonies from Charles Barkley and Condoleezza Rice as they've lobbed allegations against alleged fraudsters. One thing I've loved about journalism is that you inevitably end up in rooms you deep down feel like you have no business being in.

But this whole ordeal? This one takes the cake for "what the hell is happening?" moments.

The day after our run-in at the café with the mysterious, black-clad Ukrainians, we woke up bright and early to a text from their leader, Jack. He had made good on his promise to follow up with us. Deep down, I wished he hadn't. There was something about the guy that made me want to steer clear of him, as if there was this cloud of nefarious intentions hanging over him.

Even so, he seemed to be a proverbial "mover and shaker," and something told me we shouldn't blow him off. We still weren't really sure who he worked for, but he certainly seemed to be in with the Ukrainian military or something like that. Maybe military police? Or Ukrainian intelligence? I couldn't tell you at the time; he was playing his cards close to the vest. If he could offer a story or information that got us "under the hood" of the Ukrainian war effort, it was worth the roll of the dice.

Jack gave us a coffee shop in downtown Ivano-Frankivsk to meet him at and a sharp time. We gathered all of our belongings and rolled over in our minivan with Bryan, Pat, and Aaron. Never again would we make the mistake of going anywhere without our translator.

Our car pulled down a cobblestone road and right up to the little shop. Even in the wintertime, it had a summery feel with beige paneling and white trim. Flower baskets sat out front containing what would soon be beautiful blossoms, but for now were sad, lonely pots of dirt. The café had a Victorian-style front porch adorned with ornate designs carved into the railings. Big glass windows on the outside gave it an added modern and trendy feel.

I walked up to the front door and pushed it open, and my senses were met with a rush of warm air mixed with the scents of pastries and coffee beans. Inside, college students were sitting in groups, glancing at each other's textbooks and notes as they sipped hot beverages. An older couple sat at a small table with their legs crossed over their knees as they chuckled to themselves.

The workers behind the coffee bar were all young men and women wearing baseball caps and aprons, hurrying from the espresso machines to the pastry displays in order to fulfill the beaming-eyed customers' orders. It seemed like an out-of-character spot to meet a Bond supervillain.

Yet, sure enough, out of the corner of my eye, I saw Jack on the far side of the room. He was sitting in a red velvet chair with his head down as he appeared to twirl a sugar cube in his tea. Even in this cozy café, Jack had a way of breathing life into the word "antagonist."

He was wearing the exact same outfit he had on the night before: black combat boots, black skin-tight pants, black jacket, and black hat. If I had to go Christmas shopping for this guy, I'd know what color sweater to get him.

We approached him, and he slowly looked up. "I see you made it," he said with a dagger-like smile.

"We did," Bartley said with a smirk. Before we could get to Jack, he waved us off. "Please grab a drink; we have much to discuss."

Bartley and I looked at each other and shrugged. A coffee sounded wonderful, so we trudged over to the counter. One of the young ladies took our order at the desk and then looked at us with a warm smile. "Care for one of our pastries?" she asked in English.

"Ooh, I'll have a look," said Bartley with a hint of glee in his voice. For being a battle-hardened warzone producer, the man could never turn down a muffin. I always found that to be amusing.

Bartley picked out a blueberry muffin, and the woman handed it to him in a crinkly paper wrapper. I glanced over at him as he had this kid-in-a-candy-store look on his face. He caught me staring. "What?" he barked at me before plopping a chunk of pastry into his mouth. I just shook my head with a smile.

The lady behind the counter handed us our coffees. They were poured into small teacups with plates that had pink and green flowers painted on them. *You can't make this up*, I thought. The night before, we were being detained and interrogated; now we were having coffee and sweets in a little café.

Bartley and I grabbed our drinks, while Aaron, Pat, and Bryan had picked a table by the door to let us chat with Jack in private. I turned back toward Jack and realized he had been staring at us the entire time with a closed-mouth smile, watching our every move.

We started walking over to Jack. Four of the same red velvet chairs were sitting around a coffee table. I assumed they were all empty, but one was tall and facing away from us. To my surprise, as we approached, I realized the chair was occupied by a man wearing an olive-colored baseball cap. He leaned back into the cushions as he sipped his coffee.

"Oh, hello," said Bartley with surprise in his voice. He extended a hand to the man. "I'm Bartley."

The man nodded his head and took Bartley's hand. "Nice to meet you," the man replied. He didn't give us his name, but I brushed over that oddity because his accent was unmistakable. *An American.*

"You're from the States?" I couldn't help but blurt out.

The man gave a pursed-lip nod. "Yes, sir," he said curtly.

Bartley and I sat down in our chairs and looked over at Jack. He had a big grin on his face. Jack leaned forward and pointed his thin, bony finger at the mysterious stranger. "This man is your fellow countryman and is here to fight for Ukraine's noble cause," Jack said, beaming proudly.

No kidding, I thought. We had heard stories of American veterans planning to come to Ukraine and fight, but that was being strongly discouraged by the US government. If Americans were on the ground fighting in Ukraine, the thinking was the United States would have a difficult time making the case to Russia that they were uninvolved. Of course, the fact that the United States was sending weapons to the Ukrainians made these messy geopolitics even messier.

Now it all made sense. I stared at the man. He was a little on the short side and hadn't shaved in a few days, leaving behind a messy, scraggly beard. He wore what appeared to be a red flannel shirt underneath an olive green jacket that was similar to his hat.

"What part of the States are you from?" I asked him. He stared at me blankly and didn't say a word in response. *Dumb question, Robert.*

Jack leaned forward and chuckled. "This man would prefer not to say anything. He's afraid you'll print it!" I blushed out of embarrassment. Bartley just shook his head with a slight grin at me. Mr. Price was playing chess, and I was playing bumper cars.

Then Bartley came out of left field with a question I couldn't understand at the time. "How good is your French?" he asked with a big, coy grin as he leaned back in his chair.

The man broke his blank face and gave a smile back. "It's not bad," he replied, nodding his head. "I had about five years to learn it."

Bartley gave a little laugh. "I had a feeling you'd say that," he said. Bartley had something figured out while I sat there looking and feeling like the dumbest person in the room. Put simply, I was. "I've run into a few of your folks over the years."

"Is that so?" said the man, crossing his arms and smirking. He turned his full attention toward Bartley.

"Yup," said Bartley, ticking off a list of countries and war zones he'd been in over the last couple of decades.

"You've been all over," the man said.

"I'm sure you have too," replied Bartley. "The last time I ran across you guys I told them I didn't speak French, and an Australian told me 'no worries, mate!'"

The man chuckled at that and looked down. "Yeah, the French Foreign Legion gets recruits from all over."

Huh? One minute we're talking about Americans, then it's French and Australians? What. The Hell. Is. Happening?

Bartley didn't miss a beat. He nodded his head but didn't say a word. If I could read minds, I'd imagine Bartley internally said, "checkmate."

I had heard of the French Foreign Legion in passing but didn't really know what it was at the time. In short, it's a part of the French military containing foreigners. People come from across the globe to join. It's viewed by many as an opportunity for a fresh start in life, and if you serve long enough, they'll award you with French citizenship.

Jack leaned across the table and patted the man on the knee. "And now, he's here to fight with us," Jack said, giving Bartley a proud smile. "If you're lucky, maybe he'll give you an interview."

Ah. Now I see what's going on here. Jack wants us to do a story on this man and how the Ukrainians are recruiting people to their cause, including Americans.

I could tell Bartley wasn't sold on the story idea. "Maybe," he finally said. "Would you even have interest in that?"

The man sat there and crinkled his face as he pondered that prospect. "Not really. I'd have to think about it."

Jack was a little miffed by his answer. "Are you sure? I'm sure they could hide your face and change your voice," Jack said, looking at Bartley and me for assurance.

In theory, yeah, we *could* do that, but that's typically reserved for investigative, whistleblowing reports. Generally, it's just bad journalism to put an anonymous person on television, especially in a context like this.

The man nodded his head. "I'll think about it."

Jack smiled and patted him on the knee. "Give him time," he said, assuring Bartley, who returned a smile and a nod.

Bartley turned back toward the man. "At least tell me this. Why are you here?" A short and to the point question from Bartley. Note taken.

The man nodded his head and bobbed back and forth in his chair, suggesting that the question was well received and fair. "It's the right thing to do. I believe freedom is on the line, and I'm ready to serve." He paused, looked down for a moment, then continued on. "I think a lot of people have this all wrong. Putin isn't crazy. He's a chess player. And somebody has to stop him."

Jack looked down at Bartley's coffee cup, which was now empty, and butted in. "You need a drink, I need a drink. Come," Jack said to Bartley while glancing around the table. "You two as well?" Jack said to the man and me. We both nodded. "I'll be back," Jack said and led Bartley over to the counter.

It was clear he didn't want the man saying more than was needed. For a casual coffee and muffin meeting, there sure was a lot of strategy and gamesmanship going on in that café.

I was left all alone with the man of few words. He stared blankly ahead as he thought deeply. "Yeah, I'm sorry man, I just don't feel very comfortable doing an interview on this."

"Totally fine," I replied earnestly. I was more than happy to move on to something else anyway.

"I'm just assuming a lot of risk being here right now," the man continued. "And considering who these guys are, it might not be a good look."

I cocked my head at the man, not understanding what he was saying. "What do you mean by 'who these guys are?'" I asked in a puzzled voice.

The man gestured with his head over to the counter. "Jack." I raised my eyebrows, still struggling to understand what he was talking about. It dawned on me that finally, somebody knew who Jack was and what he did.

"Isn't he with the Ukrainian military? Or government?" I asked. The second the words left my mouth, I knew that wasn't going to be the case.

"Eh, sort of," the man said, tilting his head to the side. "He's with the Azov Battalion."

Huh?

"So . . . that's not the Ukrainian military?" I asked, hoping for a better answer or some kind of reassurance.

The man looked back, surprised, as if he assumed I knew all of this already. "They're different. More of a militant group. I'm pretty sure our country wanted to designate them a terrorist organization a few years ago."

A what?!? Terrorists? No way. I tried to quickly yet somehow discreetly open my phone to look up what all of this meant. What kind of mess have we gotten ourselves into?

I punched "Azov Battalion" into the browser and started scanning a few articles, looking for any kind of clue as to what I was dealing with. As I scrolled, my heart jolted to a halt. One single word in a paragraph stood out and sent a shiver down my spine.

Nazi.

Oh no. Surely there must be a mistake, I thought. I opened up another article to reassure myself there was a misunderstanding. The first paragraph contained the words "Neo-Nazi ideology." Another article? One more for good measure? Same words. "Nazi" and "Nazism."

By this point, I hadn't taken a breath in fifteen to twenty seconds. I couldn't move. The periphery of my vision felt like it was fading to black as I realized I had just stepped into the biggest minefield of my career. And here, sitting across from me, was this guy who willingly wanted to join up with them.

"Oh, wow," I mumbled to myself while reading, trying to be polite. I didn't know what else to say at that moment.

"Yeah, now you understand why I don't want to do an interview," the man said softly, as if he were walking on shaky ground. "A few of my friends back home said I should stay away from these guys."

Gee, I wonder why?

I abruptly sat upright and scanned the room, looking for Bartley. He was on the other side of the café, standing in line at the counter with Jack. They were talking and laughing about something. Bartley had no idea what I had discovered.

"Good luck, man," I said to the American, shaking his hand and excusing myself. He nodded his head back to me. "Same to you," he replied.

I stood up and walked over to Bartley and Jack. "Bartley, our bosses are calling us, we're gonna have to run," I lied.

Jack stood there with a warm smile as he stared at both of us. I made the mistake of looking into his eyes. They were drilling holes into the little fib I had just told.

"What a shame," Jack said.

"What's going on?" Bartley asked, confused.

"We have to go," I said, turning back to Jack. "Thank you for meeting with us," I said to him. Jack gripped my hand tightly. I didn't realize how tall he was until that moment. He towered over me and now appeared all the more intimidating.

"Of course," he said. "I'll be in touch. We have a lot of news stories for you. We've never been on American television before, so I'm excited to keep working with you."

Not happening, is what I wanted to say.

"Sounds good," I said with a smile. "Looking forward to it," I lied again. I wanted to be out of there immediately. I would have said anything to leave. I put my arm on Bartley's back and led him to the door. We walked by Aaron, Brian, and Pat who were sitting at the table right next to the exit.

"Time to go, gents," I said. That may have been the first order I gave that whole trip. Everything else came from Bartley, the team leader. The group even looked at him to make sure that was the plan.

"I guess we've got to go," said Bartley blankly, still not understanding. We quickly strolled out of the restaurant and directly to the car. As I got into the back seat, I could see Jack standing on the porch, staring at us with that soft smile of his.

"See you soon," he called out. I waved back at him. As the car fired up and rolled away, he remained standing on that porch until we were out of his line of vision.

It took a minute or two before Bartley said anything. "What the hell was that all about? You mind cluing me in?" he asked sharply.

I turned to him. We were both sitting in the back seat together. "Do you know who Jack works for?" I asked.

" . . . No," said Bartley with a tinge of curiosity.

I pulled out my phone to one of the articles I had found and handed it to him. Bartley retrieved his glasses from his pocket and placed them on his nose to read. He peered down at the phone and sat silently for a few moments.

"Oh, Jesus," he said at last. He handed the phone back to me, then sat back, staring blankly ahead. "Yeah, that's a problem," he muttered.

The rest of that drive was quiet as I sat in the back seat contemplating that morning at the café. The whole "good guy, bad guy" lines blurred before my eyes once again.

As it so happened just that week, Russian President Vladimir Putin had given some of his first public comments on justifying the war. He used words like "liberation" and "de-Nazifying" Ukraine as his reasoning to invade and continue the fighting. I had never given it that much thought and chalked it up to Russian propaganda. But maybe there was more to it after all?

I couldn't help but read more articles about Nazi influence and groups like the Azov Battalion during the rest of that drive. This has been well-documented for years but never garnered much attention in the United States from the general public. There are books out there that take a deeper dive into their origins, who they are, and what they stand for. That is not this book, but here's a rough summary.

Our friend, er, American compatriot in the café was right. In 2019, Democratic Rep. Max Rose, the chair of the House Homeland Security Subcommittee on Intelligence and Counterterrorism (since renamed the Homeland Security Subcommittee on Counterterrorism, Law Enforcement, and Intelligence), penned a letter to then US Secretary of State, Mike Pompeo, asking why certain groups had not been placed on the Foreign Terrorist Organizations list.[1]

The groups in question included several far-right organizations, including Finland's Nordic Resistance Movement, the United Kingdom's National Action, and the Azov Battalion in Ukraine. Thirty-nine members of Congress signed onto this letter. Azov did not receive any terrorist group designations by the United States in the wake of that push, but in 2024, the Nordic Resistance did. The State Department cited them as being "the largest neo-Nazi group in Sweden" and designated them "Specially Designated Global Terrorists."[2]

As the war in Ukraine carried on and the United States sent aid to the Ukrainians, there were strict carveouts that barred American weapons from going to Azov, largely due to concerns surrounding the group's origin and links to neo-Nazism. That ban, however, was lifted by the Biden administration, also in 2024. The State Department said it had concluded there was "no evidence of gross violation of human rights" by the group.[3] As such, they now have access to the same military aid as other members of the Ukrainian National Guard, of which Azov is now a part.

"This is a new page in the history of our unit," the group said in a statement shared on social media following the State Department's decision. "Azov is becoming more professional and more effective in defending Ukraine against the invaders."[4]

Azov in particular has been a focal point of criticism for Ukraine. Some, who do not believe the United States should be sending aid to the Ukrainians at all, point to Azov as an unresolved issue that needs to be addressed first. Today, Azov rejects any associations with Nazism, though they still receive allegations of having far-right extremists among their ranks.

Russia, on the other hand, *has* designated the group a terrorist organization. The Kremlin spokesperson, Dmitry Peskov, in turn accused the United States of "flirting with neo-Nazis" in an effort to suppress Russia.[5]

What we would come to find in Ukraine is that the Azov Brigade, as they are more properly referred to today, is revered by many people on the ground as being some of the country's fiercest and most effective fighters. By and large, people don't point to the controversial ideologies surrounding the group's origin or the accusations of extremism. They instead focus on the valiance with which they fought with in cities such as Mariupol.

And interestingly, there was a paradox at play here. Ukrainian President Volodymyr Zelenskyy himself is Jewish. He has publicly praised members of the group, referring to them as "heroes."[6] So like everything in Ukraine, it's not cut and dry. It's complicated, and I didn't know what to make of it back in 2022. Frankly, I still don't.

But what I did know on that cold Ukrainian day in the coffee shop was that no matter what his personally held beliefs were, I'd had my fill of Jack.

9 FROM LVIV WITH LOVE

Lviv was one of the biggest surprises for me in Ukraine. We traveled there after a week or so in Ivano-Frankivsk, and I have to tell you it is a gem of a city. While you can find many of them in Europe, something about Lviv stands out.

Founded in the thirteenth century, the place has withstood the test of time. Maybe it's the architecture. Maybe it's the history of changing hands from empire to empire and still towering over the European landscape as a thing of beauty.

The Austrians, the Russians, and the Germans would all take control of the city at certain points in history, but there were still people in Poland who believed it was truly of Polish roots. The city did belong to the Poles before the Second World War (as well as before the Habsburgs came in during the late eighteenth century), but after the war ended, the city became part of the Soviet Union. We would meet people who would insist the proper name for the place is "Lwów," which is what it was called under Polish control.[1]

If you ever think you have the world figured out and things seem black and white to you, I promise a week in Central and Eastern Europe will change your mind. The scars of the Second World War are still evident, as are plenty of tensions and unresolved issues stemming from 1945. To this day, some of the most enlightening countries I've been to include Austria, Hungary, and Poland.

The streets in the Historic Center of Lviv are all cobblestone, and every building glistens with bright splendor. The people clearly care for their history, as almost every statue was covered in tarps when we were there. Despite my naivete, I knew what that was: local officials wanted to minimize the damage done to the city's artifacts when the bombs would start falling. That stood out to me. Gone was the hope of avoiding the war entirely. Instead, it was an accepted inevitability that war would come here.

It was early March, maybe a week and a half into the war. It was also around this time that some in the international community feared Ukraine might need a contingency plan. Should Kyiv fall and the government be toppled, the initial thinking was a new government would need to be established here and Lviv would effectively become Ukraine's new capital. That shows how quickly things move at the start of the war, and while it would never come to that, Lviv was being viewed as a key city critical to Ukraine's survival.

Despite all the uncertainty and dread, folks here still made the most of life. As we strolled down the cobblestone roads leading to the center square and peeked into the restaurants, we saw white tablecloths and fine silver in some of the humblest of cafes. People sat there sipping their cups of espresso and reading articles on their tablets. One bakery was well awarded in the city for its high-end, exquisite pastries. Wouldn't you know it, despite what was happening in the country, the bakers were in there meticulously kneading dough and ordaining cakes with frosting. The simplest of pleasures can survive the hardest of times.

We kept walking, and all of a sudden we were struck by a distinct sound: laughter. Turning the corner, we saw what was an ice rink filled edge to edge with people. It was a public spot set up by the city and we watched as one eager child ignored his mother and slid full speed around the edge of the ice—berated by shouts from his parents to put his helmet on.

A little girl dressed in pink was much more apprehensive. One foot in front of the other with her white-gloved hand firmly in her father's, she was led onto the ice for what may have been the first time. A family of four handed their phone over to a stranger and asked them to take a family photo. Smiles spanning from ear to ear, they stood huddled together. Maybe that will be their Christmas card this year?

It was the first time that whole assignment we were surrounded by pure joy. The people we saw were so happy, or at least in that moment they were. Their country was besieged and their homes were under threat, but they had each other. They were a family and no amount of war could change that. Even those who weren't on the ice skating and were standing outside couldn't help but crack grins at the pure innocence. A few paces away, a woman sat alone throwing down pieces of grain for the pigeons to snack on. A sophisticated, well-dressed young couple with their pristine wool coats passed by, pointing at the whole scene. For a few moments, we let that center square consume us. I can only imagine this is what life is supposed to look like here on any given day. Smiling, giggling, relaxing in that sweet winter air.

What people will do to forget.

* * *

I wish I could tell you all of Lviv was smiling that day, but it most certainly was not. Before rolling out, the team was changing up. Aaron was set to depart as he had obligations back at school to tend to, so a new fixer and translator was brought in. We'll call him Kirk.

He was just over 6 feet tall and had curly blonde hair. He had a dark blonde goatee that he would run his fingers through when he was thinking, and wore red pants with a dark colored sweater. His English wasn't quite as good as Aaron's, but he was extremely smart. He had spent years working as a journalist and photographer for a newspaper in Ukraine, so was well versed in what we needed in order to accomplish our jobs. Kirk was probably the best fixer we had on the trip. He had strong connections to the local Ukrainian government, knew the area and geography of Ukraine well, and was a basket of information when it came to the war and Ukrainian culture. He was a great addition to the team. We met Kirk in downtown Lviv before heading out for our story that day which was to take place at the main train station near the city center.

What I could not believe is that a week and a half or so into the war, people were still struggling to get out of Ukraine. You would have to spend days to get through the land crossing to Poland and there was no indication this was going to stop. Lviv as a city played an outsized role in getting people out as it became a main hub for people fleeing across the country. While Lviv is not a border town, there is a train station which will take you directly into Poland: a straight shot out.

The train station itself was tucked away in a corner of the city that was not easy to get to by car, so we had to park a few blocks away. The moment we foot on the cobblestone, I knew what we were walking into. There was this sound off in the distance that reminds me of being a few blocks away from a football stadium mid-game. You can't make out any distinct voices or any words, but you can hear the chorus of horns, shouts, and cries colliding. Put together, it's like a white noise.

We started walking down the empty road with that roaring hum emanating from the background. It grew louder and louder with every step we took. Finally, we turned the corner into an opening which led right to the front entryway of the train station. It stood in the center of another large, open square.

I can only describe the situation as unfettered chaos. There was a line of people stretched out the door that must have carried on for a thousand yards. They stood there anxiously bundled up in their winter coats shaking back and forth to stay warm. Some lurched up on their tip toes to get a better view of the front of the line which seemed like an eternal wait to reach. The queue would move up a pace, and everyone would take one pace forward—keeping their chests no more than a foot behind the person in front of them.

But there we were face to face with thousands of Ukrainians huddled outside of the train station. Most waited in line. Some were walking up and down the lines, appearing to try and sell items like hand warmers and bottles of water. There was a large number of Ukrainians who gave up on standing and effectively made camp on the ground—putting their belongings into a circle with their other family members and attempting to stay warm. It felt like everywhere we went, we saw people focused solely on surviving.

Kirk stood up on a bench to see the individual faces in the crowd, then picked out a young woman with a guitar case and stringy brown hair. Her face was pale, and she stood there with an aimless look on her face as she stared forward toward

FIGURE 9.1 The line of people at the train station in Lviv, Ukraine, attempting to flee the country. Photo by Robert Sherman.

the front of the line. She looked miserable and barely gave any expression when Kirk approached her.

"How long have you been waiting here?" Kirk asked.

She turned toward him. "Four hours," she said in English, clearly too exhausted to provide a flicker more of emotion. She was maybe three-quarters of the way back in line. There was a long day of waiting yet ahead for her. "It took me a week to get a ticket, so I guess I'm lucky."

"Where are you from?" asked Kirk.

"Kharkiv," she answered, still without emotion.

Now I understood. Every day there were headlines coming out of Kharkiv as the city was brutally bombed to pieces. The Ukrainians refused to give up any ground in that highly strategic area near the Russian border, causing some of the most brutal fighting of the war to take hold there. Before the fighting, it was Ukraine's second-largest city. Centuries of history were turned to rubble and much of the city became unlivable in a matter of days.

"It's been intense," the woman said with a sigh. "We got bombed while we were at the train station. All the people ducked and covered their heads."

The woman explained she traveled from Kharkiv to Lviv by train earlier and was now trying to just get out of the country. Poland would be her starting point, and then she would figure out her next step later. Many Ukrainians had the same strategy: survive any way possible, then come up with a long-term plan.

"I hope it's going to be a month or two, this whole war," she said. "Then it will end, and I'll come back." It's remarkable to hear people in the early days of the war holding onto hope that the pain and displacement would be short-lived. Obviously, things did not play out that way. We walked up the line toward the front and saw much more of the same. Anxiety. Fear. Dejection. Agony. Uncertainty. You didn't even need to ask most folks—their faces told the whole story.

We made it to the front, being careful to make clear to everyone we weren't trying to cut in ahead of anyone in line. Kirk walked up to a man who was all the way at the front door. He stood there with a heavy coat and a bowling hat. This gentleman did not speak English, so Kirk spoke with him in Ukrainian. Whatever the man said, it was filled with defeat. His shoulders were drooped. His hand gestures never rose above his waist. He struggled to make eye contact.

Kirk turned to us and explained. "He's waited eight hours to get to this point. Inside, he expects another three more. He's hoping there will be space to get on a train to Poland today."

Eleven hours in total to maybe get on a train? Then again, what other choice did these people have?

We saw a woman wearing a blue coat get off one of the trains and start making her way outside. Kirk stopped her to ask a few questions. When she turned toward us, I saw the tears welling in her eyes. Kirk said something, and she began to melt right in front of us.

"Our city has centuries of history, and they're destroying it!" she exclaimed, through Kirk's translation. "It's unbelievable. It's unbelievable. They're animals." She couldn't bear to say any more as she wiped the tears from her eyes. Shaking her head, she picked up her bags and walked off before we could ask her any more questions.

But then a husband and wife approached us, seeing our microphone and camera. They must have been in their 40s, and both were wearing heavy, winter coats with fur. "You are journalists, yes?" We responded affirmatively, explaining we were from the United States. The man did not speak English well so looked at Kirk and asked if he could translate. He then proceeded to tell us their story of escape in Ukraine. They lived in a small town in Eastern Ukraine which was invaded by the Russians. The man claimed they hid in their basement as the Russian tanks rolled into town.

"One tank stopped in front of our house," Kirk translated on their behalf. "And they started shooting. Then some soldiers entered our house. They opened fire on our windows and broke in our doors. We screamed 'there are small children here! Please, do not shoot!'"

He stared at the ground, shaking his head as he recalled the chilling details. They heard Russian soldiers break into their home and tear their living room apart. When nightfall set in, they made their escape and fled for Lviv. They never thought the Russians would seriously invade, and now they never expect to see their home again.

FIGURE 9.2 With no sense of certainty as to when, or if, they shall return to their country, Ukrainians pack up their livelihoods and most essential possessions before making their exodus. Photo by Robert Sherman.

The woman chimed into the conversation. "It's impossible. It's the twenty-first century, and people are being shot and houses are being burned? It must be stopped," She said.

I was stunned by the couple's harrowing tale of escape. We quickly realized that very few of the people here at this train station were actually from Lviv. Those who were from here and wanted to leave were already gone. Everyone here was *already* a refugee. In these early days of the war, there was such a focus on refugees who had already fled Ukraine to other parts of Europe. Millions of people did get out. But what was often overlooked by politicians and journalists alike were the millions more who were displaced *within* Ukraine. Lviv was viewed as a safe haven, and many arrived with little to nothing except for a single suitcase and pennies to their names.

We thanked the couple for sharing their story and wished them luck. Standing at the front of the line, we turned back around to see the queue stretching down the street. It was so long you couldn't pinpoint exactly where it began. Adding to that, bright yellow and red buses would pull up next to the line at their respective stops. Long columns of bundled-up people would trudge down the stairs and make a hard right turn to get into line. The already eternally long line was getting longer and longer as more people were coming than going.

But then, everything changed. The clattering of voices was drowned out.

Tuh-dum-dee-dum-dee-dum-dee-dah

A melodic tune that could only be made by a piano started to belt out over the crowd. It was coming from nearby. We turned and saw a small huddle of people gathered around one of the pillars that stood outside the station.

FIGURE 9.3 In the midst of chaos, a piano man attempts to serenade and soothe the line of distressed Ukrainians as they prepare to make their escape. Photo by Robert Sherman.

Strolling over to see what was happening, the crowd began to grow larger and larger. A man had brought a piano to the train station and was playing away. Beethoven classics. Brahms' Lullaby. Some of the more common songs you'll hear on a piano.

But even if the crowd had heard all these songs before, it may as well have been a newly minted masterpiece. Those who stayed and listened were transfixed by the sequencing of chords and tapping of keys.

A father stood there with his two children under each arm—clutched tightly. Another child with a small red suitcase seemed to fall asleep while sitting at their parent's feet as the notes carried out. There was even a smile or two visible in the crowd.

Most ignored the music entirely, especially those in line. They were too focused on the mission at hand and getting on a train any way possible. But some broke off from the line and came over. Despite all the shouting and chattering that created a wall of indiscernible sound, the piano music pierced through the air.

The pianist was a man draped in a puffy winter jacket and wearing a beanie to stay warm. I don't know how he was able to get enough circulation to his fingers, but his hands moved swiftly from key to key without lingering. He played with passion like it was his first time on stage at Carnegie Hall. His eyes were closed and he let the melody carry his body from one ditty to the next.

Even I was mesmerized at this point. The music was beautiful, but even more so comforting. I can't explain it, but I swear the cold didn't feel as cold while listening to the piano man tap along. The pandemonium didn't seem so overwhelming. In the midst of an invasion and desperate attempts at fleeing, for the first time everything seemed like it would be all right. This went on for a few minutes until he wrapped up his performance. The small crowd clapped enthusiastically. Some of the parents pointed at the piano man while making happy faces to their children. It was a brief reprieve from the chaos, just like the ice rink.

Bartley approached the man, who happened to speak English as well, and asked him what he was doing. He looked at Bartley for a moment and paused, then glanced at the people who gathered. Finally, he returned his gaze to us and said, "there's a lot of people here having a bad day. I wanted to make it better, so I brought my piano."

The pianist explained every day since the invasion he had been down here performing free little concerts for those waiting in line to escape Ukraine. He had no intention to leave. This is where he belonged in that moment. We asked to interview him, but he declined. He didn't want the attention, just to help soothe the pain so many were feeling. I had a theater teacher in high school who told me, with conviction, "there are no small roles in theater. Just small actors."

A life lesson learned which applies here: in moments of crisis, we all have a role to play—and none are small.

10 THE MOST INNOCENT OF ALL

There is a phrase that gets thrown around our culture which is "never forget the little people." Inevitably, when discussing a subject like war, you think of the heads of state. You think of the powers that be. You think of the soldiers. But the little people? Despite best intentions, they are sometimes an afterthought. And in this case, making a clear definition here, I do not use "little" to mean insignificant.

I mean "little" as in the children. And for this story, to be more specific, I mean the orphaned children. What happens to an orphanage when a city is bombed? I sure couldn't have answered that question when we first arrived in the country. A worse admission? I didn't even think to ask.

Bartley came through on this one. He was able to find a contact who set us up with an orphanage in Lviv. The story was the orphanage was busting at the seams with children because they took so many in from cities like Kharkiv and other regions that bore the brunt of the Russian invasion. At the time, Mariupol and Kherson had already fallen to the Russian military. Some of these children got out just in time.

Our car pulled up to the orphanage which looked like many elementary schools I've seen in the United States. Faded brick that became a yellowish-red color, windows that were dark and uninviting, and a fence around the building to keep unwelcome visitors away. We stepped out of the car and I felt the crunch of leaves underneath my feet. Autumn had come and gone, but some of the fallen leaves remained scattered across the driveway. One of many chores that appeared to have gone untended at this place.

A man dressed in a dark wool coat came out. He had gray hair and a warm but goofy smile that was reassuring. He took out a key, unbolted the lock and removed the chain that held the gate closed. We entered, and were led to the front door. As we got right up close to it, we could hear the sound of children playfully screaming on the other side. The man smiled, and without breaking eye contact with us, pushed the door open. The sounds of laughter barreled through the opening.

"Come in, come in," said the man. Pat, Kirk, Bartley and I stepped foot into the hall which was poorly lit. Tile flooring that must have been there for forty years was peeling away underneath our winter boots. The walls had small paper drawings all over them. Dragons, princesses, and flowers sketched out in color pencils brought the innocence of children into this somber place.

A woman came down the hall and greeted us in Ukrainian. Kirk responded and translated for us, explaining her name was Susan and she was the deputy director of the orphanage. She had her dark hair combed into a center part and cut to a medium length, and wore a sweater that had purple, black and white stripes. What struck me the most was the look of existential dread on her face. It could have been from the diligent task of caring for dozens of children, or maybe it was the stress the bombings inevitably take on you. In hindsight, it was probably a lot of both.

Before we met the children, she wanted to speak with us first and explain the situation. She led us upstairs to an empty classroom. Like much of the building, it was poorly lit. Desks were scattered and stacked in the corners and the chalk board was old and crumbling apart.

Susan looked around and gave a sigh, holding out her arms as if to say "this is what we're working with." Kirk was tasked with translating the entire exchange, but unprompted, Susan just started talking before I could even ask a question. She had a lot to say, but none of it was angry or even sad. It was like a cry for help, and in fact it was.

"It's scary," Kirk explained, translating for Susan. "When they arrive, you look at these children and they're scared. They're shaking, screaming and hysterical, and don't understand what is happening here."

Kirk added that twenty children alone had come in these recent weeks with likely more on the way. For an organization that was already trying to make do with what they had, twenty extra mouths to feed was no short order.

"There are those here who already have their own traumas, and this new situation is amplifying it," She said. Then, Susan paused, as if she were picking carefully what her one wish would be. "We have everything we need here. We only need peace. We need to have confidence in the future. We need your support to understand we are not alone in this world."

That was her big plea. For the war to end and the nightmare to cease: a sentiment shared by many. I could only imagine what she was talking about. These "amplified traumas" for the children. This is a part of the war I didn't want to think about. The emotional tolls suffered by the most innocent of souls. As suspected, many came from cities like Kharkiv, Kyiv, Mariupol which were ground zero for the war. Susan was clearly holding back tears at this point, and then said something to Kirk in Ukrainian. It was pretty quiet, as if she was sharing a secret she didn't want too many people to hear.

Kirk turned to us and said, "she has family in Russia. They support the war. It's a very sore subject for her." Susan stood there with her head pointed to the ground with disappointment.

This reminded me a lot of what Olivia, the Ukrainian mother, had to say. Some Ukrainians are very close with the Russian people or even have Russians in their close family. Many, of course, saw the war through a political lens, but when it hits so close to home, I had to imagine Susan took it personally. Family members supporting the war as you try to get children out of conflict zones? Just from looking at Susan as she made mention of this, I could tell it was emotionally eating her alive.

Susan didn't want to speak any more on the subject, and decided to take us downstairs and through the hall back the way we came. The sound of laughter growing louder and louder as we retraced our steps. I looked at the walls and couldn't take my eyes off of some of the sketches made by the children that I had seen earlier. Princesses and dragons seemed like a remarkably innocent thing to doodle considering how their lives had been turned upside down.

Susan finally brought us to a brown wooden door with a white paper sign on it that appeared to be written in water color. She smiled, gave a little knock which was greeted by excited clamoring on the other side. A young woman with dark hair, bright eyes and a big smile opened the door. We'll call her Jasmine.

"Ah, you're here!" she exclaimed. "Come on in!" The door swung open fully and we were greeted by thirty of the most wide eyed faces I'd ever seen. Children were sprawled over the floor playing on their hands and knees when we came in— quickly springing to their feet and surrounding us.

Pat quickly pulled out his cell phone and started recording. I'll give him credit, he handled it as well as one could considering so many of the kiddos were getting scooting right into the camera lens for their close up. Some even leaped up and swung on his arms as he tried to hold the device steady. It was cute to watch.

Later I would see some of the footage of the children. They would get right in front of the phone, puff out their cheeks, stick out their tongues, and make wobbly movements with their eyes. It was nothing shy of adorable. These kids seemingly came alive once we arrived.

Nobody, however, was more excited than Jasmine. She must have been in her late teens or early 20s, and clearly loved each and every child. She made it a point to go around and point out each child and say their name, say what she loved about them.

"And this is Sophie. I love her smile! And this is Sasha. She is *so* funny!" Jasmine would go around and around, unable to get her fill. It's such a joy to see someone so in love with their work and their job commit themselves fully. By the time she ticked off the third child's name, I had lost track of everyone. It was an absolute frenzy of children running around, skipping, hooting and hollering. Jasmine then picked up one of the little girls wearing a pink hoodie with rainbow colored shoulders. "I mean look at these eyes! It's just diamonds!" she proclaimed in her best English.

She was so proud to show off her little treasures. Without question, she was the happiest most joyful person we met in Ukraine. Those children, in that moment anyways, were all tied for a close second.

"I really like those little eyes," she said, referencing the child she was holding and unable to contain her own giggles. "And that smile." Jasmine was one of the teachers and caretakers at the orphanage, and spent most of her week there with the children. "They need love," Jasmine emphasized. "They need just people who will be with them. Together. That's all."

She held on to hope that every child would be adopted any day now. Susan, who stood off in the corner, was more concerned the children would be safe. She told Kirk that she was currently working on an emergency plan in case the frontlines of the war came here. If need be, she was prepared to get them over the Polish border and out of the country all together. You could tell by the way she stood there gazing at the children that she was doing her absolute best to hold in her fears and worries. It was like she didn't want to spoil the innocent joy both Jasmine and all of the children had.

It felt similar to what Olivia said from the perspective of a mother, that in times like these it's up to a mother to put on a smile and good face for her child. Susan was trying to do that for thirty different ones.

That was one of my favorite days in Ukraine, and I'm pretty confident the same could be said for the rest of the team. We turned Pat loose and let him run around with the children, videotaping anything and everything he wanted. He was crawling under tables, playing "peek-a-boo" with the camera. For a brief moment, we were all able to forget about things like war and missiles and focus on the small things. The laughter of a child. The joy of a teacher fully committed to her work.

Sadly, that wasn't the only orphanage dealing with juggling the needs of children without parents mixed in with an invasion. There are countless organizations throughout Europe and the United States who were working to get as many out as possible. Some reached out to us after this story aired as they wanted to be more involved or share their own struggles.

We departed the orphanage shortly thereafter and made the children the focus of our evening reports that day. I don't know what happened to those smiling faces there, but I hope they're still smiling, wherever they may be.

11 POLAND ON THE BRINK

It's all fun and games until somebody gets hurt.

I cannot explain it to you. I really wish I could. But it didn't matter how many distraught faces I saw, how many times I had to run into an air raid shelter, or how many times I saw groups of Ukrainian soldiers walking down the street and militia members manning the various checkpoints. It never really sunk in that I was in an active warzone. A lot of that is my fault. I was still far too immature and caught up in the adventure. *What great stories I'll have to tell my friends when I'm home*, I would at times think to myself. I know my mom was worried sick and my friends back home feared for my safety. Despite all of that, I'm ashamed to say in my heart, I was actually having some degree of "fun." My life had never seemed so exciting.

For example, the first time I saw a rocket launcher rolling out into the field, I was awestruck by the caliber of weaponry before my eyes. It doesn't hit you at the moment that behind that missile is a human being, surely with loved ones, who believes firing that missile accurately and swiftly will give him or her the best chance at returning home. It also doesn't hit you that if the soldier does their job, they will be taking a life or multiple lives at once. The movies and video games that occupy our culture have done an excellent job of ripping the humanity from war.

All of these concepts slipped past me at the time, and this is where I'm so grateful to have been with Bartley. As I was losing sight of the big story and the devastation that was around us, he got me back into line. One example was a night in which we thought Lviv was going to get bombed pretty hard. Our team was sitting in the conference room of the hotel waiting to get our security update. "It's not good," Bartley announced, going on to explain that several of the other news teams from other networks were on high alert. "The thinking is, we could get hit tonight."

Brian was in charge of making sure all security measures were in check, so he left to put together a plan. Pat and Kirk stayed where they were. Kirk seemed a bit nervous, twiddling his brown curly hair, and stroking his goatee. Pat just nodded his head with pursed lips. This was a serious situation that no one was taking lightly. Everyone was on the same page that it was time to buckle up and be prepared for the worst.

Everyone except me, that is.

"Can we wear the vests tonight?" I blurted out. I couldn't see my own face but I'm sure it had a stupid, beaming smile plastered across it. Up to this point, the bullet-proof vests had stayed packed up in the car. Bartley was old-school and didn't believe in hyping things up more than they needed to be. When I said that, Bartley just looked at me with a puzzled stare. I may as well have shouted out "Yahtzee!"

"No," Bartley said in a tone of certainty. The way a parent talks to their kid when they ask for a new toy.

"Oh come on!" I said, sounding like the aforementioned child asking for a new Lego set. "Now's our chance!"

"No," Bartley said more sternly. He was giving a clear hint for me to shut up. It went right over my head. Or, I just simply ignored it. Either way, wrong move.

"You're so lame. Who put you in charge anyway?" I said while laughing. I was genuinely just trying to be funny at this point and tease Bartley like I always had. Pat and Kirk both cracked slight smiles.

Bartley wasn't in the mood for nonsense. He spun around, grabbed hold of the door by its edge, and slammed it shut on the way out.

Kirk didn't say a word. Pat's eyes bulged out of his sockets like an insect. I just kept laughing, brushing the whole exchange off. I assumed Bartley wasn't being serious. A few moments later I felt my phone buzz. It was a text from Bartley. Before I even opened my phone, I felt my back tighten with tension. I knew a "wake up" moment was coming, I could feel it. I was afraid to look at my phone knowing Bartley was upset. Finally, after composing myself, I picked it up and opened up his message. I've kept it to this very day.

"It's adult time. You need to take this seriously."

I immediately shut down after reading that and felt utterly ashamed of myself. I had lost my grip on what was happening. That night I went up to see Bartley and profusely apologized. To my surprise, he wasn't angry. He was understanding that I was getting carried away, but made clear that he would not tolerate any childish antics from me, especially as the situation now started to look legitimately dangerous.

It was the shoulder shaking I needed because what came next really rocked the whole team. The morning after, news broke that one of the reporting teams for another American cable network had been hit. We didn't know much in the moment, but later we would come to find out that the cameraman and fixer were killed. The correspondent survived, but was permanently disfigured. Finally, my bubble of blissful ignorance had been popped. We were pretty conservative in our risk-taking since making the cross into Ukraine. But now, the simple act of being on the streets was worrisome.

It was no surprise to us that later in the day we were given the order by our Chicago headquarters to pull back to Poland. We didn't protest as the war just became real to us. I really appreciated NewsNation's dedication and commitment to safety. We checked out of our hotel and packed up the blue minivan. Kirk, Brian, Bartley, and I weren't wasting any time. We had about a six hour drive ahead to get back to Polish soil and we knew we'd have to stop at a dozen checkpoints along the way. The key was to get home before nightfall.

The somber tone of our retreat was broken with a small issue: what do we do with Pat? Two days earlier we had "fired" him but we still needed to get him out of Ukraine.

The Ukrainian government had just banned the sale and distribution of alcohol in the country while the war was going on, so getting a drink at a restaurant wasn't a possibility. Not that it was a necessity, but there is something to be said for a cold beer to relax during downtime.

The company we were going through which provided the team to us, including Pat, decided to send us a "care package" filled with supplies. Snacks, medical kits, toiletries, and yes, alcohol. Pat was in charge of going to collect the supply kit early in the morning and we never thought twice about it since we were busy putting our reports together. But that night we had plans on a big dinner at the hotel we were staying in, and the thought of a drink was more than well awaited. By this point, it had been a dry week or two in Ukraine.

Dinner was served, the food was hot, and Pat came strolling in with the goods. He set a small bottle of vodka and two small bottles of beer down on the dinner table. That was for six people.

"Where's the rest of it?" Bartley asked.

Pat shrugged his shoulders. "That's all they sent us."

"That's it?" Bartley asked again. Pat nodded.

None of us expected the Budweiser Clydesdales to pull into Lviv with a cart full of libations, and of course we did have bigger priorities, but two beers and a small bottle of vodka was paltry for six people to last the rest of the month.

Consider this: how is beer distributed in the United States? Unless you're buying a single bottle from a gas station, it never comes in those quantities. You almost always buy a six pack, a twelve pack, or a twenty-four pack. And yes, when I was in Greencastle, Indiana going to college, the holy grail "30-rack" of Hamm's Special Light was an option.

I'm no Sherlock Holmes, and I am not armed with a shred of proof, but I stand here today firmly convinced that clown drank it all. If the production company sent a six pack, Pat drank four. If it was a twelve pack, Pat drank ten. Or hoarded them.

What kind of person does that to the team that has hired them? Pat. That's who. Our fleeting suspicions were confirmed, or at the very least stoked when two nights in a row Pat showed up to our reports absolutely wasted—despite there being no alcohol to be found in Ukraine. Incoherent and rambling on about unicorns, singing songs about rainbows. You think I'm exaggerating. I wish I was. All true. I've never seen Bartley so angry. When he fired Pat at around two o'clock in the morning, the man was so drunk it all went in one ear and out the other.

So, as we were preparing to make our exodus from Ukraine, Bartley had to deal with the Pat problem.

"He's not sitting in that car with us," I overheard Bartley bark into his phone. On the other end of the line was the head of the production company who provided us with the crew and logistics. I could overhear the man pleading with Bartley, saying something to the effect of, "It will make things much easier to get him home if he rides in the car with you all. He won't say a word, I promise."

"I don't care!" Fired back Bartley. "He is *not* riding with us."

"He's very sorry and embarrassed," added the man.

"Good," said Bartley.

"If he doesn't ride with you we'll have to send another car to get him, and that could—"

"Perfect." Bartley wouldn't give an inch. A word to the wise: never try and argue with Bartley Price after he's made up his mind.

The man on the other end of the phone was silent, trying to think up any strategy to convince Bartley to relent. Finally, he gave in. "We'll send another car." The vibrations of defeat could be felt from Warsaw to Kyiv.

"Sounds good. See you in Poland!" Bartley added with a charming flare to the end.

Before I die, I hope to add Bartley's skill of looking someone in the eye and smiling while telling them to pound sand. Granted, this was over the phone, but I've seen him do it a thousand times. My Midwestern politeness would have been eaten alive.

Rolling out of Lviv was a surreal moment. I looked back at all the beautiful stone buildings and gorgeous statues. Through it all, the Western Ukrainian city remained standing. I thought back on all of the people we met there.

Despite my spurts of immaturity, I was abundantly aware of the fact that we stepped into their situation for a matter of days and were able to leave. For them, this was the nightmare reality they couldn't escape.

When we reached the last leg of our exodus, some of the towns near the border came into focus. We were on the road where just a few days earlier cars were lined up for miles on end. After a few weeks of frantic evacuations the roads were now empty, but there were hundreds of cars off to the side left behind.

It reminded me of those post-apocalyptic films where cities were left abandoned overnight. Families had picked up their lives and left: dropping what they were doing in that moment and leaving the small remedial tasks unfinished.

As we passed all those cars, I felt each one told an unwritten story of survival. Maybe a desperate family fleeing the war. Maybe a newlywed couple hoping love and a prayer could get them through. Who knows.

We made it all the way up to the port of entry. There was a short line to get into Poland, but nothing compared to what we saw just days earlier. The wait time was maybe an hour. Finally, our car pulled up to the border guards and immigration officers. We handed them our stack of passports. After briefly fiddling through our documents, he gave each one a stamp, then returned them.

"Welcome to Poland," he said with a nod, before waving us through.

I never knew hearing those words could cause such a sense of relief to an American. I can only imagine what they meant to a Ukrainian refugee.

* * *

Throughout the first month of the war, there was this lingering question: where does it all end? If Russia rolls through Ukraine, who will be in the crosshairs next? A NATO country formerly with Soviet ties like Estonia? Latvia? Lithuania? What about Finland? Maybe Poland?

Many of us Americans do not have a grasp on European geography—much less Eastern European. But, if you look at a map, it puts a lot of this into perspective.

For example, Poland shares a border with Ukraine. By this point in the book, you are more than well aware of that. But did you know if you picked up a rental car in Berlin, Germany and drove nonstop you'd be in Ukraine in about eight hours? *Eight.*

Prague? The capital of the Czech Republic? Similar story. It'll take you about seven hours. How about Venice? A stunning, Western European city in the beautiful country of Italy? Ten hours if you go through Hungary.

Now, let's switch it up. How long will it take you to drive across the state of Texas? Twelve hours. That's right, El Paso to the Gulf of Mexico is a longer drive than Ukraine from these European countries we've conjured up as being "safe" and "removed" from war.

When you really focus on the geography, it's much easier to understand why so many people living across Europe were on edge and worried about their own futures. Ukraine and Germany might seem like worlds apart in one's mind if you hail from the Western hemisphere, but geography shows that's not exactly the case.

Add in another factor: Poland is a country that knows invasion all too well. September 1, 1939, German forces rolled into their neighbor's land from the west. Shortly after, the Soviet Union followed from the east. But even beyond that obvious example, Poland has seen armies bearing foreign standards enter its territory time and time again throughout the previous centuries.

FIGURE 11.1 The center square of Zamość, Poland, as Europe braces to take in millions of refugees while fearing the war may come to their doorstep. Photo by Robert Sherman.

It's no surprise then that many Poles we met were apprehensive. "If it happened to Ukraine, it could happen to us" was a common sentiment.

We woke up bright and early and departed our hotel on the outskirts of Zamość, Poland and made our way into town. It's easy to get lost in these cities due to their beauty. At the heart of the town was an open forum.

Standing in the center was the city hall which, to this day, is one of the most stunning buildings I have seen in Europe. A pearly white clock tower that the sun radiantly dances off hulks over the square. The average building there couldn't have been more than five stories tall, so compared to those the structure was enormous. It had a pair of grand staircases flowing from the front door down to the forum. Trimmed with a pink, tan color, the white stone emanated this sense of purity.

The buildings that made up the perimeter of the square each were their own unique color. A bright yellow building would be followed by a blue one, then green, then red, and the variance would continue on.

The population of Zamość stands at around 60,000 residents. The center square was quiet save for a couple of folks sipping espressos at a nearby café. We saw a man and woman pushing a stroller across the forum and decided to go speak with them. It was a young couple. The woman wore a fluffy headband and scarf that covered much of her dark hair tied in a ponytail. The man wore a gray skiing jacket and dark pants. They told us their names and said they were open to chatting with us for a few minutes. We'll call them Christine and Pete.

The young couple was very up to date on the war and told us how sad they felt it had come to this level of fighting. They added Ukrainian refugees were coming through their town every day.

"Do you fear Poland could be invaded?" I finally asked. The couple stood there in silence. Their hearts sank as they considered that prospect.

"Yes, such thoughts come to us," Christine said finally. "We are afraid that Poland will be next, but we hope that the war will end and there will be peace."

Then Christine looked down at their one-year-old daughter, who was sitting in the stroller: ogling and giggling at the conversation. She brought a sense of innocence to a difficult discussion. Christine looked back up at us then finished. "We are worried about living in such a country. We just want to live in peace." She nodded her head when she finished as if to say she was satisfied with what she said. We thanked her, and they went on their way.

Another couple walked up to us. Both young as well. A woman with dirty blonde hair and a man wearing a black leather jacket, white t-shirt, and beanie cap. We'll call them Veronica and Derek. They told us they were both students in Poland and keeping a very close eye on what was happening across the border. "In general it's making me nervous," Veronica explained. "It's a terrible situation. People are dying. It's just wrong." Veronica was a bit tepid about going into whether she thought Poland should take in all Ukrainian refugees. This was a conversation happening at the time in Poland. Could they take in some refugees? Most Poles were on board. But millions? Not necessarily. She wanted to steer clear of going into that.

Derek was a bit more outspoken on what he wanted from other NATO members, particularly the US, as the war inched closer to their doorstep. "I think right now in Poland, we are the supporting country for the Ukrainian people. So we do have help from the US, but we need more help," said Derek.

"Yes, we are just regular people. We can't do much, but President Biden can do more," Veronica chimed in.

Derek nodded his head in agreement. He was a bit more optimistic about Poland's security amid the conflict.

"I think because we are in NATO, if Russia attacks us there will be a World War. So, I think we are in a safe position," Derek said. "The poor people from Ukraine are coming here, so we need to help them. Right now we kind of feel safe here. I am from the Ukrainian border, so there are a lot of people getting out of Ukraine to have a normal life. I think we need more support to support them."

And then there was John, a tall, athletic Pole who wore a white Nike baseball cap and a red jacket. We stopped him as he was passing by, and his English was about as close to perfect as could be. John, however, was growing more frustrated with countries like the United States who didn't have to deal with the war so imminently.

"It's happening. The atrocities are happening. The West should know it's true. It's right next door to us, and it could come closer," John said, gesturing passionately. "I've talked to my friends in America who say this topic is not as important for us right here, right now. So, I'd like that message to spread and to see more support from citizens around the world."

Those conversations continued on throughout the afternoon. Pole after Pole told us they were at the very least on edge with what was happening in Ukraine next door. Zamość also played a critical role as it was a point where many Ukrainian refugees staged before heading to other parts of Europe. Millions crossed through this region of Poland. We were able to secure an interview with the mayor to speak to this issue. Andrzej Wnuk was his name. He had slicked back hair tightly cut on either side and wore a navy pea coat with a steel colored scarf. He spoke with meticulous intent—choosing his words carefully. On the one hand, he wanted to voice every concern he had. On the other, he did not want to cause panic in his community.

When speaking with us, he focused his attention on the refugee crisis.

"We have never seen a refugee crisis like this since the second World War," Wnuk said. "We need help. Two million have already crossed into Poland. They will need long-term accommodations."

Pressing him for more perspective, we asked what kind of help they needed here and if that included NATO forces on the ground. He paused briefly, calculating his answer, before saying help from the West is what they needed, but clarifying he did not think his city was in the path of imminent danger. "The people know they are protected from the aggressive policy of the Kremlin," he said at last. "We don't want war, but we're not afraid of it either. We will fight for our land in the case of war."

As such, he like many Polish leaders wanted NATO forces on the ground to ensure none of the fighting spilled from Ukraine. An effective show of force. Wnuk was the first Polish official we spoke with in-person. That's when the clear tightrope game of trying to be in support of Ukraine but not become adversarial with Russia became evident. Poland wanted peace, and did not want the fighting to continue in Ukraine. They also wanted their sovereignty to not be infringed upon and for any advances toward their country to be deterred. The uncertainty surrounding Russia's long-term objectives muddied all of this.

Little did we know it was just a matter of time before boots would really hit the ground.

12 HOME AT LAST

Allow me to set the scene for you. Imagine you're sitting in a Polish café. It's late morning, teetering on lunchtime. The sun is up, the spring afternoon temperatures are starting to punch through the frigid air, and towns that have gone into hibernation for months are starting to see life again.

You're sitting at the café table with your work colleagues as the server pours a scalding hot cup of coffee and slips a shallow bowl full of pierogis on your table. Despite your best intentions, you're lulled into a sense of comfort. The world seems normal. The simple things in life are the most magical. War seems like an unworldly concept. And then, like an ominous string quartet bowing a nefarious villain's entrance, or the jagged melody of the "Jaws" theme, peace is disturbed. The coffee in your mug begins to ripple. The table in front of you rattles. You feel the vibration coursing from the floorboards through your legs and up your spine.

Turning around and peering through the cloudy window, you see it: a column of tanks and Humvees rolling down the Polish highway with their dark metal glistening in the spring sun and treads trampling the pavement. You can't see the end of the line, but the tip of the spear is heading right toward you. That was our situation one Polish morning as our team sat in a diner just off the highway. The café was comparable to a truck stop as it had a big parking lot. One by one, the Humvees and trucks pulled in as the tanks proceeded down the road.

The fleet of vehicles came to a halt and the roaring motors pattered off. We knew who these people were before their combat boots hit the pavement. Once the first soldier stepped out and that flag of freedom could be seen plastered on his shoulder, there was no mistaking it: home had arrived.

Just days earlier, President Biden had addressed the nation in the State of the Union. As the world anxiously rocked in its seat waiting to see how the war in Ukraine would shake out around the globe, the President attempted to quell those fears. "And as I've made crystal clear, the United States and our Allies will defend every inch of territory that is NATO territory with the full force of our collective power—every single inch," President Biden declared.[1]

As such, the American military, as well as other NATO forces, were deployed to the Polish border in case the war moved any further west and violated Poland's sovereignty. We were now standing face to face with the president's red line.

FIGURE 12.1 US military equipment rolling down the streets in Eastern Poland after President Biden vowed the United States will protect all of its NATO allies. Photo by Robert Sherman.

The trucks emptied and American soldiers filed out of the back: hooting, hollering, and laughing. I understand why Europeans accuse Americans of being loud and obnoxious, but in that moment I was proud to be an American and see our armed forces deployed in person. Dozens of soldiers entered the café with big smiles wrapped around their faces. Most went straight for the restroom or stood in line to pick up coffee and lunch. One soldier, a bit short and stocky, straggled in last, his eyes darting around the café. He seemed excited, taking it all in.

"Where are you from, man?" I asked with a smile.

He turned to me with a bewildered look on his face. "Jesus Christ, you speak English?" he asked in disbelief.

"Yes sir, we're from the States," I responded.

"God damn, you scared me! I ain't heard nothin' but Polish for days," he said to me with a sigh of relief. He then gathered himself. "I'm from New Smyrna Beach, Florida."

"No kidding! I used to live in Orlando, maybe an hour from New Smyrna," I replied. It is true, New Smyrna is one of America's finest beach towns that folks outside of Florida likely haven't heard of. I secretly hope it stays an undiscovered gem to most.

"Aw hell yeah, brother!" he said, giving me a fist bump. "I'll tell you what, I'd much rather be there than here today. It's cold as hell here. But in a few weeks I'll be on leave and back home sipping beers on the water." Another life lesson right there: sometimes a cold beer is the only incentive you need at the finish line to get you through the race.

FIGURE 12.2 A Humvee passing by the US military base established in Eastern Poland. Photo by Robert Sherman.

I looked around the café which had become abuzz with the arrival of the soldiers. Some locals came up and shook their hands and bought them their morning coffee. Seeing American armed forces arriving in their hometowns was well received and welcomed. It was certainly preferred to seeing the Russians here, I can tell you that much.

We departed the café and set off to find where the soldiers were stationed. Our hope was to see if we could meet some of the leadership and talk about the situation here in Poland. I had very low hopes they would bother to meet with us, for the sake of national security and military defense, but it was worth asking.

We got into our car and rolled down the highway. We didn't have to go far to find the base. The big giveaway? The PATRIOT Missile defense systems scattered throughout an open field. These things were massive and pointed at the sky—ready to pick off any enemy missiles that entered Polish airspace. I say "enemy," but really at the time, the United States and NATO were trying their hardest to thread the needle between arming the Ukrainians and staying out of the conflict. Nevertheless, to see such powerful machines of warfare on full display was a pretty surreal experience.

While Bartley and I did make it onto the US base, I won't go into detail as to what happened as we were told very directly that the second we set foot on that ground, everything was off the record which I'll adhere to. What I can tell you is that day we met some of the leadership, and while we were given a few details about NATO operations in Eastern Poland, no interviews were granted.

I did walk away with a deeper understanding of this: tensions were high around the world with what was happening in Ukraine, and nobody knew what Russia's endgame was. That's why people were so nervous about how the war would shake out. One question people always ask me about Ukraine is, "how serious is the war?" I always interpret that to mean, "should I really care about this conflict?" As an American, it's a question I do understand. There are plenty of domestic issues the United States is currently grappling with, so why should one be concerned with a war between two countries on the other side of the globe? The logic makes sense.

Here's what that day, seeing the US military up close and watching missiles being unloaded and transported along the front lines, taught me: we are all one day away from waking up to a completely different world.

I pray that day never comes.

*   *   *

Things really changed for us once we left Ukraine and were back in Poland. Aside from our run-in with those American troops, it felt like we had traveled to a completely different universe—one free of war and conflict. The disconnect was most pronounced once we left the Polish border towns and traveled back to Warsaw, which is several hours away.

I remember in 2020 when the coronavirus pandemic was at its apex of uncertainty and hurricane season was in full force. The states of Louisiana and Alabama would go on to be pounded multiple times that year by major storms. Heading into that season, the conversations we were having revolved around safety. How could reporters cover the hurricanes in Louisiana while avoiding travel and staying in New York and Washington, DC, to reduce the chance of spreading or contracting Covid?

The short answer is, they cannot. Unless you are on the ground living and breathing the day to day, it's impossible to do the viewer justice. You can't report from the outside; you have to be in the middle of it.

That's how I felt about Ukraine. It became increasingly difficult to report on much of anything from Poland except for the refugee crisis. To be clear, that was a highly important story. Millions of Ukrainians fled their homeland and made their way to countries such as Poland to take refuge. Some would never go home to Ukraine and would remain permanently displaced or just try to start life all over again in a different country. We would cover the refugee crisis in Poland for about a week—telling the stories of people who lost everything due to a geopolitical crisis they couldn't control.

But it was evident we would not be going back to Ukraine due to safety concerns. I understood this and appreciated such care and dedication for our safety, but by that same token, I also firmly believe that it's irresponsible of me to continue reporting on a story like this without being able to touch, see, and feel it for myself. With that no longer being possible, the decision was made to bring us home.

Bartley and I wrapped up our final live reports from downtown Warsaw right by the Presidential Palace. After all of our reports were concluded, I heard him give a little shout. "And that's a wrap," he enthusiastically quipped, holding his arms above his head. Then he came up to me and gave me a hug. "Nice work, brother." That meant the world to me coming from the guy whose Humvee in Afghanistan had been hit by a rocket and he made it out alive. By comparison, this assignment surely must have been a piece of cake for him.

I'm glad I didn't let him down. I'm also shocked he didn't kill me while we were over there. We had been on the road together for six weeks, including our trip along the US–Mexico border. That's a lot of time spent together. Probably too much. After a brief stop-off in London, we then flew back to the United States. Bartley set a course for his home in Connecticut while I was being recalled to Chicago for a few days at our headquarters to debrief and have meetings.

But first, I had to make a connection in New York City. The flight from London to JFK was uneventful, but I spent much of it staring out the window gazing at the clouds. I distinctly remember being consumed with a sense of guilt. Despite my initial obliviousness stemming from immaturity, it became apparent to me that while in Ukraine I was one of the most fortunate people in the country. The reason being was simple: I got to leave and go home. For many of the Ukrainian people, they would be lucky if they had a home to return to.

I tried my best to stop thinking about Ukraine, knowing there would come a time for an internal audit and reflection. Eventually, I did fall asleep on the flight back across the pond—awakened by the rude but well received *thump* of the wheels pounding the tarmac. I looked out the window and saw all the familiar sights. Domestic airlines, signs written in English, grounds crews hurrying about. Some of them wearing New York Yankees and Mets caps. It didn't take long until I saw my first American flag. US soil at last.

The plane pulled into the gate slowly. I was seated right by the door and as the plane arrived and the seatbelt sign came off, I sprang out of my chair and bolted for the jetway the second the door opened. Those first footsteps felt different, like long awaited strides. The jetway led to the JFK halls which shepherded everyone to Customs and Passport Control. It was a *long* line, but I had an hour and a half until my flight to Chicago so was not too worried about making the connection.

I looked around to see all the Americans who were returning home as well. There were a lot of people in those Customs lines jockeying for position as they slowly made their way toward the kiosks to be granted access back to their home country. Yet even so, I couldn't help but wonder about their travels and how they compared to my own. *What was their story? Family vacations to Italy? Business trips to China? Hawaiian shirts? They must have been in the Caribbean. Maybe a cruise.*

The same way life carried on for some people in Ukraine, life carried on outside the country. It was business as usual at JFK. The pandemic at the time was taking its last breathe and the skies were returning to their rampant state.

I wondered how many of these people had been following the war? Did they even care? It certainly seemed like the most important thing in the world to me. The way folks carried on in that line, joking and laughing, it was as if nothing I had seen was even on their radar. Maybe it wasn't, and maybe it shouldn't have been, but the way the situation in Ukraine dominated my mind and every coffee shop conversation in Ukraine and Poland. I perhaps naively assumed that would be the case everywhere.

The line slowly trudged forward and I made my way up toward the front of the Customs area. I was in the US citizen line so it moved along pretty quickly. Little to no conversation was being had between the Customs officers and the travelers ahead. Just a "where did you go?" and a "did you bring anything with you?" before hearing the best words in international travel: "Welcome home."

I was excited to finally hear those words. At long last I made my way to the desks and handed my passport to the agent. He was well built with red hair and a beard. He threw the booklet through the scanner staring at his screen—not even bothering to look me in the eye. It all seemed routine.

Moments later I saw his facial expression change and knew something was awry. He was puzzled, then looked back down at my booklet.

"Where did you come from?" He asked incredulously.

"I was in Poland, Ukraine, and the United Kingdom," I said shyly.

"Ukraine?" he responded.

". . . Yeah," I said even more timidly than my previous answer.

"You're gonna need to come with us," he said, motioning for a security agent to come forward. *You've got to be kidding me. Again?*

The security agent was a big, intimidating fellow. I didn't say a single word as he led me, his hand on my back, to an interrogation room. *What the Hell is going on?*

"Wait here," the man said. He took my passport in his hand and closed the door behind him.

Oh no, was the only thing that could come to mind. I had been detained multiple times in Ukraine, now here I was back on US soil in the same predicament. *Am I in trouble? Are they going to punish me for ignoring the state department guidance which clearly said to not go to Ukraine? Is that even against the law? I thought that was a guideline. Are they not going to let me in to my home country?*

By this point, you the intuitive reader have likely picked up the fact my mind goes a mile a minute in stressful situations and my thoughts quickly race toward the worst case scenario. I sat at that table for what must have been twenty minutes. Finally, the door swung open and a woman in her 40s walked in. Her hair was pulled into a tight pony tail and she wore a button down shirt and a sweater. She introduced herself as an investigator for the Federal government.

Her pleasantries were short, as she then she sat down and pulled out a blue plastic envelope with my passport in it. She removed the booklet and flipped through it briefly, then got right to the point.

"How much time do you have until your flight?" she asked sternly.

I looked at my phone to check the time. "It's about to board," I said earnestly.

"Well, hopefully you make it," she tersely responded.

Gulp. Here we go, I thought.

"I need you to tell me everything about Ukraine," she said. She pulled out a legal pad and a pen and prepared to take notes.

"Ok," I responded, feeling like a cornered mouse staring into the jaws of a cat. "What do you want to know?"

She asked me a series of questions. Who did I travel with? When did I enter the country? When did I leave? Where did I stay and specific addresses? Who did I meet? A lot of it made sense in hindsight, but at the time I was nervous I had broken some kind of law and tried to answer earnestly, honestly, but carefully. Then, she started asking me about the Ukrainian military. Where I saw them, if they were just walking around the cities, where they were stationed, what kind of resources they had. She was very curious about all the checkpoints, asking me to try and remember where I encountered them and how many people were stationed there.

She wanted to know about the morale of the Ukrainian people and their thoughts on the war. What it was like to travel around the country. Were the roads dangerous or safe. If they were dangerous, which ones and why. I answered all of her questions as best as I could, but to this day I have no idea where that information went. The way she asked her questions made it feel like this was important intelligence she was gaining, though I couldn't possibly imagine how little old me could possibly offer them any valuable insight.

That said, this woman was no nonsense. She was hellbent on squeezing every detail out of me she could about the ongoings in Ukraine. The questioning lasted maybe thirty minutes. She glanced through her notes a few times and nodded her head seeming satisfied.

"Ok," she finally said. "Security will escort you back to passport control." She placed my passport back into the blue, plastic folder and handed it to me. The door then swung open and the same security guard who brought me in said something to the effect of "come with me." I grabbed my backpack and headed for the door. Before I left the woman turned to me and said, "thank you, and safe travels."

"You got it," I responded. What I really wanted to say is "You got it, mystery woman whom I have no idea who you are or what you want." But that's neither here nor there. I just wanted to get home and not go to jail. The security guard walked me back to the same Customs officer who pulled me aside before. I went right to the front of the line as he took one more look at my passport, peered up at me, then handed it back.

"Welcome home," he said with a smile. *About damn time,* I thought. I officially crossed back onto American soil and boarded my connecting flight with newfound perspective and a more grateful disposition toward the world.

One warzone was enough. I learned all I needed to learn, saw all I needed to see and officially closed the chapter on my war reporting career.

Or so I thought.

PART II

THE MIDDLE EAST

13 INTO THE FIRE

"Where were you on October 7?" I've been asked many times.

It's an important date in world history now. For the people of Israel, it's the equivalent of asking, "where were you on 9/11?" Much like that horrific day in 2001, "Black Saturday" of 2023 changed the global landscape as we know it.

Me? I was in London, specifically on a tour of the Tower of London with my parents. This was a family vacation we had planned for months—our first time overseas together. We had just wrapped up treks across Scotland and Ireland, but it was London we were most excited for. To this day, it's one of my favorite cities: the culture, the fashion, the architecture. I couldn't get enough of it all. And frankly, neither could my parents. The last time they were in London was more than thirty years prior. It's a city my mother is especially enchanted by. We stepped through the mighty entryway into the tower itself, where our tour was about to begin. Out sprang a Beefeater, clad in her black and red uniform and hat, who would be leading us on the tour.

"'Ello lovely people," she said in a voice that sounded like Audrey Hepburn's take on Eliza Doolittle at the beginning of *My Fair Lady*. We'll call her Mary.

"I'm your tour guide for the day, indeed I am. And today, I'm here to take you through the Tower of London . . . and on a journey through the Monarchy's bloody past!" Mary said with her eyes flickering in delight. People in the crowd were smiling and muttering amongst themselves as if it were a deeply held secret; they wanted to know all the gory details of the Tudors and Stuarts. Full disclosure: I'm one of them. Takes one to know one, I suppose. Mary beckoned us to follow her as we marched into the castle. She had full command of England's history, I'll give her that. With such attention to detail and a flair for the dramatic, she recounted story after story of who was murdered here, who died here, who disappeared in the middle of the night there. It was truly fascinating as she toured us around the yard.

I felt my phone vibrate in my pocket so I retrieved the device—letting out an "oh" as the screen flicked to life. It was a news push alert saying Hamas, recognized as a terrorist organization by the United States, had carried out an attack on Israel. There was no indication of what had happened or if there were any injuries. I thought very little of it. A few months earlier, my travels took me to Tel Aviv and Jerusalem. While we were there and biking down the Mediterranean, we stopped in our tracks when we heard a loud *BOOM*. Looking up at the sky, we could see a trail of exhaust left behind from a rocket intercepted by the Iron Dome—which is one of Israel's air defense systems. This carried on while we were there as Hamas fired hundreds of rockets at Israel, though I never felt unsafe due to the defense systems.

"Welcome to Israel," our taxi driver even said that night. "This is a part of life here."

All of that to say, when I got the notification on my phone that an attack had been carried out, I hardly batted an eye. Instead, I zoned back into the Beefeater tour and slid my phone back into my pocket to hear Mary hit the crescendo of another story. "And then the children were never seen again!" she exclaimed. "Rumor has it their spirits still haunt their old living quarters to this day." Oohs and aahs emanated from the crowd again. Mary was working the crowd and nailing it. A true pro.

My phone started vibrating again. I pulled it back out and saw more push alerts from different outlets saying the same thing: Israel had been attacked. One said, "casualties suspected." Now it was starting to get serious. More news alerts were flowing in with one standing out above the rest, articulating a statement from Israeli prime minister Benjamin Netanyahu: "We are at war." In a matter of minutes, things escalated drastically, though people outside of the Middle East still didn't fully comprehend the situation. A few of the other tour attendees around us were getting the same news alerts as they showed their phone screens to friends and loved ones. That's when I knew with certainty that this *was* a big deal.

I quickly fired off a text message to my boss—volunteering to go if we needed to send a team to the Middle East. If this was as big a story as I thought it would be, I felt I needed to be there. Why? Maybe a bit of ego considering I had been branded as the network's de facto "war correspondent" with precisely one war zone worth of experience. I'm not entirely sure why I felt so compelled to be a part of this, but I did.

A few minutes later, my phone started to ring. It was Bartley Price calling. I answered.

"Here we go again," he said. That's when I knew: I was about to head back to the Middle East. The date was October 7, and the marching orders were straightforward: Get to Israel as soon as possible.

"It's about to be a mess," Bartley warned. "They're going to start shutting down flights if they haven't already."

"Understood. I'll figure it out," I told Bartley, hanging up the phone.

And just like that, the innocent family vacation was over. I turned around and saw my parents standing there, pointing at a map, trying to figure out where to go next. Now it was time to break the news to them. As I approached, they knew something was going on.

"I've been summoned," I said sheepishly. My parents gave me a blank look back.

"Summoned to where?" asked my dad.

"Israel."

"Ok," he said with a nod, looking at my mom. It was as if they had somewhat expected this reality. "When are you going?"

"As soon as I can. Likely tomorrow morning," I replied.

"All right, well let's go," my dad said. My mom gave me a pat on the back and squeezed my shirt. *That's it? No resistance?* I shouldn't really be surprised. My parents are the two most supportive people in my life.

I took one last look at Mary the Beefeater before departing. She was pointing to a jail behind her. "This is where the monarchy would keep all their prisoners before lopping their heads off!" she said, running her pointer finger along her neck. "Thankfully, we don't do that anymore!" Everyone thought that was so funny and started laughing. I, however, did not and gave a big nervous gulp at that one.

Maybe the British don't chop people's heads off, but I'm pretty sure there are a few terrorist groups in the Middle East that still do, I thought.

Oh, well. Let's hope it doesn't come to that.

* * *

That night was easily one of the worst sleeps of my life. If I drifted into slumber at all, it certainly wasn't even for an hour. I had stayed up the night before drinking gin and tonics with my parents as a final sendoff. I could tell my mother was nervous that I was leaving. My dad, on the other hand, had a "if Robert's not worried, I'm not worried" kind of attitude.

On the surface, I kept my poker face intact. Deep down, however, I of course had my concerns about going back into an active war zone. This was made worse by the fact that I had booked four different flights on various airlines to Tel Aviv, and three of the flights had already been cancelled. Few commercial airlines wanted to take the risk. The one flight that wasn't cancelled would have me connect in Istanbul, then travel onward to Tel Aviv, but I had little optimism at the time that even that second flight was going to actually go.

I grabbed my phone off the nightstand. The clock showed 2:15 a.m. The alarm was supposed to go off at 2:30 a.m. Nevertheless, I waved the white flag of surrender and got up. Rolling over and putting my feet on the floor, I clenched my toes to try to wake myself. My bags were already packed from the night before, so it was just a matter of hailing a cab and heading to London Heathrow Airport. I sent my mom a quick text to let her know I was up and about to head down. Moments later, she pinged back—affirming she was heading down. Of course, she was already up. I'm sure she got even less sleep than me.

My dad, cool as a cucumber, was asleep. He wasn't even going to bother seeing me off to the airport. "I'll see you when you get home," he said the night before. I admired his unflappable confidence amid the tumult. I stepped inside the elevator as the door shut behind me. Descending, I felt the muscles tightening in my neck again as if my body was signaling to me, "there's still time to turn around."

When the elevator slid open, a part of me wanted to stay. I saw my mother there in the lobby with tears running down her face. She really didn't want me to go. *Maybe I should stay after all? Make up an excuse as to why I couldn't make it to Israel?* I gave her a hug and walked with her to the front of the hotel, where taxis were lined up, waiting to take guests to the airport. We set foot outside, and my mom hugged me again, pressing her chin into my shoulder. She didn't have to say a word. I knew what was on her mind. She was truly, to her core, worried this was the last time she'd see her son.

The last time. Something nobody ever wants to think about. The worst part is that it sneaks up on you with the most sophisticated stealth. You seldom *know* when it will be the last time for anything. The last time you see a friend. The last time you drive down that road. The last time you visit that place. You don't really plan it out that way, it just happens. My mother and I broke our embrace as my black London-style taxi rolled forward. The big headlamps and rounded roofs are such an iconic look. A man in black slacks and a black coat stepped out. "Taxi?" he asked.

"Yes. Heathrow," I chirped back.

He nodded his head and popped the trunk open. I slid my suitcase over to him. He hoisted it into the trunk with a bit of a grunt, then slammed the hatch shut. My mother took that as her cue. "Good luck," she said. One final hug, then I turned to my cab, slid into the back seat, and let the taxi man roll me away. I watched my mom's shape disappear from the rearview mirror, her gaze never breaking until I was out of her line of vision.

"Where are you headed today, my friend?" the driver asked.

I gave a pause—knowing exactly how this conversation was going to go as I tried to decide if I wanted to have it.

Relenting, I responded, "Israel," I said somberly.

"Israel?" he asked. "Why the hell are you going there? Didn't you hear about what happened?"

My point exactly. Couldn't have scripted it better myself.

"That's why I'm going," I tried to explain. "I'm a journalist."

The man paused. "Well, don't get yourself blown up, you hear?"

Awesome. Just an awesome thing to say in that moment, I thought sarcastically. I pressed my head back into the headrest as imposter syndrome started to rattle around my skull.

Ok, maybe I really shouldn't be going, I pondered. Hamas had fired thousands of rockets at Israel the day before, and there was no indication they would stop anytime soon.

I gave a glance down at my hands resting on my knees. I turned them over until they were palm side up and started to inspect each finger individually, one through ten, to make sure they still worked. Then I looked down at my legs, and on to my feet—tapping away at the floor of the car in a rhythm concocted from randomness. For whatever reason, this one thought could not escape me: *I hope I come back with all these body parts still intact.*

Now, you, the savvy reader, may be listening to these inner thoughts and thinking this is a bit overkill and perhaps an exaggeration. Especially considering Hamas doesn't have the capabilities Russia has and Israel has more fortifications than Ukraine, not to mention everything we know regarding the destruction of Gaza that would shortly follow October 7. I give you all of that.

But on October 8, 2023, the world was filled with uncertainty. I hadn't a clue what was coming, but what I did know was this: the probability of, as my taxi driver so eloquently put it, being "blown up" was certainly not zero. There was no textbook I read in school just a few years prior that prepared me for that. I shut my eyes and somehow was able to drift off into a doze as the taxi cab rolled along. When I finally regained consciousness, the car was pulling up to the terminal at Heathrow.

Even at such an early hour, the airport was packed and the check-in line for my flight stretched all the way around the periphery of the room. It took about an hour before I was able to make my way up to the desk where a young lady was checking passengers in. "Hello there," I said, handing her my passport. "Final destination: Tel Aviv, please."

She smiled and took hold of my passport. Pecking away at the keyboards, she kept her gaze down. She punched the "enter" button, and her pleasant smile became a puzzled grimace. "Uh, there seems to be a problem, sir." *Of course, there is.* "The system is saying there's an issue with the flight from Istanbul to Tel Aviv. Must be weather or something." I sat there blankly. *Was that a joke? Or does she really have no idea what the issue in Israel is?*

She handed me my passport. "Can you go stand over there and we'll figure something out," she said, pointing to a space on the other side of the counters all the way at the end. I slung my backpack over my shoulders and marched down.

Time passed by rapidly as I waited. Fifteen minutes. Thirty minutes. An hour I stood there. Now it was becoming less of a question of whether this issue with flights would be resolved and more of whether I would I even make the flight at all. Maybe this was the universe's way of telling me to stay in London and try the Beefeater tour again.

The line trickled down, down, and down. Each check-in felt like another drip of alcohol on an open wound. Finally, there were only four people left, including myself. The other three were clearly journalists as well. One was a short, stocky man with a brown horseshoe hairline that left the top of his scalp exposed. He was wheeling a cart that had a large television camera. A photojournalist if I've ever seen one. We'll call him Ronny.

The second gentleman was a big fellow. Well over six feet tall, broad shoulders, large biceps. His head was shaven, and his attire was what you would expect from a hit man: black leather jacket, black slacks, black combat boots. My best guess was he was the security detail, and I ultimately was right. We'll call him Ian.

Lastly was the guy who I knew right off the bat was the correspondent. If you live in Britain, you've seen him on television. Brown hair, glasses, an olive green jacket, and khakis with brown leather boots. He was working the check-in counter folks with a smile and coy charisma. Clark is what we'll call him.

Clark turned away from the desk and looked back at Ian and Ronny—giving a shrug. "Not looking good, mates," he said in a dejected tone.

"Surely somebody can figure something out. Besides, there has to be another way to Israel," Ian said with easing certainty.

"I can assure you there isn't," Clark responded, not having any of the flippant optimism.

"It seems like we're all going to the same place," I chimed in.

The three looked at me, bewildered. "Israel for you as well? Journo?" Clark asked.

"Yes sir," I replied.

"American, I see. You've been before?"

"Second time to Israel, second war zone. Ukraine last year," I said with admittedly a bit of a chip in my step. For whatever reason, saying that made me feel like I had some degree of credibility to be a part of that conversation. Never mind the fact Clark had me beat by thirty or forty conflicts.

"At your age? You're mad, brother. Mad!" Clark declared, patting me on the shoulder. "I love it. Today you're with us. We're all in this one together."

As an aside, I'll take a moment here to say most people don't understand the relationship between journalists in the field. And how could you, really? You've surely seen a prime-time commentator bashing a host on another network. It's common. That's not what happens in the field, though. The networks may be rivals on paper or even on television, but in person, everyone is friends. And in a situation like this, it goes far beyond that. There is an indescribable sense of camaraderie between journalists in a war zone. Sure, everybody wants to get the best video and content for their respective network, but everyone also wants to see each other go home to their families.

When I was in Ukraine, news crews were constantly talking to one another about where they were, what they were seeing, what the danger levels were, and more. All that said, it wasn't a surprise that this British crew took me under their wing, but it did make a huge difference in reassuring me everything would be all right.

"Hello everyone!" piped up the check-in desk woman, trying to get our attention. "We have a *slight* problem."

On second thought, maybe this won't be all right.

We all huddled up around the check-in counter. "So, the flight to Istanbul is good. It's the flight to Tel Aviv that the system is having problems with. There must be severe weather or a technical problem with the plane. You know how things go," she said with an innocent, schoolyard smile.

The four of us turned to one another. Now I *know* she has no clue what's going on in the Middle East. Honestly, maybe she's the smartest one of all of us. There are plenty of days that go by where I wish I was blissfully ignorant.

"So we're going to cancel the reservation, and I suggest you wait here in London until the weather clears or the plane is fixed," she said in a chipper tone—about to reach for the computer.

"Whoa, whoa, whoa!" We all said in unison as the lady jolted back in fear.

"Hang on, hang on," Clark said with a smile. "You can't do that. The problem isn't weather. It's a terrorist attack."

The woman's eyes shot open as she covered her mouth with her hand. *Yup, she had no clue.*

"This is the only flight to Israel, so if you take us off, we'll have no way to get there, and it could be weeks."

The woman paused. "I see."

"Istanbul. Let's start with Istanbul," piped up Ian.

"Yes, Istanbul. Can we get on that plane to Istanbul?" Clark asked.

"Not unless we cancel the second leg," she replied.

"Fine. Just get us to Istanbul." Clark was now getting impatient.

The woman started frantically pecking away at the computer. I looked down at my watch. The plane was already boarding, and doors would shut in maybe fifteen minutes.

"Passports, now!" she sternly barked. We all without hesitation threw them onto the counter. One by one, she picked up the booklets, peeking her head over her shoulder at the clock.

Tapping away frantically, she tossed our passports back. "Ok, you're all set. Now run!" she said with a smile.

Are you kidding me?

The four of us looked at one another. Ian snagged the camera out of Ronny's cart and hoisted it onto one shoulder while grabbing the cart with his other hand. It was like watching a running back in football mentally preparing to carry three linebackers into the end zone.

"Gents, I'd love to chat, but I believe we have a plane to catch. Step lively," Ian chuckled.

Don't have to tell me twice. Thankfully, our friend at the check-in counter was courteous enough to call ahead and let the flight crew know we were on our way. They held the doors for us, and we made the flight.

I wish I could tell you that was the end of our troubles.

* * *

Every moment of sleep lost the night before was made up on that flight to Istanbul. After finding my seat and sitting down, I was out in a matter of seconds. It wasn't until touching down in Turkey that I woke up.

"Morning, sunshine," I heard behind me. I turned around, and it was Clark who happened to be sitting in the seat one row back. "Now's where the fun begins."

"Why is that?" I asked, confused.

He smiled. "Istanbul is the easy part. Now we have to find a way to Tel Aviv. And it's not looking good. Do you fancy a drive?"

"A drive?" I asked.

"Well, the way I see it is if we can't fly to Tel Aviv, we could go into Amman and drive. Maybe Cairo."

Geez. This is not what I had in mind. Is it even safe to drive through that part of Egypt? I'm pretty sure it isn't.

"Something to keep in mind," I acknowledged. Deep down, I really did not want to end up driving into Israel.

Clark smiled back and gave me a playful smack on the shoulder. "We'll manage something, I'm sure."

I hope so. Our plane taxied to the gate and came to a lurching halt. I stood up and retrieved my backpack from under my seat. The passengers ahead slowly trudged forward, and one by one, we were off.

Clark and his team followed close behind me. The lone corridor we were in led us straight to Passport Control and Customs. Despite all the issues we had that day, there were no problems there. In and out within a few minutes. Since the airline had canceled the second leg of our journey to Tel Aviv, we needed to purchase new tickets in order to get to Israel, so our first stop was the check-in counter. A tall, lanky man with short dirty blonde hair and stubble stood at an open section of the counter. He greeted us with a smile.

"We need to purchase new tickets to Tel Aviv," I tried to explain. The man started pecking away at his computer, then paused and looked at us.

"You are aware of the problem in Israel, yes?"

"Well bloody aware," piped up Ian in the back. He was the most anxious of all of us. Ronny just stood there with a stone face and hardly said a word. Clark leaned on the counter, hoping for good news.

"It's no good," the man said. "Flights are not running normally to Israel."

"So they are running?" Clark queried.

The man paused, trying to pick his English carefully. "Well, yes, but most flights are cancelled. We're consolidating everyone onto a few flights."

"Superb!" exclaimed Clark. "We'd all like to book flights on the next flight with availability."

The man laughed nervously. "Eh, it's not like that. It's first come, first serve."

We all looked at each other. "What the hell does that mean?" asked Ian.

"Well, we have everyone in one corner of the airport and every few hours we fill a plane and try to fly to Israel."

"Oh sweet Jesus," Ian said in disbelief.

I had never heard of such a thing. We could buy a ticket, but there was no guarantee we were going to get on the plane. That meant it was going to be a mad dash to get to Israel.

"We have no choice. Four tickets, please," said Clark, taking command of the situation.

The man nodded, patted away at his keyboard, and after a few minutes gave us our tickets.

I stepped away from the counter and intuitively took a deep breath. I didn't even need to see the airport to know what was coming: pandemonium.

We made our way to the gate, which was on a lower level of the airport. Even while standing on the mezzanine, I could hear people screaming, shouting, and crying. It was like that first step into a football stadium where thousands of echoes collide.

"Say your prayers, gents. Into the fire," quipped Clark.

As the escalator descended, I was struck by the magnitude of the situation. There were four gates in this section of the airport, each one reserved for flights to Israel. You couldn't actually get to the gates, however, as they were roped off. That meant a sea of people was moshed into the middle of the small concourse: jostling, pushing, shoving, standing on tiptoes with passports in hand, hoping to get on a flight. I couldn't possibly tell you how many people were there, but it was certainly in the thousands.

Some were clearly journalists trying to do the exact same thing as us. Almost everyone else was an Israeli hoping to get home—and that seemed to be in doubt. Everywhere you looked, people were crying. Some were sitting on the floors, sobbing uncontrollably as they flipped through their phones and looked at images from the October 7 attack.

"My son is dead, let me through!" shouted a man pointing to a photo of his son in an Israel Defense Forces (IDF) uniform as he tried to make his way toward the rope line. People tried to part the sea to allow him through.

I could overhear a woman hysterically shouting into the phone, "I haven't heard from her since Friday, I don't know where she is." It finally hit me in that moment: it wasn't a normal airport mad dash to get home. People didn't even know if they'd have a home to return to. Life as they knew it was on the brink of oblivion.

"Let us through!" shouted a man at the rope line, shaking it violently.

"There is no plane! Do you not understand that? There is no plane here!" barked the Turkish airport attendant back.

Ian huddled us all together and showed us a series of security alerts on his phone. "Here's the problem," he said. "The airport in Tel Aviv is currently being bombed."

"Bloody hell," remarked Clark.

"A flight from Heathrow was about to land, and they turned the thing around. It's heading back to London now," Ian explained.

"That's five hours each way," exclaimed Clark with a gasp. That would have sunk us. Hours to get on a plane, five hours of flight only to be unable to land and turn around back to London.

If you're a frequent flyer, your first thought might be to ask why the plane couldn't just be diverted and land at a nearby airport. The Middle East isn't that simple. Most countries don't even recognize Israel diplomatically. Sure, Beirut is geographically close, but good luck putting a plane full of Israelis down on Lebanese soil.

"The same thing just happened to a flight from France," Ian continued. "Almost every airline is shutting down service to Israel." It became clear in my mind that our only option was to get on one of these planes in Istanbul.

Ian then motioned toward the crowd. "We need to position ourselves toward the front. When a plane does come, we have to be ready."

We gathered our things and started making our way through the crowd. Some had given up on standing and sat on the ground, making effective camps out of their suitcases. We slid our way through any crease of bodies we could find before making our way up close to the front of the rope line.

In that moment, a plane did start to arrive, which was met by cheers. In seeming unison, everyone in that small terminal got to their feet and started trying to push their way toward us. Ian moved us in front of him as he held his ground to stop people from jostling into our backs. He refused to budge or give an inch to the mass.

An airport attendant then came up to the crowd. "Who here is supposed to be on this flight to Tel Aviv?" Everyone's hands shot up, and they started clamoring with variations of "I am" and "me." The poor guy looked overwhelmed by the response and retreated to his podium. We were all still held back from getting up close to the specific gate where the flight was leaving from by the rope barrier.

The math started to make sense in my head. This plane had a few hundred seats. There were at least a thousand people here. The vast majority were not getting on this plane, and we needed to be among the ones that did.

A different airport attendant came up to the line of people and approached an older woman who was standing there silently and politely. He asked for her passport, and she gave it to him. He looked it over and pulled her through the line to the gate. I knew at that moment she was the first passenger getting on the flight. One spot gone.

The woman was now sitting alone at the gate in one of the chairs in front of the podium. The airport attendant walked back to the crowd. He appeared to be the boss and was running this operation. He picked out a family of four with small children and asked for their passports. Same deal. They followed him under the rope line and over to the gate. Five seats gone now.

If it sounds like some twisted game show, believe me, that's how it felt. But instead of there being a jackpot or a brand new car at the end, for many, it was the right to go home and put their lives back together. No laughing matter.

This continued for a few minutes as people were seemingly selected at random. When the attendant returned once more, people started holding out their passports, trying to get him to take them back to the gate. The attendant thought for a moment, then one by one began to take hold of the passports—picking them out of the air like they were berries off a tree.

Ian immediately recognized what was going on. "Give me your passports!" he barked at us. We all handed ours over. The attendant had already passed by us, so Ian, without a thought in the world for common courtesy, started pushing and shoving his way down the line—much to the protest of some of the other people there. Having almost reached the attendant from behind, he slapped the passports into the attendant's outstretched hands. It looked like a windmill dunk in a basketball game. The attendant turned to him in shock but clearly didn't have time to say anything to Ian.

Ian came back to us with a bit of a smirk on his face. Perhaps a bit aggressive of a move, but I knew he just might have gotten us on the plane.

The poor airport attendant now had his arms quite literally overflowing with passports as he took them back to the podium. Placing each one into several tall stacks, he started going through the booklets one by one. Then, he would call a name individually to give them their new ticket.

This went on for forty-five minutes or so as seats on the plane started to fill up at a dramatically slow pace. It was like watching a bucket of water fill drop by drop.

Minutes later, Clark, Ian, and Ronny's names were called. They grabbed their things and were about to make their way forward when Ian asked the attendant, "What about him?" pointing at me. "He's with us?"

"American?" he asked.

"Yes," I replied.

"Name?"

"Sherman."

The attendant had a puzzled look on his face and went back to the stack of passports. He was sifting through them rapidly—pulling each one out individually to give a quick inspection. He kept on digging until he retrieved one blue booklet and opened it up, then rapidly motioned me forward. The whole group followed up to the podium, and the attendant handed us our passports with tickets enclosed inside them. "Good luck," he said.

I nodded my head back and stepped onto the jetway.

"Thank you," I said to Ian, patting him on the back.

"Don't mention it, mate," Ian replied with a smile. "It's what I'm here for. Passage provided by one of His Majesty's finest."

I laughed at that one. We made our way down the jetway and onto the plane where almost every seat was already full. Finding mine, I plopped myself down and tried to make myself as small as possible—fearing someone at the airport would think my finding a way onto that flight was somehow a mistake. The PA system cracked to life as the Captain introduced himself—first in Turkish, then in English. The normal pleasantries off the top—flight time, weather, et cetera.

"I'd just briefly like to take a moment and say our hearts are with all of you impacted by what happened yesterday," the Captain said. "We're going to try our best to get you in to Israel—but know if it gets too dangerous we'll have to turn around."

Everyone on the plane was nodding in acknowledgment of the situation. As the Captain was saying all of this, notifications were going off on my phone, which said the airport was currently being bombed again. There were already videos already circling online of people dropping to the ground and seeking shelter inside the main terminal in Tel Aviv. Nobody on that plane really knew what they would be walking into when they landed. By then, the Israeli death toll was already approaching a thousand, with hundreds taken hostage or considered missing. I didn't even want to think about how many people on that plane knew someone who was killed. As I would later come to comprehend, Israel is such a small country that effectively everybody knew someone who died or was taken that day.

Our plane sat on the tarmac for well over an hour. Finally, the PA system cracked to life again and the captain informed us we were clear for takeoff. I was lucky enough to have a window seat and stared out as our plane rolled onto the runway.

From the moment the plane took off to its descent, I didn't stop looking out that window. It was a short flight, maybe an hour in length, but it felt like years being in the air. I could finally see lights on the ground as the Israeli landscape came into view and watched as our plane drifted down in its approach.

I've been on enough flights that I've never once worried about a takeoff or landing—until this one. I couldn't bear to look out the window any longer, so I shut my eyes tightly, waiting for my eyeballs to explode and pop right out of my skull. I listened intently as I heard the jet engines switching speeds and the landing gear deploy. I felt the way the aircraft bobbed back and forth as it attempted to stabilize on its way to the ground.

With my eyes closed, I couldn't see my knuckles, but I knew they must have looked bone white as my fingernails dug into the front lip of my seat.

Waiting. Anticipating. And then—*thump.*

The intense vibration coursed through my body as the tires slammed into the tarmac. First the back wheels, then the front, as the plane slowly brought its speed down on the ground. It wasn't until I heard loud cheers that I knew we had made it. The whole plane was clapping and whistling in celebration of a successful landing.

Despite all the turmoil, the chaos, and everything that went wrong, we were in Israel.

* * *

I had only been to Israel once before. As it so happened, it was in May of that year for a short vacation. One thing I found is that the people of Israel tend to be upbeat and strikingly positive. Rockets would explode overhead and folks would shrug. "That's life," I heard time and time again. But that unflappable optimism was not present when I arrived in Israel on October 8. In fact, it was anything but. Everywhere you turned, you saw people on their phones in tears.

I tried to put that all aside for the moment and focus on getting out of the airport and to my hotel. Many taxi drivers weren't working that day, as too many people were fearful of the present situation. That meant the line to get a ride out of the airport was long.

The whole time I stood there waiting for a cab, I looked anxiously over my shoulder in case someone started running toward us with an explosive vest to carry out another terrorist attack. Again, you probably read that and think my fears were excessive. They were shared by everyone in that line. On October 8, all bets were off.

After waiting for thirty minutes or so, a cab arrived for me. I threw my things into the trunk and slid into the back seat—instructing the driver to take me to my hotel. As the cab rolled out of the airport, I could see flashing first responder lights everywhere. There were checkpoints every few miles that you had to drive through, where heavily armored police scanned passports to make sure everyone was who they said they were.

"Israel will never be the same," my driver said to me.

"I'm so sorry," I responded. I didn't really know what to say. What could I say?

"Where are you from?" he asked.

"The United States."

"America," he said with a smile. "Why are you here?"

"I'm a journalist."

"Ah. You're here for the war."

"I am."

My driver then pulled out his phone and opened it up as he waited for us to go through the checkpoint. "Look at these," he said, handing the device to me.

My stomach instantly hit the floor. His phone was filled with photos and videos of people killed in the October 7 attack. Bodies butchered. Clips of Hamas members laughing as they kidnapped an old woman. Another video showed them pointing and laughing at a pile of Asian male bodies.

"Thai workers," he explained intuitively. "In the south. They came here to work in the fields and have a better life. They had no place in this fight. Gone."

I couldn't bear to keep scrolling through these videos and photos—handing them back before I got sicker.

"Every Israeli has been sharing these with one another. The world doesn't care," he said, putting his phone away. As the car remained stopped while waiting on the checkpoint, he turned around in his seat and looked me in the eyes. "When you report, you report the truth. Don't lie."

I looked him dead in the pupils. I could see the intensity in his eyes. "I will," I said, once more not really knowing what to say.

"Just remember. You get to go home."

That last line hit me the hardest. I slumped back into the seat and laid my head back to process that last sentence. The exact same one I mulled over on my flight back from Ukraine. *I got to go home.*

You've probably figured out by now that I'm a lover of adventure. What I enjoy most in this life is hopping on planes, exploring new places, and seeing new things. But one constant I've found after every adventure is that no matter where I go, I return with a newfound appreciation for home. Nevertheless, despite my best intentions, I'd come to take it for granted and just assumed home would always be there.

October 7th changed that for me. Seeing all those Israelis who would do anything to get back to Israel, hoping and praying they could see their loved ones one last time, really shook my inner soul. It's a sad reality: what you've always had could be blasted to pieces at a moment's notice. Before you even get a chance to say goodbye, it's slipped through your fingers. A hard lesson to learn firsthand: home may not always be there. One day, without you even realizing, it will be your *final* time going home. Your *final* time experiencing home as you've always known it.

Never take home for granted.

14 TEL AVIV TREMBLED

My toes curled into tight fists as the alarm blared. Head throbbing from just four or so hours of sleep, I rolled over and repeatedly bashed the screen on my phone until it silenced, then pressed my shoulders back into bed. I was awake and there was no going back, despite my desperation to slip away again. My eyes were locked on the ceiling above me as I didn't have the energy or willingness to avert my gaze in a less convenient direction. It was smooth and beige. Painfully ordinary.

I slid my legs under the white bedsheets seeking new, untouched cool spots. *This all felt so familiar*, I thought to myself. When you spend more than 300 nights a year in hotel rooms, they all start to look and feel the same. The texture of the bedsheets, the rigidness of the towels, the seat of a desk chair all seem practically identical once you experience enough of them. My eyes were still struggling to adjust to the light and, as a result, my vision was still blurry. Not quite alert enough to be awake, but too far gone to fall back asleep. A purgatory of sorts I've come to despise.

I mustered up enough energy to roll back over and tap the screen again. As it blared back to life, I tried to make out the words atop the screen: "Monday, October 9."

The world started to come back to me a bit. While that hotel might have seemed familiar to me at the time, it was no motel in Warner Robins, Georgia. What I didn't realize was the prying open of my eyes was the beginning of the first day in my new home for the next few months: Tel Aviv, Israel. There really is no city in the world quite like it. The closest comparison I can come up with is Miami, but at face value that doesn't quite fit. Sure, both cities sit atop stunning coastlines and are known for their sunshine and beaches. And yes, both are consummate melting pots of the world bringing in a wide array of culture. A stroll down Dizengoff Street in the heart of Tel Aviv and you'll come across Brits, Kiwis, and Aussies who you'll meet in Swedish coffee shops or French bakeries and then agree to see for dinner at the Russian restaurant down the road that has a server from Ukraine and a bartender from Los Angeles.

But that's where my perceived parallels between the two cities end. Tel Aviv doesn't have nearly the flash. Many of the buildings are outdated and the restaurants don't try to impress you with trendy facades. If Miami were the big shot banker in a designer suit, Tel Aviv is the modest entrepreneur in a t-shirt who doesn't feel the need to impress you.

That's not at all a knock on the city. It calls a booming tech scene home and the people on the streets are fit and stylish. The mandatory military service commitments all citizens must go through surely play a role in that.

Like Miami, Tel Aviv is a party city. It gets wild every Thursday night at the many rooftop bars—not Friday or Saturday due to Shabbat. It's much more secular than Jerusalem, but religious observances are still visible. A lot of young, Jewish college students flock to the city from the United States while on Summer break to trace their heritage and have some fun. You'd be amazed how many people you see on the streets with t-shirts that say "Michigan Swimming" or "UCLA Basketball" on them.

But as I waddled over to the balcony window in my hotel room and peered down on the city a dozen stories down, it was what I wanted to be at that moment: asleep. Our hotel was situated right on the beach boardwalk which was empty. The normally busy highway right next to us was strikingly quiet save for the occasional motorbike or ambulance. Cities like Tel Aviv don't rest, but it did that day.

The whole world was watching this place intently. Two days earlier, Hamas attacked Israel on October 7 and still nobody knew the extent of what had happened. In fact, by the time I arrived, the IDF had still yet to regain operational control of Israeli territory. Heavy fighting was taking place still in Southern Israel as soldiers were going door to door looking for Hamas fighters. The death toll numbers were so fluid that it was unclear exactly how bad the attack was. They would rise sharply by the hour, as would hostage totals. It would take weeks until becoming clear that over 1,200 Israelis died that day and more than 200 were taken back to Gaza by Hamas.

We had a lot of work to do, and it was time to get started. I quickly got dressed and went downstairs. The elevator went straight to the ground floor and when the doors opened I saw a familiar face. It was my first producer assigned to the Middle East with me. We'll call him Adam. He was tall with long hair styled in a manner that some famous singer named Justin made popular a decade earlier. He had a trimmed beard and moustache and always spoke in a chipper tone.

"Hey, man," Adam said. "Good to see you made it in."

"Good to see you, I replied shaking his hand."

This was, all kidding aside, the whole team in Israel. Just me and Adam. Bartley and another crew were on the way to assist temporarily, but they were tied up with flight issues. We made our way over to the lobby area where there were some chairs and started reading through all the new reports that had come out from the Israeli government while scanning some of the top headlines from the war.

It was just like the first few days of the war in Ukraine. Everyone was scared, nobody knew what was going on, and nobody could look away. It dawned on me that we were there, right in the heart of the world's watchful eyes.

If you ever feel like you have a firm grasp on the world, spend a week in the Middle East during a crisis. You quickly realize the globe is a complicated place, none more-so than this region. Even Israelis acknowledge it when you ask them. Israel becoming a country in 1948? It's complicated. The West Bank? Very complicated. Gaza? Definitely complicated. Relations with Egypt? They recognize each other, but they don't like each other. It's complicated. Does Iran recognize Israel? No. Does Saudi Arabia recognize Israel? No. So Iran and Saudi Arabia must be allies? Not really. They are in agreement on some issues, strong disagreement on others, so not really pals. Why? It's complicated. Then there's the political division in Israel that was taking place leading up to October 7. People were participating in large-scale protests, some of which turned ugly, as the government pushed for wide-ranging judicial reform that would give them more control over the Supreme Court.

Not to mention that Israel doesn't exactly function like the United States. Instead of two major political parties, there are multiple coalitions. Instead of a constitution that seeks to separate church and state, Israel is unabashedly the Jewish State. It's because of religion that the Israeli flag-carrying airline El Al doesn't fly while observing the sabbath. My point is, I felt utterly overwhelmed sitting in that lobby trying to piece all of this together. It's like trying to cram several millenniums worth of world history into your brain.

Thank goodness I had Adam with me. He was truly a blessing my first two weeks in Israel because he spent so much time covering foreign affairs at another network, and he was more than willing to help fill in the sizable knowledge gaps I had. The world had changed just 48 hours prior and I was right there at the forefront of history. I needed to dive into this and get a handle on what was happening.

But that would have to wait. All of the sudden, I heard that sound I knew all too well from Ukraine. That pale, whaling sound in the distance that builds by the millisecond in intensity.

Sirens. Tel Aviv was under attack.

"Move! Move! Move!" Came a voice. I turned and it was one of the hotel staffers waving us to follow him. "Come! Quickly, please."

Adam and I looked at each other, then dropped all of our things and hurried after the hotel staffer. He led us down a back hallway toward a stairwell which was surrounded on four sides by a concrete wall. I stepped inside and quickly realized we weren't alone. There were fifteen to twenty people huddled there, waiting out the attack. One woman was holding her dog. Another was crouched in the corner facing the wall with her head tucked down as she prayed. Adam and I nestled our way into the crowd and stood there, listening to the howling roar of those sirens. Not even the concrete walls could completely muffle them.

BOOM. A loud explosion could be heard above us.

FIGURE 14.1 Israel's air defense system attempts to intercept a rocket fired by Hamas at Tel Aviv. Photo by Robert Sherman.

BOOM-BOOM-BOOM.

Three more in quick succession. The woman in the corner started to scream, and a child, tucked in her mother's arms, began crying. A short, stocky man standing next to me, dressed in construction clothes, began shouting, holding his fist above his head. He was angry and hoped they could hear his curses all the way in Gaza City. The explosions continued for a few moments, slowly fading into the distance. "Please wait here until it is safe," the hotel staffer said. He quickly stepped out of the stairwell and disappeared around the corner. The roughly two dozen of us stood in tense silence.

Finally, the stocky man in construction gear turned to me and started shouting while pointing his bony finger into my chest. He was speaking in Hebrew, so I couldn't make out a single word except one: "American."

"I'm sorry?" I awkwardly replied, caught off guard.

He switched to English. "You Americans have no idea what is happening here! Do you understand what they did to us?"

"Yes," I earnestly responded.

"No! No! You don't!" The man then reached into his pocket and pulled out his cell phone. He opened it up and showed me a picture of a young woman. My best guess was she was late teens or early twenties. "This right here is my niece. Those animals took her! They took her! To Gaza!"

I was stunned speechless. It was becoming quite apparent that everyone in Israel, a country of roughly ten million, was impacted by the October 7 attack. I remained silent and let him continue.

"Why are you here? Why did you come here?" the man demanded, getting closer to my face. I didn't know what to do. I couldn't remove myself from the situation, on the one hand out of respect for his loss, but on the other hand because the all-clear hadn't been given.

"I'm a journalist," I meekly responded.

"Gah! A journalist? A journalist?! You all *love* the Palestinians! You all *hate* us! Look at her face!" He shouted, putting the phone right in front of my eyes. "She was at a party, listening to music, just twenty years old. And they *took* her! You understand me?"

I nodded my head. No words could come out.

"They are killing us! They want us all dead! They butcher us like animals! But no more!" he yelled, making a firm sweeping motion with his hand. Then he looked me in the eyes as his pupils contracted, beaming right into my gaze. "*This* is the *last* time. This time, we end it for good." Then he stormed out of the stairwell in a fit of rage, right as the hotel staffer came back in to give the all clear.

Everyone started making their way for the exit except me and Adam. I couldn't move an inch as I replayed what the man had said to me in my head again and again. One by one, the people huddled in that stairwell departed until it was me, Adam, and the woman who was praying in the corner. She got to her feet and kept her head down, walking toward the doorway before stopping. She then turned to me so I could see her face for the first time. She must have been in her 40s with dark hair and olive skin. Her eyes were bloodshot red, presumably from tears welling up inside of them. I met her gaze for a moment before she muttered three words at me in English.

"Tell the truth."

With that, she stepped out and was gone. There they were again. Those three words the taxi driver said to me that punched me in the soul. I didn't want to show my face to anybody in that hotel. I just put my head down, walked straight out of the stairwell, and back to the chairs that Adam and I were sitting in. With my face still angled toward the ground I sat down and just stared.

"It's okay, man," Adam said, trying to reassure me.

What did she mean by that? "Tell the truth?"

It was one of those moments when you realize you're not "covering a story." It's not a game or a cycle of political talking points. It's people's lives, trauma and pain. It's one thing to see a situation play out like this on television, but it's another to be there.

And in that moment, I felt like an imposter that didn't belong. Clarissa Ward of CNN was staying right down the road from us. Trey Yingst of Fox News lived a few blocks away. I wasn't worthy of breathing their air that day and felt like I needed to go home. But that was not an option. I was here, this assignment was too important, and I needed to dig deep because put simply, this little imposter syndrome thing I was dealing with really paled in comparison to the pain people were feeling 40 miles down the road where their loved ones were slaughtered.

Shut up and get a grip, I thought to myself. Yet still, the woman's words kept replaying in my head over and over. *Tell the truth. Tell the truth. How do you tell the truth when you feel utterly over your head and don't really understand what is happening?* I still don't have a good answer to that question.

But sitting in that lobby chair, I made a promise to myself: I would only tell people what I saw and what I knew was true.

Everything else? It's complicated.

15 CLAUSEWITZ COULDN'T IMAGINE

You hear it all the time from kids in school. "When am I ever going to use this lesson in the real world?" The Pythagorean theorem? The mitochondria is the "powerhouse of the cell." Pi is 3.14159265 . . .

It is true that there are a lot of facts and figures from textbooks over the years I have yet to apply to the "real world." Yet somehow, they are forever imprinted into my long-term memory.

There was one particular class in high school, however, that I am forever grateful for, and I use the lessons taught in it every day. "Strategy, Diplomacy, and War." The instructor was a retired US Army colonel who had commanded Special Forces, and the material was dense, featuring works by the likes of Sun Tzu, the Chinese military general and philosopher known for the book *The Art of War.* Sometimes classroom discussions would be replaced with simulations of how real-world diplomacy played out in history. It was a fascinating class that analyzed some of the world's most pivotal moments.

One of the readings that has stuck with me was an excerpt from *On War,* written by Carl von Clausewitz, a Prussian general who coined the term "Fog of War," which, since the October 7 attack, has been a favorite phrase of every pundit to take the place of the words "who knows what's really going on?"

Although Clausewitz never used the exact term "Fog of War," it was a paraphrase of the following excerpt:

> War is the realm of uncertainty; three quarters of the factors on which action in war is based are wrapped in a fog of greater or lesser uncertainty.[1]

Nevertheless, you get the idea. In wartime, there is a finite amount of information at your disposal, and you can only make decisions based on what you know.

Clausewitz wrote that in the early nineteenth century so his teachings sorely predated airplanes, drones, satellites, thermal cameras, and more. As such, you might think the "Fog of War" might be obsolete, or maybe reduced to a slight haze thanks to the advancement of technology. I may have briefly thought that too, until the day the Israeli Air Force bombed a hospital, killing 500 people.

Or at least, that's what Hamas said, and social media ran wild with it.

We were standing on the balcony of our live shot position in Tel Aviv when Adam noticed something on social media.

"Hey man, this might be nothing, but people are saying a hospital just got hit with an airstrike in Gaza City," Adam politely informed me, being careful not to press the issue. He was the experienced one on foreign affairs, and I trusted his judgment.

"Oh really?" I responded.

"Again, it may be nothing. But it's what people are saying and worth keeping an eye on," he said. An airstrike on a hospital would certainly be a major development in the war. Israeli forces had been shelling Gaza City, the major metro area inside the enclave and a notorious Hamas stronghold, rather incessantly since October 7.

The date was now October 17th, and already there was a clear emphasis on the humanitarian situation in Gaza starting to take hold. Not nearly to the level of "Ceasefire Now" chants and demonstrations that would engulf college campuses in the Spring of 2024, but in ten days, the public sentiment tide was starting to make its first turn.

The guidance from the top of our network was clear on how to cover every development in this war: be accurate on every detail, even if it means not being first. That's a big part of the reason I've been so proud to call NewsNation home: news, not noise, accuracy, and impartiality above all else.

This was a moment in which we were heavily constrained as to how to handle it. Did the Israeli Air Force really strike a hospital? I couldn't be certain because I was standing 40 to 50 miles away. Ten days into the war, nobody was getting into Gaza in any capacity if they had a journalism badge. The best you could hope for would be to stand along the Israeli–Gaza border, which is *closer* but still doesn't solve the problem of seeing what's happening in Gaza firsthand.

"We'll definitely keep an eye on it," I told Adam. That's all we could do. A random social media account or two were not nearly enough to report something like this.

But within an hour, that all started to change. It was no longer just one or two random accounts online, but now semi-news accounts and small tabloids out of the Middle East were picking it up. Some American and British journalists were acknowledging "rumblings" online that they were looking into—a means of addressing a rumor without reporting it as fact or tying oneself to it. Several minutes later, the next domino fell: the Gaza Health Ministry, which make no mistake about it, is still under the Hamas umbrella government in the enclave, put out a statement saying 500 people were dead as the result of an Israeli airstrike.

We live in a world of big numbers, where people talk about having 100 thousand followers, one million subscribers, or scoring ten million views on a single video posted online. Sometimes, people lose sight of numbers like 500 people killed. That's a massive number in a single explosion. But right off the bat, there was something that didn't track with us: how could the Gaza Health Ministry, within an hour of the explosion, already have a death toll? In my mind, it would have been impossible for the best rescue crews in the world to determine 500 people were killed less than an hour ago. It's not as if they could have pulled that many bodies out of the rubble in such a span. Or at least, that was my thinking, which spurred my hesitation.

Adam and I were in agreement: we weren't ready to go to air with anything. We hadn't even heard from the Israelis yet, despite our pestering them for some kind of comment. It was complete silence from their communications teams, which made one thing clear to us: this was a highly pivotal and sensitive moment in the first ten days of the war.

But all of a sudden, several highly reputable news outlets, some from the United States and others from Europe, began running with the 500 killed number while placing the blame on an alleged Israeli airstrike. I won't name them here, but you can find it online to this day.

So now, there we were, 40 miles away from Gaza as this highly critical incident was playing out in Gaza City that we could not see with our own eyes. I couldn't confirm or deny what was happening. The sources we had were as silent as the grave, yet the fury and anger pouring out on social media and certain news outlets were hitting a roar.

Some were already on television accusing the Israelis of war crimes. Others were calling on the United States to immediately suspend any support for Israel. It's amazing how quickly a snowball can pick up steam in situations like this.

All I can recall in that moment was feeling utterly helpless. I was the guy sent overseas to be the boots on the ground and tell the viewers exactly what was happening. And I couldn't tell them a damn thing other than "here's what people are saying on social media." The imposter syndrome was rearing its ugly head once again.

"What do we do?" I asked Adam.

"Just stay the course, man," Adam replied firmly. "Keep monitoring it. We don't report anything until we know something."

But in television news, it's not that easy. Our phones were ringing from Chicago, and they wanted us in front of the camera immediately to give an update on what was happening—anything that we could.

I always joke that whenever I go on television, I black out and whatever comes out of my mouth is what it is. It's seldom that I ever get a case of the nerves before being on air. But in the moments leading up to that live report, my shoulder blades would not unlock. Despite standing upright, it felt as though a small car was pressing onto my rib cage. The tissue in-between my teeth and my lips was bone dry as my tongue turned to sandpaper. I hadn't had those feelings since my first local television job in Birmingham, Alabama.

"Just tell them what you know, and be honest about what you don't, man," Adam said reassuringly. Once more, my gratitude for Adam being there could not be greater. I repeated that in my head over and over. *Just tell them what you know. Just tell them what you know. Just tell them what you know.* What did I know exactly? Not a whole lot. So let's run through the facts.

We knew that the Al-Ahli Al-Mahdi hospital in Gaza was treating patients injured from the war. We knew there was a major explosion there that evening. The information about what exactly transpired was unconfirmed and came from the Gaza Health Ministry under Hamas. They claimed there were 500 people killed and placed the blame on an Israeli airstrike. Israel had not yet given any indication about whether they were involved or not. That's it.

Don't say 500 killed. Don't say Israeli airstrike. Those were the last words that went through my head before the lights came on and I heard the anchor give the floor to me. There was no script, and there was no time to put one together. It was just me, the camera, and however many thousands of people were watching. My joke about blacking out wasn't so whimsical because I do not remember those two minutes I was on television at all. I went back days later and looked at what I said, and I did somehow manage to follow the plan we had set out. It was a bit more put together than I thought it would be, but I still walked away feeling like I had given our viewers, who were putting their trust in me, the biggest supersized "nothingburger" one could cook up.

"That was really, really great, man. You told the people the truth. You told them what we know and what we don't," Adam said reassuringly. I still felt like a waste of a plane ticket. We were able to pull up the stream of one of our competitors. I can't recall whether it was a reporter or a pundit, but they were talking about how the Israelis need to be brought to justice and that 500 people killed was one of the, if not the biggest airstrikes on civilians in the history of modern warfare. *Very different from what we said.*

I decided to start scanning social media to see if anything of interest was popping up. That just made my anxiety worse. There were some accounts posting videos of what appeared to be a missile whizzing through the air, creating a loud explosion. There were other videos showing fighter jets and bombers flying overhead Gaza and people claiming to be eyewitnesses saying those were the planes that dropped the bombs on the hospital.

Some of the videos did look to be rather compelling, and I was starting to believe everything was true and this is what was really happening inside Gaza.

Reporters love to play detective and piece together clues to get to the truth. But I quickly reminded myself that I didn't go to West Point, I didn't serve in the armed forces, and I've been in the Middle East less than ten days. That *could* be a missile, but I couldn't tell with the naked eye the difference between that and a homemade rocket. Those *could* be Israeli bombers, and the videos I'm looking at *could* be of Gaza City, but I didn't know for sure.

What the hell do I know? I'm just a dumb kid from Cleveland in over his head. I have officially outkicked my coverage, I thought to myself.

"We have a statement from the Israelis," Adam shouted while hunched over his computer at a table behind me. I turned quickly and hustled over to him. *Finally, something.*

It was a video, posted to social media by Rear Admiral Daniel Hagari, who was one of the most prominent faces of the IDF's military operations and their lead spokesperson. The statement was heavily scripted, and he was clearly reading from a teleprompter. He too was picking his words with the utmost precision:

> I want to give you an announcement of the event that occurred in the hospital in Gaza. I can confirm that an analysis of the IDF operational systems indicates that a barrage of rockets was fired by terrorists in Gaza, passing in close proximity to the Al-Ahli Al-Mahdi hospital in Gaza at the time it was hit. Intelligence from few sources that we have in our hands indicates that the [Palestinian] Islamic Jihad is responsible for the failed rocket launch which hit the hospital in Gaza. I repeat. This is the responsibility of the [Palestinian] Islamic Jihad that killed innocents in the hospital in Gaza.[2]

The Israelis were now outright denying they struck the hospital at all. The Palestinian Islamic Jihad is another group that operates around the region, including Gaza. Separate from Hamas but allied with them, as well as groups such as Hezbollah in Lebanon.

Despite all the advancements of modern technology, the Fog of War was thicker than ever, and a major geopolitical crisis had devolved into a "he said, she said" situation.

Nevertheless, it was a major development. Already dozens of outlets were placing the blame on the IDF for the strike based on one statement released by the Gaza Health Ministry, and now it was clear that it was *possible* they were all wrong. As such, the importance on my end of picking each word carefully and getting every detail right was higher than ever before.

The news cycle was exploding. Some reporters and outlets were walking back their stories that 500 people were killed in an Israeli airstrike. A few pundits, not many, were doubling down, calling the Israelis liars without offering any evidence to support that. The pendulum was swinging both ways.

Adam once more assured me that it was best to stay the course: tell them what we know, and be honest about what we don't. That's how we carried on the rest of the night, being very careful to source every fact we had and explain what wasn't confirmed. It was a long night filled with very tense moments for fear we would miss something or inaccurately report a detail. Looking back on it now, we remained disciplined throughout the night, and I went to bed that evening thinking I hadn't royally screwed anything up. A small victory.

It was the day after that really opened my eyes to what this war would become. The sun had risen, and with it had come new clarity. The Israelis were right. They did not strike that hospital. The Palestinian Islamic Jihad did have rocket misfires causing a massive explosion. The reason for such a blast, according to intelligence agencies throughout North America and Europe, was that weapons were likely being stored inside by terrorists. The estimated death toll was disputed by several Western intelligence agencies but placed much lower than 500.

What struck me the most was the reaction from a bevy of news outlets. One of the most premier newspapers in the world had to issue an effective mea culpa, acknowledging shortcomings in its reporting. There were retractions and apologies from some, while others acknowledged their original numbers were wrong but peddled the blame onto Hamas and, you guessed it, "the fog of war."

Many major outlets around the globe got it wrong that night. One of the few exceptions? NewsNation: Adam, Robert, and their feverishly flipping fingers on their computer keyboards.

How much did it matter? Not a whole lot. Because of so many errors in news coverage, millions around the world to this day believe Israel blew up that hospital. In the immediate aftermath of the incident, leaders of some militant groups called for "a day of rage," leading to mass demonstrations around the Middle East. The damage was done, and there was no putting the toothpaste back into the tube.

But journalists worldwide learned a pretty valuable lesson that day: this fog of war was different from anything anyone had seen. Some of the photos of casualties that started to rapidly circulate that night weren't from Gaza but rather from Syria a decade earlier. Some of the videos that claimed to capture the airstrike on camera came from totally separate incidents around the region.

The Palestinian Islamic Jihad may have misfired those rockets, but social media dropped the biggest bomb of all that night. Since that moment, every reporter has been much more wary about taking statements and wire reports at face value henceforth. In many cases, journalists still keep that cluster in the back of their minds when any new information comes out of Gaza. This isn't to say civilians didn't die in Gaza as a result of Israeli airstrikes. Many have, but not in this incident. Every fact matters, especially when it comes to life, death, and war.

I felt over my head that day. But I take a little solace in knowing that if Carl von Clausewitz were on that balcony with me that night, he'd be drowning in uncertainty just the same.

16 SECONDS COUNT

Have you ever considered the value of a single moment in time?

If you have, you are far wiser than me. Time is that commodity everyone longs for more of. "There just aren't enough hours in a day" is a phrase I hear all too often. "Oh, what I wouldn't give to turn back the clock" is another.

Yes, I too am guilty of waving the white flag and fantasizing of an hourglass that sand can't seep through. As I write these words while watching the sun rise and set on the other side of the globe, the prospect of time weighs on me. With the acceptance of time comes the embracing of change as well. There will come a day when the sun rises and your whole world will be different. Friends and family you've come to rely on will be gone and, in the end, it will just be you and the person in the mirror.

Despite my best intentions, I think about this often. And as someone proudly and unabashedly still in the midst of his "quarter-life crisis," I don't see Father Time's hushed whisper dissipating anytime soon.

We've all let the concept of time slipping away enter our minds, but how many of us have taken tangible action to course-correct? More pointedly, how many of us have put our minds through a renaissance of perspective to shift from longing for more time to vehemently defending it with every muscle in our body?

For me? Maybe a little, but certainly not enough. Despite the way ticking clocks rattle inside my skull, I am the first to say I don't take adequate action to preserve my time.

Seconds, minutes, even hours are flippantly discarded in exchange for mind-numbing activities like scrolling through social media or browsing utterly nonsensical videos online that, for whatever reason, pique our interest just after midnight. How could we, as human beings, acknowledge the way time slips away from us, long for more of it, yet so carelessly toss it to the wind? My hypothesis is this: we don't fully recognize the opportunity cost of wasting time. For whatever reason, deep down, we wrongly believe time is endless.

So I ask you again: Have you ever considered the value of a single moment in time?

I have. Our assignment in Ashkelon has taught me seconds can make the difference between life and death.

About a month had gone by since October 7. Adam left to return to DC, and Bartley stopped off to join us in Israel for a week or so with one of the network anchors. He departed as well, so that just left me and my new producer by my side: Will Budkins.

We had worked together maybe once or twice. He was one year younger than me, but what I love about working with him is he has an insatiable sense of curiosity and a longing to understand the world. Adding to that, the kid works his tail off. Little did I know Will and I would be on the ground in Israel for about a year together. I couldn't ask for anyone better to spend that much time with.

Despite the fact I had only been in Israel for a few weeks, from my perspective, this war was very different from Ukraine. There you could be hundreds of miles away from the frontlines and still face a very real threat of Russian missiles and airstrikes. In Israel, Tel Aviv was just over 40 miles from the Gaza Strip. It may as well have been a different world as the fortifications allowed life to somewhat carry on. People were certainly scared and most businesses were shuttered due to the war, but life was still moving forward to some degree. On any given afternoon, you could find people taking walks on the beach or working out at the gym. The same couldn't be said for southern Israel. And then of course in Gaza City, people were just hoping to live to see tomorrow

Our plan was to go to Ashkelon—a city in southern Israel roughly 10 miles from the Gaza Strip. From what I had heard, Ashkelon was getting hit with more Hamas rockets than anywhere in Israel. Thousands of refugees from there were calling Tel Aviv home in the meantime.

I got dressed and was prepared to head downstairs before I remembered to grab the black canvas bag sitting in the corner of my room. I zipped it open to reveal three navy bulletproof vests and Kevlar helmets, each one brand new, still in their plastic wrap.

Gonna need these, I nervously thought. It dawned on me that in Ukraine I was begging for an opportunity to put our haphazardly spray-painted vests on. This time around, there was no such childish fascination.

It's one thing to put on protective gear when deep down, you know you won't need it. It's another thing to put it on knowing you will need it, but it won't do you any good. Bullets weren't the concern. It was rockets. And in this part of Israel, Hamas would let them fly indiscriminately every day.

I hoisted the bag onto my shoulders. *Geez, this is heavy*, I thought. Three vests and three helmets may as well have been a bag of cinderblocks. I took the short walk to the elevator and made my way downstairs. The door slid open, and standing right there in the lobby was Will with his floppy brown hair and full beard wearing an olive colored button down. He was locked in conversation with two men.

The first one, slim and older. Probably in his 50s with pepper speckled gray hair and tan skin. We'll call him Ron. He was the freelance cameraman we had brought in that day. Apparently, he took the job not knowing what we were doing. When he was informed we were going to Ashkelon, his jaw dropped.

"Ashkelon? Are you kidding me?" Not the kind of response I was looking for. "Wish I would have known," he told Will sarcastically, mumbling about how he didn't bring his own protective vest with him. Thankfully, we had a spare.

The other man was our fixer, who we'll call Derek. Just under 6 feet tall, but athletically built. He had a shaved head and a pair of arms sleeved in tattoos. He gripped my hand firmly and looked me square in the eyes with a piercing gaze.

Derek was the real deal. He was a retired war correspondent in Israel who had gotten bored of all the rockets and artillery, so decided to start making documentaries instead. I'm not kidding. That's not an exaggeration. The man thought the sounds of war were dull, so started making long-form content focused on telling stories about the everyday people who live this reality. Meanwhile, with a comparatively meager two war zones (including this one) under my belt, I still get the shivers every time I hear a siren blare.

"Are you ready?" Derek asked after a few pleasantries were exchanged. He was no nonsense. I loved that. Not a single moment was affordable for waste.

"I guess so," I said with a shrug. He led us over to his car which was four door, silver sedan. Will and I piled into the back seat. Derek took the wheel and Ron rode shotgun. I slid into the seat feeling every fiber of the canvas covering wrap around my back.

Derek impaled the ignition with his key and cranked it on. The engine hummed to life right before he slapped the car into drive and we were off. I turned around and watched out of the rear window as our hotel faded into Tel Aviv's sprawling skyline. Minutes later, the city itself disappeared from view. What replaced it was a mix of suburban and rural. To my right, I would look out and see farmland rolling off across the landscape. To my left, I would see things that reminded me of what the outskirts of Cleveland—or for that matter, any American city—looked like. I noticed shipping depots, truck stops, gas stations and even outlet shopping malls.

"This is Israel," Derek said sarcastically. I could see the corner of his smile poking out from his face. He was proud of his country—for all the good and bad.

The drive was about an hour in length. It was hard to gauge where we were as all the signs were written in Hebrew—a language I couldn't begin to decipher. That whole drive I stared out the window. We were outside of the safety of Tel Aviv, but from everything I could see Israel looked like a normal country. Still, I couldn't get Bartley's last minute words of wisdom out of my head. "If the sirens start blaring, be sure to duck!" he told me on the phone the night before—the sarcasm dripping off his words. A brilliant "Plan B" if I've ever heard one.

Derek pulled the car off the highway. The sign above the exit was written in both English and Hebrew. "Ashkelon" it said. We had finally made it.

Our first stop was to go visit some scenes of rocket strikes in the city. The damage was relatively fresh—maybe a day or two old. Our plan was to park the car in downtown Ashkelon and start walking.

Derek pulled off onto the main drag that led us directly to the heart of the city. Before we could enter, there was a checkpoint. Four IDF soldiers standing there with large, metal barricades staggered so you couldn't drive right through. To get in the city, you'd have to take a left around one barricade, then weave right, and back left again.

"This is weird," Derek said.

Again, not what I wanted to hear. "What do you mean?" I asked.

He shook his head. "To see the military here? In Ashkelon? Maybe Sderot, but never here," he said. Not exactly a vote of confidence. The whole country was still on edge and everybody was a threat until proven otherwise: similar to Ukraine.

The car slowly rolled to a stop in front of the checkpoint. A female soldier brandishing a military grade rifle walked up to the driver's side and beckoned Derek to roll down the window. The two exchanged words in Hebrew, then she craned her head inside the car to see who all was inside. I couldn't make eye contact with her as she had on sporty sunglasses, but I could feel her pupils piercing my soul nevertheless.

The soldier then barked a question at Derek to which he produced some kind of identification card in response. She nodded her head seeming satisfied and waved us through. Derek lurched the car forward and spun it through the labyrinth of barriers.

The 2020 coronavirus pandemic feels like a blur. Everyone in my generation can attest to feeling like valuable years of life were sapped from our futures as we stayed inside, hunkered down, and watched the hours, days, weeks and months fly right by us. For me, there are entire seasons that run together without notable memories to distinguish them. But one image that stays with me is watching network television in the early days of Covid and seeing Times Square in New York empty. Not a soul to be found. If you drove your car into downtown New York, you'd have the whole road to yourself.

That's what Ashkelon looked like as we made our way into the city. Whole shopping centers were boarded up and the sidewalks were without a single pedestrian in sight. A beach town situated right on the Mediterranean on a hot sunny day? Could've fooled me. Nobody was there. Aside from the occasional news vehicle rolling down the street, I would have assumed the entire city of over 100,000 packed up and skipped town. The reality is, that was only mostly true. Maybe a couple thousand stubborn residents stuck around.

Derek pulled the car into an empty parking space near city hall and threw the car into park. He yanked the keys out of the ignition and gave a brief sigh. I could tell, despite his best efforts at fortitude, the environment weighed on him. Ashkelon was a city he had visited many times before, but never under these conditions. He took a deep breath then popped the door open. We all filed out after him.

Leading us back to the trunk which was already open, we all grabbed our vests. I slipped mine over my head and immediately felt the weight drip down from my shoulders. Encumbered would be putting it lightly. Now I know why the hare is faster than the tortoise. Everybody had their vests on now and we started walking. If I didn't already feel out of place enough, I could make out a sound I've never heard while walking around a city: an echo. Every footstep. Every clank of our cameras. Every conversation bounced and rattled from building to building. We were, in every sense of the word, walking through a ghost town.

Our team turned the corner and I immediately understood why people here were on edge. I was staring at an apartment building, maybe four stories tall in the middle of a courtyard. There were identical buildings on each side of it. The one I was looking at, however, was impossible to miss. The entire second floor was blown out and the ground in front of it was covered in rubble. It was such an odd sight to see. The building couldn't have been more than two or three years old, but it had this gaping hole in it. Even as I was a few hundred feet away, I could make out what appeared to be the remnants of a kitchen. The giveaway was the sink dangling out the side of the building.

We all stood there for a brief moment, and then I made a move toward the building. I put one foot down on the grass out front and was startled by a crackling sound. I picked my foot off the ground to see the entire area was covered in tiny shards of glass. The strength of the blast so powerful it blew debris hundreds of feet outward. Everywhere you looked, reflections of sunlight emanated from the glass fragments on the ground. I put my boot back down on the ground, thinking it was fine, and continued walking toward the building. *Crack-crack-crack* went my shoes with every step I took.

I could see the ground level door to the apartment was open as everyone in the building had apparently moved out. We reached the front entrance where it was clear the inside was pitch black. The light that was supposed to make it possible to see was blown out and dangling from the ceiling by a wire. Derek slid past me and took the lead—striding forward toward a door on the other side of the entry way. This one was closed but he was able to ease it open. The little bit of sunlight seeping in allowed me to see it was a concrete staircase with nothing more than the first few steps visible.

We each pulled out our cellphones and flipped the lights on so we could see. Step by step, we marched upward until we reached the second floor. There, we came to another door. Derek tried to pull it open but I could see it was dented by the blast, so he had to use a bit of muscle to get it to dislodge. It gave way after a tug or two, and a burst of light came through. As we stepped in, we understood why: there was no wall left to keep the sun out. Everything was left exposed by the rocket blast which tore apart the front of the building. This section had two individual apartments, split down the middle by a hallway. The doorways still held their shapes with right angle corners, but the frames were ripped off. The doors themselves in shambles.

We exited the stairwell and I could feel the unevenness underneath my shoes as the debris settled underneath me. Each step feeling wobblier than the last.

Derek led us to the apartment on the right side of the hall and we made our way inside. Piles of debris were on the floor as the entire front façade was annihilated. It would've looked like an unfinished construction site with all the jagged stones on the floor.

But then, as I looked down, it was possible to make out small trinkets that were not completely gone. Family photos where the glass of the picture frame was shattered but the photographs themselves remained mostly unscorched. Plastic boxes filled with pencils and scissors. The furniture half survived, and by that, I mean quite literally the couch in the living room was half obliterated and half standing. One thing that stood out to me was a lone shoe. Judging by the size, it clearly belonged to a child and was left sitting in the rubble underneath a few layers of debris. A place of innocence. A home for play. Gone.

The living room was at the front of the apartment which clearly took the worst of it. The kitchen was set off to the side and was blown open as well. I could now get a clearer view of the sink as it drooped down outside the building with a few pipes and coils holding it in place. Aside from the refrigerator, nothing else could be made out in that part of the unit. Seeing scenes like this up close reminds you of the lethality of war.

"Thankfully, the people who lived here evacuated town," Derek said. "The owner told me we could come to look at it. He hasn't even seen it."

FIGURE 16.1 Inspecting the damage of a rocket attack up close in Ashkelon, Israel. Photo by NewsNation.

"Oh, he wasn't here?" I clarified. "That's good."

"Yes. He picked up his mom, and they left twenty minutes before the attack."

Twenty minutes? Talk about a close call.

Derek led us back down the hall toward the bedroom, which was around the corner. The wall was knocked out here too, but much of the furniture survived as it was deeper in the home. Still unlivable, but I at least had some reassurance in my mind that a human being could have, at one point, called this place home. On the other side of the bedroom was a metal door. This was interesting as it appeared to be completely unscathed save for a few dings. I opened it up where there wasn't much room inside, maybe five feet by five feet. There wasn't any furniture or anything in it either. It seemed like an empty walk-in closet without a place to hang anything.

"The bomb shelter," Derek said intuitively. I had been told these are pretty standard for every newly built home. In the United States, if you asked somebody to construct a bunker in your home, people would look at you as if you had a serpent's head. Here, they'd look at you as weird if you decided *not* to include one in your home. A stark contrast from what I was used to.

We cut Ron loose and had him shoot some video around the apartment. I was just taken aback by how the destruction was so contained. On the second floor of this building, everything was gone. One building over? Untouched. Heck, even one floor up, people still had their home intact.

"So Derek, how did this rocket get through? How come the Iron Dome didn't stop it?" I asked. The Iron Dome was well-renowned for its accuracy in stopping thousands of rocket and missile attacks. Back home in the United States, for those who knew about it, there was this perception it could not be breached. That would be an inaccurate assumption. Exhibit A: the apartment I was standing in.

Derek cocked his head as if to say it was a fair question. "You've been staying in Tel Aviv, yes?"

"Yeah," I responded.

"Well, Tel Aviv is 30–40 miles north of us. So, the Iron Dome has more time to react," Derek explained. "It takes two minutes for rockets to reach Tel Aviv. Here, you get thirty seconds."

"Thirty seconds?" I blurted out. "From the time the rocket is fired to the time it makes impact, you get thirty seconds?"

Derek pursed his lips as he pondered that. "Maybe. If you're lucky."

If you're lucky? I couldn't believe that. In fact, I didn't completely. I was certain he was exaggerating.

"So, because there's less time, the Iron Dome can't respond as accurately," Derek carried on.

Logically, that does make sense. But thirty seconds seemed like nonsense. Imagine thirty seconds in your day-to-day life and how casually that time goes by the wayside. It takes me more than thirty seconds to check out at the grocery store if there's no line and I only have one item. That's the difference between life and death? No way. I tried not to think of that exchange. And ironically, despite walking through a blast site, I still believed it was next to impossible for us to be in any danger.

Giving the apartment one last glance, I then scurried after the group as they marched down the stairs. All four of us had our phone lights out to guide our way. It was a quick walk to the ground floor when we stepped back into the foyer and returned to the sunlight outside.

Looking back up at the sky, it was a clear day with the sun beaming down on us. The beach, just a few blocks away, looked inviting as if this place wasn't being bombed daily. We walked back over to Derek's car. I wanted to take a look at some of the footage we shot so slid into the back seat, buckled up, and pulled out my laptop. Derek and Ron left us alone for a few minutes and strolled off as Will and I flipped through the clips.

"Dude, that was crazy," Will said. It was, no two ways about it. And looking at some of the footage as well on my laptop, it was pretty amazing the level of destruction wrought on that place.

Granted, this was my second war zone. It was Will's first, so everything seemed new to him. Still, I was pretty stunned by how in an instant a home like that could be annihilated. You hear stories of tornados shredding communities in a matter of minutes, but this felt very different. At least in those situations you had an idea of which day a tornado *could* strike. People in the South gear up for severe weather days in advance. This, on the other hand, you had to always be on guard.

And then, as if I had willed it into existence with my thoughts, it happened. I heard this slow build-up of sound from behind me. Like a wolf's howl that in split seconds grew from a whisper to a deafening blast. That distinct sound you can't unhear.

Sirens started blaring all over Ashkelon. But this was different than Tel Aviv where you hear them a few blocks away echoing throughout the air. These sirens were right next to us and they were deafening.

In that moment, a few thoughts and bad habits popped into my head. *Here we go again. How inconvenient. Do I even need to seek shelter?*

"Run!" I heard Derek scream a few hundred feet away from us. That answered that question.

Will jerked out of the car in panic and took off back the way we came. Intuitively, all my arrogant non-believing was gone. *30 seconds.* I started counting in my head, remembering an old elementary school trick to keep track of time.

One thousand one. I was still in that damn car. I needed to go. *Now.*

One thousand two. I threw the laptop onto the seat next to me and lunged my body out the car, only to be jerked back inside. I still had my seatbelt on.

One thousand three. *Of course I still have my seatbelt on. Where the hell is that damn buckle?* I thought.

One thousand four. *Isn't this the cliché crutch every horror film director uses? They're trying to escape the man with the chainsaw but the car won't start? Shut up, Robert. Focus. Where is that damn buckle?*

One thousand five. *There it is. I've got my fingers on it. Click.* The seatbelt burst loose and I was free. I was outside the car standing on the sidewalk as that siren howled.

One thousand six. *Where the hell is Will?* I looked back around and saw him a few paces away from me waiting as he jumped up and down to get me to follow. *There he is.*

One thousand seven. *What do I do? Do I get down on the ground?*

One thousand eight. "Run!" I heard Derek yell again. I saw him in the distance. He was by the corner pointing for us to follow him back toward the apartment complex we were just in.

One thousand nine. *Run, you idiot.* I took off sprinting with everything I had. Will was motioning for me to follow. I was right on his heels as we made a beeline for Derek who was spinning his arms like a third base coach in baseball telling his player to "go home."

One thousand ten. Full steam ahead. I was almost to Derek. Now he was turning and burning around the corner. I followed him.

One thousand eleven. I made the turn and the apartment building was in sight. *Why were we running for the apartment again? Doesn't matter, keep running.*

One thousand twelve. "Go to the stairwell!" Derek yelled. *Yes, the stairwell. It's made of concrete. That should be safe.*

One thousand thirteen. *Wait, which building is it? They all look the same!* I was approaching the apartments and I couldn't remember which one it was, though in the heat of the moment I didn't think to look up and seek out the one with the unmistakable hole in it.

One thousand fourteen. I turned around. There was Will. He had broken off and was heading for a different building than I was. *Should I follow him? Does he know where he's going? Is that the right building?*

One thousand fifteen. *No time! Run idiot, run! Follow Will.* Derek was heading for that building too. I shifted course and was in hot pursuit of them.

One thousand sixteen. *I'm almost there. Less than a hundred feet from the building. The door is open. Just go for the door.*

One thousand seventeen. *I'm so close. I'm so freaking close. I'm gonna ma—*
Boom.

One thousand eighteen. The loudest explosion I have heard in my life. Right over top of me. *What the hell was that? Doesn't matter, keep running. Almost there.*

One thousand nineteen. *I'm at the door. Get inside! Get inside! Move legs, move.*

Boom.

One thousand twenty. Another huge explosion. Right over us again. I'm now inside the foyer. *This looks familiar. Wait, where's Will? Where's Derek? Where's Ron?*

One thousand twenty-one. "Come on!" Came a voice. It was Derek's as he, Ron and Will were all poking their heads out from behind the door leading to the stairwell. *The team's all there. I just have to make it through the foyer. Only a couple of feet to go.*

One thousand twenty-two. I've reached the stairwell entrance and am now leaping inside to the ground. The momentum of my body carrying me to the far wall. I brace for impact as my hand stops me from going head first into the concrete.

One thousand twenty-three. Derek slams the door behind.

Boom-boom-boom-boom.

One thousand twenty-four. Multiple explosions overhead, now muffled by the closed door.

One thousand twenty-five. My heart is going a mile a minute. The adrenaline is pumping with everything it has. All I can hear is *thump-thump-thump* as my pulse beats in my ears.

One thousand twenty-six. Ron is crouched in the corner with his head down. Will, I didn't realize, was sitting right next to me. Both of our backs pressed against the wall as we slid down to the floor.

One thousand twenty-seven. Derek was bracing the door shut. Not sure that was necessary in hindsight, but at the moment I feared something was going to rip through and blow the door off its hinges.

One thousand twenty-eight. The echoes of the explosion are now fading off into the distance. *How many more are coming?* I thought. *Thump-thump-thump* went my heart. It felt like every vein in my body was vibrating as blood couldn't pump fast enough.

One thousand twenty-nine. Nothing. Complete silence, save for the panting as our lungs gasped for oxygen. The sound of our breath echoing in that stairwell.

One thousand thirty. Derek turned toward me. First a concerned look on his face to make sure we were all right. *I'm ok. Well, at least I think I'm ok. I don't think any bones are broken. I don't think anything hit me. I'm pretty sure I'm ok.* I was, but the adrenaline was flowing so swiftly if I had been hurt I would have never known.

I looked back up at Derek and gave him a nod. He glanced around the room to make sure everyone was okay as well. A single nod back was all he needed. Derek then turned back to me as a smile cracked across his face.

"That," he said, struggling to get the words out as he was panting. "Was *not* thirty seconds."

Everybody laughed at that one. It is true. The first explosion came less than twenty seconds after the sirens first roared to life. We all sat there for a few moments laughing with one another. The nervous kind of laugh you make when you finally know everything is going to be all right.

Derek raised himself up off the floor and reached out his arms to both Will and me. We each took hold of one arm as he hoisted us onto our feet. I dusted myself off and recomposed.

"Shall we carry on, gentlemen?" Derek asked in a chipper tone. I nodded, and he led us back outside.

I couldn't help but look up. There in the sky were over a half dozen plumes of smoke. The Iron Dome had picked them all off. No rockets made impact in that barrage. I had by this point made it through a few rocket attacks in Israel. Back in Tel Aviv, you'd typically see the interceptions take place thousands of feet in the sky. These plumes were just a couple hundred feet above us.

Derek hastened his pace back toward the car and we followed him. Now I know why he always felt time was of the essence. We made it back to the car and I slid into the back seat, not bothering to remove my vest. Will hopped in next to me as we each slammed our respective doors shut. His eyes met mine and we both smiled. I knew exactly what he was thinking. *Not a chance in hell we're telling our parents about what happened today.* If I told mom she'd be on the next plane to Tel Aviv to drag me back to Ohio personally.

Derek popped into the driver's seat as Ron retook the passenger seat up front. "Everybody good?" Derek asked. We all nodded our heads. "Okay, let's go." He flipped on the ignition and rolled the car into drive. Just like that, Derek had already moved on with his life. I admired his ability to just shake it off and press on.

I, however, was not so mentally ready to do just that. It amazed me how right Derek was. You have to be ready to go at all times. It also dawned on me that I was awake and alert while all of that happened. Now, imagine being asleep and having just a few seconds to get up, roll out of bed, and find shelter after the sirens started blaring.

Take it a step further: consider being a civilian in Gaza who doesn't have the benefit of a warning siren. Their clock has even fewer ticks and even then, there's no air defense system to fall back on. The twenty seconds or so I was afforded would be greatly welcomed by some of the people in Gaza City, I can assure you.

As I said, that day in Ashkelon was the first time I considered what a moment is really worth. Now, I think about that constantly. Time is that one resource we long for more of yet can't get back.

Life lesson learned: protect your time with everything you have. You never know when those moments will count the most. Years. Months. Weeks. Days. Hours. Minutes. Seconds. They all add up.

I looked down at my watch as the hands lurched around the face.

Tick-tick-tick.

Three seconds tossed to the wind right there. But I guarantee you: Somewhere, somebody's life just changed forever—and they'd love to have those seconds back. I haven't looked at my watch the same ever since.

17 WHEN THE FOG CLEARS

"There are two sides to every story."

You didn't have to go to journalism school or study communications to know that one. I felt that phrase running through my head seemingly every day in the Middle East

That hospital incident discussed in Chapter 15 serves as the perfect example. Many *thought* they had it all figured out as to what happened that night, but they were wrong. Many were *certain* they had gotten to the heart of it, yet they had missed the mark. And our trip to a hospital in Ashkelon truly articulated to me that if you don't have both halves, you don't even have half an understanding.

The hospital in question is called Barzilai University Medical Center. On October 7, the medical staff there was at the forefront of the attack, working tirelessly to care for the wounded. The videos that came out of this hospital that day illustrated a sense of pandemonium as ambulances barreled in, bringing a column of stretchers.

The day we visited, a little less than a month had passed. Much of the day-to-day chaos had subsided, but the scars remained. And, as we quickly found out, October 7 was hardly the last of the action the medical workers here would face.

Will and I stepped through the glass sliding doors and were hit with palpable tension immediately. We set foot in the waiting room, which was full, though not everyone was a patient. To our left was a group of police officers with their equipment lying across their laps. They briefly looked up to meet our gaze, then their stares returned to the ground. To our right was a trio of medical first responders who were sitting on the floor. Their heads were angled back toward the wall as they tried to catch a moment of rest. There were some patients seated in the waiting room chairs, and each was keeping quiet, minding their own business. No one was saying a word.

A pair of metal automatic doors swung open, and out stepped a woman with messy light brown hair, dressed in dark clothes. This was the contact we had been set up with here at the medical center, who was a hospital administrator. We'll call her Tanya. She approached us with the same sunken facial expression everyone in that hospital exhibited. Dark circles clung to her eyes that seemed practically lifeless. I can't imagine anyone there had been sleeping well since October 7.

Tanya extended her hand to introduce herself. "You picked a difficult time to visit," she said in a somber tone. "Every day here is a new crisis." We promised her we wouldn't take too much of her time and were hoping she could share some perspective on what the medical response was like on October 7.

She nodded her head in understanding. "It was one word: a massacre," she muttered, then pointed to the ground where we stood. "The floor had these huge spots of blood, and I was walking there and there was blood here and blood there. I had my gym shoes on, which are very bright . . . and they are not bright anymore." She paused one more time. "They are just red."

An entire hospital turned into a battlefield infirmary with patients rushed to emergency surgery. And while this was a substantial medical center complex, it was hardly the size of major hospitals in Tel Aviv, for example. Compare it to a semi-rural hospital in the United States being thrust into the midst of an attack that claimed over a thousand lives. No level of training really prepares you for that.

Tanya led us down the pale white corridors of the hospital, pointing out where blood used to be or where patients had been treated for their injuries. She seemed to have a patient story for each corner and crevice. Some made it; others did not. She didn't know their names, but she could vividly recall their cases: a boy who lost his arm here and a woman whose husband passed there. Each open space told its own tale of tragedy.

We arrived at an area that was different from the rest of the hospital. It looked like a greenhouse, with each of the walls covered in glass windows. It wound around a courtyard that opened up to a grassy area. What took me off guard, however, was that there was debris everywhere. Many of the windows were blown out, and steel pipes littered the floor. Amid all of the debris were bright red, orange, and yellow children's toys.

"This is the children's center," Tanya said, intuitively answering my question. "It was hit by a rocket just a few days ago. God forbid, there were no children here because usually they are here."

My ears perked up at this, and I turned to her in shock. "Your hospital was bombed?" I asked, the words falling out of my mouth in surprise.

Tanya nodded her head. "Four times, actually."

Four times? A hospital in southern Israel was struck by rockets on four separate occasions? Why wasn't anybody talking about this?

"You are the first Western journalists here. Aside from a few local television reporters and newspapers, nobody else has come to visit this place." Tanya then pulled out her phone and handed it to me. I hit play and saw a beige-white corridor, just like the one I had walked through, but with medical equipment scattered around.

When hitting play, the volume on the video was loud as I could hear the sound of alarms blaring and the spraying of water. The camera panned around to show pipes bursting and an entire lobby area blown to pieces. The only way I knew that's what it was, was because half of the ceiling had fallen onto the chairs, and the sliding glass door was ripped off its hinges and shattered. I was looking at direct hits from rockets in multiple parts of the hospital complex.

As I watched the video, Tanya craned her head over my shoulder—shaking her head the whole time.

"If I may ask you a question?" she said, breaking her silence. "What is a hospital? What is a medical center? It's a place where we're supposed to take care of patients. That's the only thing we should do here, take care of patients. In this case, children. You don't see a headquarters of the IDF here."

International law is at face value straightforward when it comes to hospitals. The Rome Statute of the International Criminal Court under Article 8, Section 2 says:

> (b) Other serious violations of the laws and customs applicable in international armed conflict, within the established framework of international law, namely, any of the following acts:
>
> (ix) Intentionally directing attacks against buildings dedicated to religion, education, art, science or charitable purposes, historic monuments, hospitals and places where the sick and wounded are collected, provided they are not military objectives.[1]

That last caveat is the most critical: "provided they are not military objectives." At this particular time in the war, this was becoming a heatedly debated topic in Gaza. The Israelis were accusing Hamas of using hospitals, schools, and mosques as military positions to barricade troops and store weapons. The United States and other Western nations came to Israel's defense on this—corroborating the claim. As such, the IDF's position was that if a hospital in Gaza was being used as a military site for Hamas, it was fair game to be raided.

This would play out multiple times throughout the war as the Israelis would give hospital staffers notice that the raid was coming, then troops would move in. Each time this happened, the United Nations and certain humanitarian groups inside Gaza would outspokenly condemn the action.

But this hospital in Ashkelon? Nobody was calling this a military site. The IDF was not planning out their invasion of Gaza from the basement of the hospital to try and hide behind civilians. Nobody, not even Israel's harshest critics, was accusing medical staffers at Barzilai of harboring troops or stockpiling weapons.

And yet, this hospital was bombed four times in recent weeks, and the international community was silent. I didn't understand that one.

But I didn't have time to ponder it any longer because that shrill shriek I had heard so many times started to echo in the distance—building into a crescendo that sliced through the air. The sirens were going off again, and once more Ashkelon and this hospital found themselves in the line of fire.

"Do *not* panic," Tanya ordered, holding up a hand to our crew. "Stay calm and follow me." I was taken aback by her coolness. She smoothly led us over to a door near the courtyard, which she popped open to reveal a stairwell. No lights were on to illuminate it, so we pulled out our phones as we carefully moved forward—descending step by step into the dark.

We reached the bottom of the staircase and came upon another door, which Tanya had to put her shoulder into in order to crack it open. Behind this door was what appeared to be a storage room filled with boxes and old furniture coated in a thick layer of dust. There were still no lights, so it was just me, Tanya, and our crew in the pitch blackness.

"And now, we wait," Tanya said, her arms crossed, her lips twisted like a corkscrew as she appeared to be focused on her thoughts. She bobbed up and down, her eyes slowly sliding from side to side. Based on her body language, you would think she was waiting for the elevator, not for a barrage of rockets to pass.

On cue: *Boom-Boom-Boom.*

The sound of three rockets exploding overhead—intercepted by the Iron dome—took us by surprise, but not Tanya. She refused to break her cold, firm stance and didn't react in the slightest.

Following the explosions, we stood in silence for a few moments, waiting to get the all-clear. Finally, I broke the tension.

"It concerns me how calm you are right now," I commented to Tanya.

Her face remained facing forward, but her eyes darted to the corner of their sockets to make contact with mine.

"I am *not* calm," she replied firmly. "Believe me, I am not calm right now." She paused for a moment, then took a deep breath. "We don't have a choice. We really don't have a choice."

I understood exactly what she meant. If she didn't remain strong, if she didn't offer a steady hand, who would? That was the mindset of many people in Israel at the time. Shelve your fears until the crisis is in the past. Easier said than done, but never once did I consider that beneath Tanya's firm exterior was a woman locked in silent panic.

We stayed down in that basement for a few more minutes before Tanya's phone notified her that the all-clear had been given. She looked back up with her lips pursed, then turned back to me. "Okay, let's go."

I could tell something specific was weighing on her mind, but she was picking her words carefully. She led us back up the stairs where daylight was creeping in from the courtyard. I haven't been so relieved to be back above ground since the night Bartley and I spent in that Ukrainian bunker just a year and a half earlier. There is an inherent sense of helplessness when sheltering underground. You don't have control of anything; you can't see what's happening; you are completely at the mercy of what transpires in the world above.

I walked shoulder to shoulder with her, but she remained silent, her eyes facing forward with a locked gaze on the path ahead.

"Do you think all of these rocket attacks on your hospital are intentional?" I asked earnestly. She kept walking forward, at first giving no indication she had even heard the question. Then, she abruptly stopped, turned to me, and gave a bit of a shrug.

"There is some worry that we've been targeted and chosen as a target," she acknowledged, cocking her head to the side as if she were weighing the likelihood in her head. "We can't know, but four times we've been hit by rockets, so . . . it probably means something."

An even-handed response. Only the top brass at Hamas could answer whether they had intentionally put that hospital in their crosshairs. Yet nevertheless, four bombings was four bombings. Perhaps a brazen war crime, perhaps an accident or coincidence. You may insert the "fog of war" line here.

Tanya, seeming not to want to elaborate further on the subject, then proceeded forward without giving me an opportunity to ask anything more. I could only imagine what was going through her head. October 7 was a traumatic day for medical workers here unlike any other—then add to that the possibility a rocket may fall on them if they showed up to work any morning going forward.

We arrived at another courtyard near the main lobby area where we had entered. Tanya stopped me and pointed to the corner of a building that was surrounded by excavation equipment. She stood there and shook her head again, explaining that what we were looking at was not a renovation project but emergency repairs being conducted due to one of the bombs that had fallen on the hospital.

She pointed to the blasted-out windows and exposed inner walls where the rocket made an impact. "The missile came like this," she said, motioning with her hand. "Crossed over, ruined everything, fell here." Tanya threw her hands up as if to say, "unbelievable," then spun back around in a mix of frustration and anger.

I tried to catch up with her as she stormed back into the lobby through the sliding glass doors. As she made her way halfway through the waiting room back toward the main entrance, she turned around and extended her hand to tell us goodbye. She needed to get back to work, and judging by what I saw that day, there was no shortage of it to go around.

"One last question for you," I interjected. "Based on what you've seen, what would you like people around the world to know?"

She gave a polite smile, then dropped her gaze to the floor to think about that one. After a few moments, she looked back up and explained she wished people could see what she saw on October 7 and the chaos that ensued at her hospital:

the faces of innocent victims, the gruesome injuries they sustained, the families broken.

"It's very hard to understand the cruelty. There really are no words to explain this kind of cruelty," she concluded, looking me in the eyes and holding my gaze.

Seeing the aftermath was one thing, but being there on Black Saturday with pools of blood on the floor and people dying in the corridors was something incomprehensible to me.

We thanked her for her time. She gave us one final handshake and a smile, then departed. We set off back outside into the crisp southern Israeli night, got into our car, and started heading north to Tel Aviv.

Once more, I left a place in the Middle East where I had seen plenty and somehow walked away feeling like my grasp on this subject had more holes than I'd given credence to. How different the world looks from a 40,000-foot view compared to looking people right in their eyes.

And everything we felt like we started to understand now seemed flimsy at best. What exactly happened at that hospital explosion in Gaza? I don't know; I wasn't there. Were the rocket attacks at this hospital in Ashkelon intentional? You'd have to ask Hamas. Why was there outrage for one hospital being caught in the midst of the fray, yet indifference toward another despite what international law says? No clue.

But I did feel comfortable drawing one conclusion: the idea that war can be clean and neat is a fallacy. War is inherently messy, with everyday people like Tanya, who just want to do their jobs and save lives, caught right in the middle.

And there's no escaping it.

18 HEROES SHIVER TOO

Lay on the ground and pray you don't die.

That was the takeaway from the "safety briefing" with our fixer, Derek. I hoped he was joking. He wasn't. I could tell by the way he looked at Will and me with sternness—refusing to break eye contact until satisfied we understood his words clearly.

That was our game plan in case we came under attack while in Sderot, an Israeli city that is just off the Gaza Strip. So close, in fact you can see it from a hill in town just a mile or two away. The overlook was a common spot for journalists to report live from because you could see the smoke plumes inside Gaza over the correspondent's shoulder. Bartley told us "TV hill," as he called it, was worth inspecting for ourselves.

"TV hill?" scoffed Derek. "It's called 'death hill.' That's where you have the best chance of dying." I think we could have done without that correction.

Ashkelon set the tone for us in that a few moments can make the difference between life or death. But Sderot was a different ballgame. Since it's farther south, eight seconds is all you get to take cover. Ten if you're lucky. So, with that context in mind, you'll understand that "lay on the ground and pray you don't die" isn't a cheeky quip. It's "Plan A." There is no "Plan B."

Sderot before October 7 had a population of roughly 30,000 people. Hardly a sprawling metropolis, but certainly the largest city that was caught directly in Hamas' crosshairs. As we made our way south, we pressed on until I saw something unmistakable in the sky: thick, black smoke.

It came more and more into view the farther we went. What seemed like a stream of smoke became a more massive plume hanging over Gaza. When we got close, Derek pulled the car over so we could get a better view. Watching from a distance, it seemed it could be confused with the smog that comes from a factory chimney. It was that constant. Wood, foliage, homes, and worldly possessions were being evaporated into charred black clouds instantaneously.

Boom.

My gaze was interrupted by a loud blast. I jolted around and saw that just past a thin tree line maybe 20 feet from the road we parked on was an Israeli artillery battery. Through the leaves I could make out the barrel—still smoldering.

Moments later, two IDF troops came sprinting out of the woods directly toward us. Derek walked past me to meet them head-on. As the troops made it to our fixer, I could see them pointing emphatically at us, then off into the distance behind us. It didn't take a rocket scientist to tell we were being told to take a hike.

Derek put his hands up, giving the universal hand gesture for "okay, relax" and turned back toward us. "We have to go," he said. "The Army doesn't want us here. Too dangerous."

Boom. Another blast. *No argument here.*

Derek started the car back up and quickly sped off. I turned around to see the IDF troops watching us drive away until we were out of their line of sight.

We were without question in the war zone now and hadn't even made it all the way to Sderot. Derek's words started to make more sense. It was evident that the danger was very real. But, what I would quickly come to understand is that, compared to the people who lived through October 7, I hadn't a clue what danger even was.

Our car entered Sderot, which was strikingly empty. There wasn't a single person on the street or soul to be found. Within moments, the reason for this became clear. One of the first buildings we saw was a hollowed out gray and charred structure. It had several craters in the side of it with the windows blown out.

"That's the police station," explained Derek. "Hamas entered the city and destroyed it." This was our first time in a place where Hamas put boots on the ground to carry out their attack. The police station was hit by several rocket-propelled grenades (RPGs) from close range. What wasn't blown to pieces burned.

By this point, the October 7 attack had happened about a month ago. Emergency crews had already come and gone, and bodies of both civilians and terrorists had been removed.

Left behind is what I can only describe as a shell of a city devoid of its life and energy. A few subtle reminders here and there gave the indication that people used to call this place home, such as the empty playgrounds and shawarma shops with plates and cutlery still sitting on the outdoor tables.

As our car rolled closer, we finally saw a handful of what appeared to be residents, each one wearing a bulletproof vest. Derek would later explain to me that in this community, everyone had protective gear of some kind.

We pulled the car over and got out. There were maybe a dozen people in total, a collection of men and women standing across the street from the old police station. They kept staring at the building with their hands on their hips as they took it all in.

Derek shut his door behind him and took the lead in approaching the group. One woman standing on the outside of the gathering turned and gave a smile. She was short, with dirty blonde hair and tan skin.

The woman waddled up to Derek and, without saying anything, gave him a big hug. Clearly knowing one another, the two held their embrace for several moments. Finally, they let go, and their eyes met each other's. We'll call the woman Gina.

"I'm glad to see you're okay," Derek said.

"I am doing as well as I can," she said with a sigh.

Derek then turned to us. "This is my friend, Gina. She was here on October 7 and survived the attack."

"I guess I'm one of the lucky ones," she shrugged, then walked up to us. I attempted to extend my hand, but she went straight for a hug. I could feel her hanging onto my shoulders. It was as if the weight of the world was pulling her down. She released, let out a big sigh, and began to explain.

"The terrorists came to my home," Gina said. "It was the 7th of October. We were at home and we heard the sirens. We went to the shelter and we stayed in the shelter. I took my baby and we sat on the floor. We know the sound of rockets. But then I heard shooting," Gina paused, regathering herself as her hand gestures intensified. "All of a sudden we heard more and more sirens so we stayed in the shelter. After one hour, a lot a lot a lot of shooting. We opened our phones and could see the terrorists came to Sderot."

Practically everyone in Israel has some kind of application on their cell phone that lets them know when and where rocket alerts are activated, if there are drones in the air or terrorists on the ground. We found it became normal for people to check their phones regularly for this reason. Any time they would hear the alerts, it was a snap reaction.

"I take my baby and I say 'shh, be quiet,'" continuing on with her story. As she recalled every detail, you could hear the anxiousness in her voice. "I go to the kitchen and I take a knife, and I came back to the shelter and all you hear is 'doo doo doo doo doo,'" mimicking the sound of gunfire.

This was when people here, including Gina, realized this was far from a normal rocket attack and that something was clearly wrong.

"I tell my daughter 'we're playing a game called be quiet,'" explained Gina. "After eight hours, something like that, we heard the Army. They came with guns. We started to cry because we didn't know what to do. All I had was a knife."

A sense of helplessness on the ground. Yes, homes have shelters, but they're meant to protect people from rockets, not terrorists inside the city. Thankfully for Gina, the IDF arrived in time to get her and her child out.

"Afterward, I needed to come to this place near the police station," Gina said, motioning to a community center that was used to reunite families. "And I see all the bodies. Murdered. And I start to cry."

Gina's English broke for a moment as the words poured out of her mouth emotionally. She then beckoned us to follow her, pointing out different areas on the ground. "Everywhere you would look, there was blood. Everything you see is blood, blood, blood. Over there, some over there," she said, pointing her finger at different spots. The stains were no longer there, but Gina spoke as if she could vividly see them.

"Everything is broke," Gina said, pausing for a moment. "Everything, it's broke in our heads," she said, pointing at her skull. "We feel afraid. We feel like all the world has died. This is what we feel all the time. We're civilians! What do we have? Knives? To what? Cut bread? It's not fair to fight like this." Her voice trailed off.

I thought about that for a moment. Here was a mother who felt helpless, as if she couldn't protect herself or her family, and didn't know if she ever could again.

"What will you do next?" I instinctively asked.

Gina let out another sigh—pondering that question for a moment.

"We don't know what to do. We want to come live here, and we want to stay in Sderot. But now we're staying in Tel Aviv because maybe there's a terrorist in my home. It's crazy."

"Could you ever see yourself feeling safe here again?" I asked.

Gina looked down at the ground, giving her next answer some thought.

"Wow. That's a big question," she said, unable to look up and make eye contact. "Something happened. The heart is broken. Something happened because we don't feel safe. You go to the street and you don't know if you'll come home."

Gina then started to emotionally raise her voice. "This is my life! Don't you understand? I go to the shop to buy ice cream here, and then you see terrorists shooting old women."

Another pause. It seemed as though Gina dreaded pondering this question.

"I want to come back. This is my country. And we try to make resilience again," her words hanging at the end of the sentence as she shook her head in disbelief. "I don't know; something broke."

Every time Gina used the word "broke," I could feel it in her soul. As if her fortitude and body were both set to give out. Everything she knew was shattered. I described Sderot as a shell of a city earlier. What I didn't realize at first is many of the people here were shells of their former selves as well.

Derek then interjected into our conversation. "We are running out of time. We need to keep moving." Derek had apparently set up conversations with other people here in Sderot.

I thanked Gina for her time. She wrapped her arms around me again. Somehow, in just a few minutes, the burden of the present situation seemed to weigh her down more. It was as if some of the last drops of stamina she had left, and her story and the tank was officially on empty.

Gina withdrew her embrace and wiped a tear from her eye. "Good luck," she said as she turned back toward her car.

Derek slid in next to me to share the gaze of her departure. "One of many," he commented, before turning around and setting off.

I followed Derek's lead as he took us away from the destroyed police station over to a nearby community center that was just down the road. Piled high outside was a mountain of supplies. Despite the fact their labels were written in Hebrew, I could make out what they were: water bottles, diapers, non-perishable food supplies, and more. There was a single guard with an automatic rifle standing by the cache. A sad reminder that in times of desperation, there's a risk people will turn to extreme measures to survive.

Derek led us inside the community center's main entrance way which brought us to a waiting area. There was a reception desk, a couple of plush chairs, and a coffee table with magazines. The floor was a classic white tile that matched the ceiling and walls. Ubiquitously bland. It looked like it could have been a small dentist's office.

"Wait here," Derek said as he quipped something in Hebrew to an IDF soldier sitting behind the reception desk. The soldier nodded his head and beckoned Derek to follow him to a back room.

Will and I were left alone in the waiting area. I turned around and noticed a glass display cabinet. It took me a moment to realize what was being displayed were not municipal awards or art projects or anything you would come to expect out of a city hall in the States. They were rockets.

Each rocket was burnt and bent in a different direction upon making impact. An accompanying white card with Hebrew written on it sat next to each rocket. Context clues helped me piece together that each card had a date and an explanation of what the rocket was or details of its impact.

The rockets showed the innovation of Hamas weaponry throughout the years. The first one looked extremely rudimentary; it could have been a pipe ripped out of the ground and turned into a projectile. The one at the opposite end was clearly much more advanced, glistening silver that was evidently manufactured to be a weapon from the beginning. It had small wires dangling from the edges, and its metal casing glistened with a modern steel color.

I heard a door open and turned around. It was Derek. "Come on," he beckoned. Will and I followed him through a doorway behind the receptionist's desk. We came to a hallway that wound around a pair of corners before arriving at a staircase that we descended. Beneath the community center was a room set up with maybe fifty chairs—each one ordered up in rows and columns. They all faced the front of the room where a presentation was ongoing.

Judging from the notebooks in each attendee's hands, I could tell they were journalists. The classic reporter's notebook is long but narrow so as to be gripped easily in a single hand. Always a dead giveaway.

What publications they worked for, I could not tell you, but each chair was filled, and each one of those reporters' eyes were trained intently on the front of the room.

Two men were standing next to a projection of several images, which were clearly photos of the aftermath of the October 7th attack. One man was leading the presentation. He had gray hair, a baggy white dress shirt, and khaki pants.

Next to him was a larger man with olive skin and narrowly cut short hair. With dark pants and an olive shirt, I didn't even have to look at the gun he had attached to his waist to know he was law enforcement. He just had that presence I've seen from countless police officers throughout my career.

What I could not take my eye off of, however, was the look on this second man's face. It was lifeless. His eyes would flicker open, and it would seem as though he couldn't maintain eye contact with anyone in the crowd, as if he were looking down at the floor in shame.

Derek leaned in and whispered in my ear, "That man is a hero. He rushed into the line of fire and saved several children."

The presentation now made a bit more sense. The projector was showing new images and videos from surveillance cameras. I watched as a half dozen terrorists roamed the main street, guns drawn, opening fire on cars passing by. One by one, I saw cars stop in their tracks and roll to a halt.

That included a black SUV where I saw one of the terrorists walk right up to the windshield and open fire—almost assuredly killing the driver. If they did survive, it was a miracle.

Then I watched as one of the Hamas fighters fired a rocket at a building. It was the destroyed police station I had seen with my own eyes a short while earlier. I marveled at how unrecognizable it was now compared to the video I was watching.

Next, we saw an officer rush onto the screen and unload several rounds at Hamas fighters who were retreating out of frame. The officer then turned and ran up to one of the cars left in the middle of the street. He went from car to car until arriving at the black SUV.

The camera angle then shifted to a body camera. The officer opened the rear driver-side door, and my heart sank. Two children, strapped into safety seats, were visibly hysterical over what had happened. Derek leaned in again. "They're saying the children's parents did not survive. They were made orphans. The officer who saved them is the one standing in the front of the room."

Indeed, it was the same man. Yet by that same token, a clearly different person. The officer in the video was full of adrenaline and energy, pushing through the street to save those children. You could hear his voice booming through the body camera microphones. The man who stood at this presentation wall looked like he couldn't even bring himself to speak. His shoulders pointed inward as his hands clasped in front of him: a big man with the stature of a mouse in that moment.

It was something about this body camera footage that stayed with me for weeks on end. War always gets framed as a chess match between two kings. An affair of adults. Something so "grown up" that children should be spared of it in conversation. And yet here I am, watching two children, sitting in their toddler seats, utterly helpless and scared as they watched their parent killed right in front of their eyes.

I felt sick to my stomach. While I was so sorry for the children, I couldn't empathize. Not because I didn't want to or didn't try. It just felt so foreign to me. One of those situations where it's so outside of your own set of experiences that you couldn't possibly begin to digest it. It started to make sense why this community, quite literally on the frontlines of Gaza for decades, was shaken in a totally different way than ever before.

Suddenly, all of the reporters stood up and started clapping. Everyone turned to the officer. His head stayed down as he stared at the floor. I couldn't imagine what he was feeling in that moment. Shame? Embarrassment? But why? He had rushed into the fray heroically.

"That officer is going to come talk to us after the presentation," Derek said. I nodded and told Will to meet us outside where it would be quieter. Derek went right up to the front of the room and politely held the officer's shoulder. He leaned in to listen to Derek, then nodded his head, agreeing to follow us out.

I retraced my steps back to the stairs, down the hallway, and out the front door. Moments later, the officer joined us—his posture still slumped over. When I shook his hand, his gaze remained angled toward the ground.

Will got the camera ready to record the interview. Derek was supposed to translate, but before I could even get a question out, the officer started talking. His tone was mumbled, nothing like what I heard in the body camera footage in the thick of the fighting. Never once did he look up during the interview. He continued on for a few moments as Derek listened intently. "I am so afraid. I am so very afraid. I don't even want to shower alone," Derek translated for us.

I thought about that for a moment. It was not the statement I had anticipated from a member of law enforcement. In my career, I've met a lot of officers, and one takeaway that I've had is that all of them have seemingly held the belief that when all else fails, they must be the immovable rock. They must be the emotionally unbreakable last line of defense. This may have been the first time I had spoken to someone in law enforcement who was past that. The untouchable had clearly been touched.

I asked him about the scene we saw inside, in which he pulled two children out of that car during the attack and saved their lives. He paused and took a deep sigh, gazing still at the ground. After a moment, he started mumbling again, which Derek translated. "I don't even have an explanation. All I saw before my eyes were two little girls. It was such a worse situation than any movie I could imagine."

I thought back to the video I saw inside as the officer rushed in, unbuckling the children hastily and hurrying them to safety. Split seconds and moments were crucial.

"It's hard for me to explain what I felt," he continued. "I wasn't afraid. When I replay in my mind everything I went through that day it's like I'm Rambo. But I'm not. At the end of the day, I go home and I'm scared to death. And I have to deal with it."

The officer paused and waved his hands at the camera as if to say "no more." We nodded our heads and assured him it was fine. He seemed to understand, shook our hands, and went back inside. Just like that, he was gone. The few moments he was with us were unbearable.

As I watched him leave, I felt the pain wafting through the air. That was a man far braver than I, and yet he was shattered into pieces in a way I have never been. It didn't matter how many people patted him on the shoulder and called him a "hero," he didn't want the title. Despite the lives he saved, it was the lives he couldn't that haunted him.

My thoughts were snapped to a halt by a voice that came crackling over a speaker system nearby. It was a garbled woman's voice speaking in Hebrew, but I knew it was urgent.

"Rockets," Derek said. He didn't shout, and there wasn't a major sense of urgency in his voice. It was more like a statement of fact, the way you might give someone the day of the week or the time of day.

In spite of Derek's calmness, or perhaps directly because of it, the muscles in my forehead went solidly tense like a rock. *Here we go again.*

"What do we do?" asked Will.

Derek stood there with an emotionless expression. Then he shrugged his shoulders and laid down on the ground. *Oh, that's really our plan A, huh?* I thought to myself. Sure enough, that was quite literally our first plan, and indeed our *only* plan. Will and I looked at each other. About three seconds had already passed by this point, so we followed Derek's lead and laid down on the ground.

Unlike Ashkelon, where we were able to find shelter, this time we were totally exposed and out in the open. I pressed my chin into the ground, feeling the shards of loose asphalt cutting into my face—stinging at their points of attack. Then I put my hands over my neck. The voice over the speaker was crackling again and even more urgently urging people to take cover.

As it so happened, the night before, I was watching videos about rocket attacks and what to do in those situations. The advice was similar: get as low as possible to avoid the up and outward spray of shrapnel.

Of course, the man in the video said words which in that moment, were not very encouraging.

"If the rocket hits you directly, don't worry about getting down. You'll already be dead."

Gulp.

I had lost count of how many seconds had passed. It must have been six or seven, which felt like months in that moment. I was lying on the ground, ready to push off and move if I needed to. But then again, what would that have done? Where would I have gone? It didn't matter. I wanted to be anywhere but there.

I did something I wasn't supposed to do and lifted my head up. In hindsight, I'm glad I did because it gave me the little bit of solace I needed. Right next to where I was lying was a small rocket crater. If you were in the United States, you would have assumed it was just a big pothole, but upon closer inspection, it clearly wasn't. There were shards of metal in the basin and burn marks on the edges—turning the dark asphalt an even deeper shade of charcoal gray.

Somehow, knowing that it was right next to me eased some concerns. It may as well have been the warzone equivalent of being struck by lightning: what are the odds the same spot gets hit twice?

Suddenly, I heard a *boom* in the distance. It was in the sky above, meaning it was an interception, not an impact. I held my breath, hoping that was the end of it. I counted for at least five seconds. Then, I saw Derek stand up. He turned around, brushed his shirt off, and looked at us with a bit of a cheeky smile.

"See?" he said, arms extended wide. "The plan worked!"

Will and I smirked back at him. What a crazy man Derek was. Always the source of optimism, even in the midst of tense moments. We pulled ourselves off the ground as Derek came over and helped us dust off.

"Now, let's get out of here before we *actually* get killed," he said.

I smiled again, acknowledging Derek's dark sense of humor. You quickly realize, in situations like war, that laughter is the light that gets you through the dark.

Pace hastened, we hustled back over to Derek's car and slid into the back seat. Derek twisted the key to ignition, the motor hummed to life, and we were off. I leaned out the window to get a better view of the sky. Sure enough, there was a small puff in the air left behind by a rocket interception.

In this part of Israel, there were a lot more rockets that got through. We were lucky, but my sense of euphoric relief didn't want to come to grips with the closeness of the call.

As we drove through the remains of downtown Sderot to get on the highway, I thought of Gina's most dagger-like words: "We try to remain resilient, but something broke." Broken is how the city looked and felt that day. Then I thought about the officer we had met, how his resolve had seemingly been broken as well. All I saw was a glimpse of their pain in one afternoon—pain that I had to imagine would stay with them for a lifetime.

As I stole one final glance at the Gaza skyline, where the smoke continued to pour without restraint, it dawned on me that this was different from anything I'd reported on before. Lives were *still* ending. The knife blade of pain was still slicing. The chills of war were causing the most rigid spines to shiver on both sides of the Israel–Gaza border.

And the word "fear" has a new meaning to me now as a result.

19 THESEUS IN THE LABYRINTH

There's something about ancient Greek mythology that has always piqued my curiosity. Their stories and fables are so dark and twisted as a means of scaring the mortal audience, yet at the same time, they instill a set of values and serve to explain why the world is the way it is.

Prime example: the story of the nymph Echo. Punished by the goddess Hera, she was cursed and only able to speak the last words spoken by others. Hence, the word "echo" we have in the English language today. How brilliant.

But one story that has always stood out to me for whatever reason is that of the labyrinth. Built by Daedalus for King Minos of Crete, he himself could barely escape the maze after its construction. The purpose of the maze? To hold the mighty Minotaur. With the head and tail of a bull but the body of a man, the beast resided at the heart of the labyrinth. Those who would enter would get lost, bewildered by the twists and turns before running smack dab into the monster—meeting a disastrous end.

It wasn't until the Athenian hero Theseus entered the labyrinth one day and successfully navigated the labyrinth that the beast was finally slain. It's a classic Ancient Greek myth that has been preserved and retold for centuries in art.

The reason I bring up this story is because one of the storylines we had been following throughout the first few months of the war was the intricacies of Hamas' tunnel network. Apparently, it was a wide-spanning construction that allegedly resembled the New York subway system. It had been described in many different ways: an undercity, a matrix, a labyrinth, a maze just to name a few.

The world started to get a clearer picture the night two of the first Israeli hostages were released. Hamas put out several videos showing their fighters giving candy bars and snacks to the two elderly women, still in their nightgowns. One was named Yocheved Lifshitz, the other Nurit Cooper. You could see the look of utter terror on their faces as they were led out of Gaza by masked Hamas terrorists. It was a big moment in the early days of the war and some of the first bits of good news since the October 7 attack for the people of Israel. Medical staffers collected Lifshitz and Cooper, then shuttled them off to a hospital where they cleared their exams. All appeared to be well.

The next day, a major press conference was held at the hospital with the hostages and their families. Cameras rolled and the world watched as Yocheved Lifshitz was pushed out in a wheelchair for dozens of lenses to see. Her face was pale. Her eyes still filled with shock. She only spoke that day in Hebrew so a family member translated to English on her behalf.

It was then we all learned that these two hostages had been to the underworld and back. Like an Ancient Greek myth, but in this case hardly a fable.

"There are a huge, huge network of tunnels underneath," explained Lifshitz' daughter Sharone speaking on her behalf. "It looks like a spider web."[1]

In that moment, the fantasy and mystique that surrounded Hamas' tunnels became chillingly real to all of us. It was no longer something the IDF mentioned in passing or propaganda purported by Hamas. It was a real place that one unfortunate enough could see, touch, and feel. Even so, it was still hard for me to totally grasp. *Could an undercity really exist in Gaza? Is this just a big exaggeration?*

That all changed for me when I saw the tunnels for myself. I'm no Theseus, and I don't believe in Minotaurs, but that day I did feel like I was one step from Hades—and I can attest: the tunnels are more real than you can imagine. I could feel the crunch of shattered glass underneath my boot as I stepped out of our car at the Erez Crossing: an entry point in southern Israel that gave direct access into Gaza.

Or, at least that's what it was before the war. On October 7, this was one of Hamas' major centers of attack. Surveillance footage from that day has widely circulated online where Hamas fighters can be seen infiltrating the crossing, going block by block and firing rockets at IDF positions.

It had now been maybe two months since October 7, but the wounds left behind hadn't begun to heal. Burnt-out cars scattered the streets with glimpses of their oil leaks clearly evident on the ground. I peered inside one office building with all of the windows blown out. The inside was charred roof to ceiling after it had been bombed and set ablaze. You could make out scraps of documents that were scattered on the ground as well as a few metal filing cabinets. Little else survived.

As I stepped back outside, a man came around the corner wearing his IDF uniform. He was short in stature and had a thick Scottish accent. Lt. Colonel Richard Hecht, who has been one of the most prominent faces of the IDF on American television networks since the October 7 attack. He would be the one taking us into Gaza that day.

The Lieutenant Colonel gathered our team around and put us through the safety briefing before heading to Gaza. His words at time difficult to understand due to his accent, so I craned my head and closed my eyes to listen as carefully as I could.

"To be clear, this is an active war zone," Hecht said. "Just the other day Hamas targeted this area again. They could attack at any moment."

Then to my surprise, Hecht said we would not be driving, but instead walking into Gaza. *Walking? How many miles?* I thought.

The Lt. Colonel then led our group forward and we turned a corner to what used to be a series of large, iron gates that had been blown open. Edges of the bars that used to form the entrance into Gaza sprayed off in different directions and were singed at their ends.

To my right, I could make out a series of large towers reminiscent of a castle. One of them had the top blown off. I remembered watching a Hamas video of a drone flying over one of those towers and dropping a bomb right on top of it. The footage was starting to take form in front of my eyes.

I felt an uneven surface below me and looked down. My boots had left the concrete pavement of Israel and were now settling into dirt. It was so uneven and shaky, comparable to walking along the high side of a powdery oceanfront beach. This dirt was darker in color, appearing to be more like an orange-red clay from a distance. I knew what the change in landscape meant: we were now officially in Gaza.

Looking up from my boots I took in the skyline. Gaza City itself was out of sight, so a dark gray smoky sky ran up to sweeping orange dunes. There was nothing else on the horizon except dirt and smog, save for a lone yellow excavator maybe a few hundred yards ahead. The same kind you'll see on the highways in the United States to fix a road. I thought little of it, until I realized that's where we were heading.

No more than ten minutes later, our group arrived at that site and I quickly understood why it was there. It sat atop a large dune which engulfed a hole in the ground. Maybe 50 feet below where we were standing was what we were there to see.

Perhaps you've walked down the street and seen construction crews in someone's yard digging for a water pipe. You'd see the rusty pipe exposed as crews worked to patch up a leak. That's what this looked like, except the "pipe" had a diameter of 10–15 feet. I quickly snapped back out of my daze and understood this was one of Hamas' tunnels, not a piece of public infrastructure. The entryway to the tunnel was massive enough you could easily drive a car through it.

There was no visible light coming from the entry to the tunnel. One IDF soldier walked down toward the gaping hole, and after he was a few paces inside, his silhouette disappeared into the pitch black abyss.

What was most shocking, however, wasn't the tunnel itself but where it was. I turned around and could very clearly see the gates of the Erez crossing we had crossed through. Hamas had built this massive tunnel structure right under Israel's nose, and it ran right up to the proverbial doorstep. Already, there were serious concerns and condemnations taking place in Israel regarding the October 7 attack, as many were incredulous Israel's highly sophisticated intelligence agencies could

FIGURE 19.1 The entrance to a Hamas tunnel in Gaza near the crossing into Israel. Photo by Robert Sherman.

not prevent it. This one particular tunnel added to that public sentiment where protests demanding resignations were common in Tel Aviv.

"Come on then," beckoned Hecht, ripping me out of my trance. He started marching his way down the dug-out crater toward the tunnel. Our team followed and after a few trudges, I almost lost my balance. The decline was steep, and the dirt underneath me kept sliding.

A pair of IDF soldiers waiting on either side of the tunnel watched us intently as we made our way to the opening. Now I could start to see what was inside. The whole circular interior was ribbed like a barrel. My first step into the structure rang with the sound of rubber meeting metal. I used each one of the ribs to prop myself up as an effective railing to avoid tumbling down to the underworld.

It wasn't until I reached the bottom of the shaft that I finally looked up and really started to take it all in. The opening of the tunnel was at least 100 feet above us, and the light shining through it seemed so distant.

A few small lanterns were set up so we could see the interior of the tunnel. Coming into this, I would have assumed "tunnel" was a loose term and envisioned something out of a prison escape Hollywood film. Instead, what I saw was impressive infrastructure. Solid concrete lined the walls and ceilings, and it was perfectly smoothed out. Above us ran a long pipe that had a diameter of about a foot, which was used for ventilation. Next to that tube were a series of thick black cables, each about an inch thick, used to bring electricity into the tunnel.

It was immediately apparent this was no rag-tag operation to build this. Forget the idea of a couple of people with shovels. This took high-level engineering, professional construction equipment, carefully done concrete pours, and more.

FIGURE 19.2 Producer Will Budkins capturing footage of the interior of a Hamas tunnel. Photo by Robert Sherman.

Turns out, my suspicions were right as Hamas put out another propaganda video shortly after to brag about their tunnels. They filmed the entire process of its construction, including the machinery used and the dozens if not hundreds of workers assigned to the project.

I walked along the walls inspecting every piece of wiring and tubing I could see. After taking 20–30 paces I came upon two IDF soldiers dressed in dark uniforms with black masks over their faces. They stood shoulder to shoulder in a way that communicated I was not allowed to pass.

"It's too dangerous to keep going," I heard Hecht say behind me. "There are still parts of the tunnel that have not been cleared."

I turned to him in shock. "You mean it's possible there are Hamas members still in here?"

Hecht shrugged. "It's possible. It's a very large tunnel."

"How far does it go?"

"Fifty meters down and about four kilometers long." Doing the quick mental math in my head, that meant this tunnel would descend 150 feet below the surface and was about two and a half miles in length.

The soldiers standing guard were part of an elite Israeli unit, which is why they couldn't show their faces. I understand now why they weren't letting us pass. While it was unlikely there were any more Hamas fighters inside, 2.5 miles is a lot of ground to sweep with plenty of nooks and crannies along the way.

FIGURE 19.3 Reporting from inside a Hamas tunnel as an Israeli soldier stands guard. Photo by Will Budkins.

"How much did this cost to build, do you think?" I asked Hecht.

He paused. "Millions," he said, his lips pursed to signify he was giving an estimate that made him bitter. I can't independently verify the validity of that figure, but I have no doubt he was right considering the size of the tunnel and the amount of concrete and metal involved.

For weeks, Israeli leadership had been using terms such as "terror dungeons" and "Gaza metro" to describe these tunnels. What I initially thought were political talking points now seemed much more on target than I had considered.

"Where does this stack up on the list of challenges the IDF is facing?" I asked Hecht.

"This is one of the biggest ones because they've been building these for so many years," he replied. *Years*, not months. Further adding to the notion that October 7 was in Hamas' playbook for a very long time.

The purposes of these tunnels were multifold. On one hand, this was military infrastructure designed to move fighters and weaponry underground and away from the prying eyes of Israeli satellites. But since October 7, they were also used to hide and imprison hostages. Yocheved Lifshitz and Nurit Cooper are just two of the many hostages since released who have attested to this.

I was uncomfortable being there for just a few moments. It was cold, damp, musky, and the word "dungeon" felt all too appropriate. A report published by the Hostages and Missing Families Forum in January of 2024 found that the conditions there caused health and respiratory issues for those who were able to make it out alive.[2] Standing there and getting a glimpse of it for myself, I don't doubt that being true.

Our time underground had come to an end. Hecht motioned us to follow him as he led us back toward the ramp leading out of the tunnel. Despite the fact the sun was unable to poke through the cloud and smog, it was near-blinding to look up.

My boot almost slipped as I was climbing out, but I was able to regather myself. I tried to take longer lunges to power through the steep ascent. Finally, we made it to the surface again, and my feet left the clanking metal of Hamas' tunnels and were back on the shifting Gazan soil.

I stopped and looked back at the Erez crossing, then down at the tunnel again. *How could Hamas have built this right under Israel's nose?* As the crow flies, we were less than a quarter of a mile away from the Israeli line. And yet somehow, Hamas had not only boldly but successfully carried out a high-level infrastructure operation.

And that was just one of the tunnels the IDF uncovered. They were all over Gaza City, Khan Younis, and the strip as a whole. Now I understood why the IDF was obsessing over these so much to the press and trying to paint this picture of an underground metro system used by Hamas to carry out their operations.

One thing about war coverage that I came to find early on is that it is so hard to distinguish between what is true and what someone wants you to think is true. I, like many, couldn't comprehend the existence of these tunnels let alone believe their sheer magnitude. Every journalist has at some point or another been told to give each word said at a press conference podium strict scrutiny.

But those tunnels? That wasn't spin. I could see them, stand in them, touch them, smell them. They were every bit real, and these terms like "labyrinths" or "mazes" weren't so hyperbolic after all. What the Ancient Greeks concocted in mythology, Hamas made into reality.

The only thing they forgot to include was the Minotaur.

20 IMAGINE A WORLD

To this day, one of my favorite songs is *Imagine* by John Lennon. I can recall hearing that song playing in my dad's car countless times as he blasted classic rock while driving down the highway. I wouldn't say I'm on board with every single lyric, but the overarching premise stands: what a world it would be if there were no wars, no fighting, and we could all live in peace. Of course, that's not the world we live in, and the Middle East is particularly the case. To understand the geopolitical landscape there, one must take into account the geography—similar to Ukraine and the European theater.

Israel is a democracy but unlike the United States very publicly does not purport a separation of church and state. It is unabashedly "The Jewish State"—the Star of David on the nation's flag leaving little mystery to that. And in that regard, it is all alone: an island amid a sea of nations that have a very different view of the world. First, let's begin with one question: what is the Middle East? Well, that depends on who you ask. Some say it includes northern Africa, others say no. Some contend Turkey should be considered part of the region, others brush that off and say it's part of Europe. How about Afghanistan? There's debate over that one as well.

Being the Yankee I am, I'm going to go with the CIA's list which is as follows: Armenia, Azerbaijan, Bahrain, Gaza, Georgia, Iran, Iraq, Israel, Jordan, Kuwait, Lebanon, Oman, Qatar, Saudi Arabia, Syria, Turkey, the United Arab Emirates (U.A.E.), the West Bank, and Yemen.[1]

For the sake of conversation, let's remove Gaza and the West Bank from that list for a moment. That leaves us seventeen countries in the "region." Some will be displeased with this grouping—possibly miffed by Georgia's inclusion or Egypt's exclusion. All fair, but this is the list we'll use for now.

Of the seventeen countries on this list, fourteen of them have populations that are at least 50 percent Muslim according to the Pew Research Center. Israel, Armenia, and Georgia would be the exceptions (the latter two majority Christian countries).[2]

Now, of the sixteen countries aside from Israel on the list, Armenia, Azerbaijan, Bahrain, Georgia, Jordan, Turkey, and the UAE recognize Israel diplomatically. The only one on that list that shares a border with Israel is Jordan. While Egypt is not included in the C.I.A. definition of the Middle East, it too shares a border with Israel and recognizes the state diplomatically. That said, it would be a severe stretch to call them "pals" as Egypt's government had threatened to annul its peace treaty with the Israelis over the situation in Gaza multiple times throughout the war.

And just a few years ago, Bahrain and the UAE would not have even been on this list. The Abraham Accords, signed under the Trump administration in 2020, finally formalized diplomatic ties between the neighboring nations.[3] That means everybody else in the region doesn't even recognize Israel's existence as a sovereign State, including two of Israel's directly bordering neighbors: Lebanon and Syria.

All of this to say that Israel is the only Jewish State in the region and most of its closest neighbors are neither friendly nor recognizing of the Israelis. Right, wrong, or indifferent, that's the way it is at the present moment. Maybe there comes a day when each of the UN member states recognizes Israel (and to be clear, there are several *not* in the region that do not have diplomatic ties with Israel either, including North Korea, Cuba, and Indonesia just to name a few). But that day has not come, and it is not presently on the visible horizon.

So, in order to fully reach the vision encapsulated in John Lennon's 1971 hit, there is still plenty of work to be done. But that doesn't mean people have given up hope.

That fact was especially prevalent in northern Israel. On October 7, Hamas attacked the south. On October 8, Hezbollah, a militant group in Lebanon, started carrying out consistent attacks on the Israeli regions near the Lebanese border in support of Hamas. The attacks have been substantial, causing back and forth firefights between the two sides that have included Israeli airstrikes on Hezbollah's positions. Seemingly every day, the growing question was "when would this explode into an all-out war?" It felt like an inevitability to many, yet not something most really wanted. The Israelis we would talk to on the streets would candidly acknowledge that a war with Hamas was one thing, but Hezbollah and its massive arsenal of missiles was a different animal. At the time Israelis firmly believed they would win a toe-to-toe fight, but it would be costly.

Something missed by many around the globe is that because of this fighting, tens of thousands of people, both in northern Israel and southern Lebanon, have had no choice but to flee their homes. Some were displaced over a year, others may never return.

We decided to go see this for ourselves in January of 2024. Our fixer for the day was a man we'll call Ike. He had long curly hair that he fixed into a ponytail, a neatly trimmed beard and a soft disposition. He picked his words carefully the same way he meticulously planned out our every move. He tried to think ahead at all times and I appreciated that.

Will and I loaded up Ike's car and made the drive north from Tel Aviv. There was a town situated right along the border called Metula that had a view of Lebanese soil from above. We took a long, winding dirt road through the mountains in order to get there.

As an aside, I'm pretty amazed by the topography of Israel. A tiny country roughly the size of New Jersey has the Mediterranean Sea, Dead Sea, deserts and mountains. All can be reached in less than a half-day drive.

Pulling up to Metula, I let out a slight "whoa" as the first thing I saw was a tank with four IDF troops huddled around it. As our car approached, the soldiers caught sight of us and immediately started moving toward us. One soldier raised his hand in the air to give the universal command of "stop."

Ike rolled down the window to talk to the first soldier who came up to us shaking his head and pointing the direction in which we came from. I didn't need to speak Hebrew to understand the conversation. "Turn the hell around and get out of here," appeared to be the loose translation I gathered from the soldier's body language.

Ike put his hand up and nodded his head as if to so "okay, understood." Then, he threw the car in reverse, turned it around and we started to make our way back down the mountain. "The army has ordered everybody to leave there. Not even residents are allowed inside," Ike explained. "They say it's too dangerous. Many rocket and missile attacks here."

This was a shock to me to see this place so locked down. Ashkelon was constantly threatened by Hamas attacks and we were able to go inside. Same with Sderot which is a stone's throw from Gaza itself. But here? This place on the opposite end of the country was an absolute no-go according to the military? It didn't make sense.

With our tails between our legs, we retreated down the mountain in search of a Plan B. Ike pulled the car over to think up a plan. We were close to showtime and needed to front a single live report from somewhere, but we weren't sure what areas up here were closed down and which were open to the public. Ike stroked his beard as he hunched over the steering wheel.

"Ok, I know where I'm going to take you," he said, throwing the car into drive and continuing down the dirt road. He pressed on a few more miles before turning down a pathway that looked like it was meant for farm equipment, not cars. We were definitely off the beaten path. Ike rolled the sedan forward maybe another quarter of a mile then pressed on the brakes. He then pointed out the passenger window. "Look at that!" He exclaimed.

I turned and saw a small hill, covered in what appeared to be a thick shrubbery similar to the wiregrass I had seen in Alabama. There was single strand of barbed wire taking the form of a short, impromptu fence separating the hill from the road. As I tried to understand what Ike was talking about, I saw it. It was a lone yellow sign with a red triangle on it tucked in the foliage maybe 10 feet back from the road.

"Danger! Mines!" It read.

We were so far away from civilization we had driven right up next to a minefield. I had never seen a sign like that before—or even for a moment considered one would exist.

"Pretty crazy, huh?" Ike said, cracking a smile. He was used to seeing stuff like this as he served in the IDF and even fought in Lebanon, so was familiar with the landscape up here. "You have to be careful in this part of Israel. Sometimes if there's a heavy rain, the mines come out of the ground and get washed into the middle of the road."

Will and I snapped our heads back to Ike in a jolt. He nodded his head while biting his lip. I had no idea land mines could be dislodged like that and *move* if it rained. There wasn't a chance in hell I was taking my eyes off the road for the rest of the day now.

With that, Ike eased off the brake and started driving forward again. We went another half mile until the road came to an end and we reached a shallow overlook. Ike parked the car and got out, and when I saw where we were I stopped in my tracks. We were about 300 yards away from a metal fence which served as the border between Israel and Lebanon.

"There it is," said Ike, pointing at the landscape on the other side of the fence. I could see a town in the distance tucked away in Lebanon's mountains maybe a mile away. The land itself was rather barren but nevertheless beautiful as orange dirt collided with farmland that ran all the way back to the gray mountain-filled skyline. Pretty astounding that a fence could separate two completely different worlds. And yet, as I looked around, nothing appeared to be all that different from the Israeli and Lebanese sides. It all looked like one single terrain with an imaginary line sliced down the middle of it.

"I'm going to move my car," Ike said, quickly sliding behind the wheel and backing his sedan up off the road and into the bushes—opposite the side of the road we saw the landmine sign.

"What did you do that for?" Will asked.

Ike let out a bit of a chuckle. "So Hezbollah doesn't see us!"

Gulp. Almost forgot for a second that there was a military group on the other side of that border that had a propensity to shoot rockets this way. We decided to be quick about our work in that spot as Will set up the live report for our morning program back in the United States. We gave a brief update on the tensions between Israel and Hezbollah, packed up our things and quickly departed.

As we got in the car and the sedan trudged its way out of the thick grass, Ike started shaking his head with a smile. "*Way* too close. That is our only risk for the day."

We decided to retreat back to civilization. The largest town nearby was Kiryat Shmona, a city that hugs the border with Lebanon and is home to a population of about 20,000 people. Or at least, that's what it was before all the fighting with

Hezbollah broke out. As our car rolled into town for the first time, we seemingly had the roads all to ourselves. We pulled off into a nearby shopping center where every parking spot was open. Each store was shuttered except for one Shawarma restaurant which appeared to be serving a few IDF troops. That was it.

In fact, it looked like it had been that way for a while. There were items of trash discarded on the shopping center's floor that looked like they had been there for weeks. As we walked along the shops, we came upon one that looked to be a restaurant with a wooden outdoor patio area. Upon closer inspection, we realized a rocket had fallen right into the business blowing out all of the doors. Those wooden railings I had seen from a distance were charred black.

I looked down at the parking lot just outside and saw a crater with blackened edges just a few feet away from the business that had been hit. It was clear multiple rockets had made an impact right in the same vicinity, though I wasn't sure if it all happened during one single barrage or if they were spaced out over time. Now I understood why people had left town.

A car pulled up and parked in the space nearest to us. Out sprang a stocky man with a bald head. He wore a light olive jacket over a salmon-red t-shirt. Flashing a smile at Ike, the two immediately shook each other's hands and exchanged pleasantries, clearly knowing one another. After a few moments, Ike turned to us.

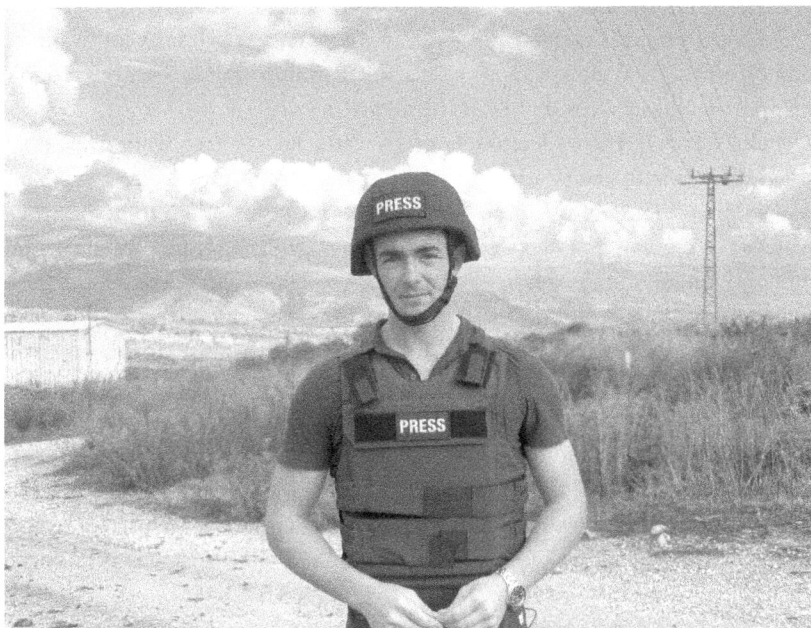

FIGURE 20.1 A live report near the Israeli–Lebanese border where attacks from Hezbollah are both common and dangerous. Photo by Will Budkins.

"This is my friend who lives here in Kiryat Shmona. He might be the only one left," Ike said with a chuckle. I didn't doubt it. This man, who we'll call Angus, was the only soul I'd seen up here not in an IDF uniform.

Angus came up to Will and me, tightly gripping our hands as he looked us intensely in the eyes. "We here in the north are *very* afraid right now for the situation." He then pointed to the mountains of Lebanon which just peaked over the buildings across the street. "Will Hezbollah come inside to kill us?" He asked rhetorically. Then gave a shrug. He had no idea what the future would hold.

People here in northern Israel and southern Lebanon had become accustomed to tensions over the years. There had been wars, bombings, airstrikes, missile attacks. And yet, all of this seemed very different. Angus made that clear.

"It is now every day," Angus said, pointing at the sky and making sound effects. "A lot of missiles, and bombs. Boom-boom-boom," he said, pointing his fingers in different directions rapidly mimicking the sound of explosions. "Wow," he concluded, letting out a sigh.

Our phones were constantly getting security alerts about this area while we were in Israel. Sometimes it was rocket barrages, other times it was drones entering the airspace above. If I had to pin one single place that got the most activity while we were there, I would have to estimate it was Kiryat Shmona. Even more than many of the communities in southern Israel.

"No more!" Exclaimed Angus. "You can speak with Hezbollah only by power," he said, slamming his closed right fist into his open left palm. "A lot of power," going on to add that at this point, he no longer wanted peace with the group or their Iranian allies. "We want to destroy them."

Angus had clearly had enough of the attacks coming from Hezbollah. In fact, some of the harshest criticisms of the Israeli government we heard came from residents of this area. They too wanted Hezbollah to be destroyed because as long as the attacks continued, they couldn't return home. We met some of them personally while living in Tel Aviv. Their children's schools were shuttered and there was little hope they'd be moved back in to get ready for the curricular year. Some lost jobs and whole livelihoods waiting for the situation to calm down.

Angus was well connected to the city of Kiryat Shmona and wanted us to meet one of the city's leaders, which was a good opportunity for us to put names to faces and get to know local officials for sourcing purposes. We arrived at the equivalent of their City Hall which overlooked the downtown. A man was waiting for us there wearing a black shirt and black sportscoat. He had olive skin and slick-backed dark hair. We'll call him Darian.

Let's just say Darian was a well-known public figure in the community and in his office he wielded a lot of power. Nevertheless, he was very welcoming as few members of the international press even bothered to come visit this town.

"We play a kind of . . . chicken game," he said with a smile, trying to piece together his English. "They hit us, we hit them back." He then shrugged. "It is our life."

Since assuming his role with Kiryat Shmona, he explained things had been very busy with the constant string of attacks. Similar to Sderot, you were looking at a span of about 10 seconds from the launch of a rocket in Lebanon to impact here. As such, the local leadership and public constantly had to be on guard.

"Do you think this is ever going to end?" I asked him earnestly. "Do you think there can ever be peace?"

He shook his head. "I hope so, but I don't think it will happen soon."

"Hezbollah says they'll stop if the war in Gaza ends," I persisted.

He gave me a polite but skeptical glance, as if he wanted to call me naïve right to my face.

"In my opinion, Hamas, Hezbollah and Iran are all the same. And what they really want is the State of Israel to disappear." He paused, then let out a sigh. He went on to explain his difficult decision to tell his citizens to evacuate and how much it broke his heart to see the city so barren.

One thing I've learned about Israelis is they do not like to run. It cuts against what they believe is central to their identity of resilience and persevering through difficult times. But in this case, Darian felt like he had no choice. The dangers were too constant and too real.

"I want my people to come back, but I want them to be safe," Darian said. Then he turned fully to me, and put his finger up to command my undivided attention. "But what I really dream of one day is building a train station."

I looked at him perplexed, but nodding my head politely to encourage him to continue.

"I want to build a train station. One where the rails run from here into Lebanon and Syria. And I dream one day, I can get on that train and go get some hummus in Beirut or Damascus," he said. Now a big smile had come across his face. "And I can sit there with them, eat lunch, and come back. Or all the way to Tel Aviv maybe." He paused again, looking me in the eyes to articulate the sincerity of his words. "That's my dream. I don't know if it will happen. But that's my dream."

Darian was one of the few people I had met in Israel who firmly held onto brighter vision of peace in the region. There are many who feel it's a lost cause and the Middle East is committed to incessant turmoil. But not Darian.

When we left Kiryat Shmona, I kept staring at the maps on my phone. Remarkably, I realized it was less than 50 miles from both Beirut and Damascus to that town. Engineering capabilities weren't what was keeping a rail line from going down. It was *physically* possible—and in fact, before 1948 you could take a train along the coast from Israel to Beirut. But of course, we live in a different time and those 50 or so odd miles separate two completely different worlds that have yet to be bridged. In fact, if you wanted to drive from Kiryat Shmona to Beirut today, you'd have to head south, cross into Jordan, then into Syria, then Lebanon. All because of geopolitics. And that's assuming not a single border guard gives you trouble along the way.

Two days after that trip, we got a call from Ike. "Remember that place right along the border we did that one live report from?"

"Of course," we answered.

"Two people just got blown up there today. A rocket from Hezbollah."

Something I learned that day: some dreams, no matter how out of reach, are worth holding onto. John Lennon and Darian's dreams will have to wait, but they're not lost.

21 THE GROUND YOU STAND ON

There are few things that put life into perspective more than standing where someone recently died. There's an unmistakable, powerful energy you feel as you take it all in. When you listen to the wind and hear the sounds of nature, it's as if time stops for a moment, and you're left in the midst of a void.

Two examples of this come to mind. One was the day we went to visit the Nova music festival site, which was effectively ground zero for the October 7th attack. We never saw it with our own eyes until a few months after Black Saturday, but I distinctly remember stepping out of the car and feeling a wave of somber energy overcome me before my boot even touched the soil.

The site itself was nothing out of the ordinary. It was an open space with uneven land and some trees, similar to the parks and festival grounds many of us have been to over the years.

And yet, when we arrived at the Nova Music Festival site, I could just feel this was different. It was a place that demanded your attention and respect, though nobody outwardly asked for it. You just knew the ground you were walking on was sacred.

Officially referred to as the Supernova Sukkot Gathering, the music festival itself took place less than five miles away from the Gaza border. It was supposed to be a celebration of friendship and love as Israelis from across the country flocked to the site to meet people, have fun, and listen to trance music.

On October 7, however, the festival was attacked by Hamas. First came the rocket barrage, which is nothing out of the ordinary for people in Southern Israel. But what came next was Hamas militants entering Israel by land on trucks and motorcycles, as well as through the air via gliders. As they surrounded the site, they fired on festivalgoers, killing hundreds and taking some hostage.

We know much of this not just from eyewitness testimonies, but because Hamas filmed the whole ordeal. It was merely hours after the attack started that bodycam videos began hitting the internet of Hamas opening fire on the crowd, blasting the toilets in case anyone was hiding there, and throwing festivalgoers on motorcycles to be taken back to Gaza.

Those videos rocked the world and captured the horrors that took place that day. To stand there myself and see where it all took place, albeit a few months later, left me speechless. How a place like that could be home to such a massacre was beyond my comprehension.

A memorial had been set up at the site which consisted of metal rods placed into the ground. Sitting atop each one was the photo of one of the victims. At their bases, mourners had left flowers, stuffed animals, and trinkets to remember their loved ones by.

If you've ever been to a place like Arlington National Cemetery, it's a similar feeling. You've been *told* many have given incalculable sacrifices serving the United States over the years, but seeing row after row of headstones makes you realize you really hadn't a clue as to the sheer magnitude.

Likewise here, you can read the articles and see the death toll numbers all you want, but looking at those metal posts and staring into all of those eyes painted a deeply wounding picture. Hundreds of sons, daughters, brothers, sisters, fathers, and mothers lost in one day. And how many people did they touch? How many family members and friends did they leave behind? Israel is a country of about ten million people as of this writing, and without exaggeration, I still have yet to meet one person who *did not* know someone who died, was injured or taken hostage that day.

FIGURE 21.1 A memorial established at the site of the festival grounds attacked by Hamas on October 7th. Photo by Robert Sherman

While I didn't know anyone myself, there were several people I heard from in the United States who did. Just hours after the attack, one of my friends texted me saying her aunt just watched her neighbors die. Another said they knew one of the American–Israelis taken hostage. The impacts were felt by people across the globe.

That was one instance of my soul being touched after visiting the places where people died. The other one came just weeks after the attack and was a few miles down the road from the festival. We were invited to visit the remnants of Kibbutz Be'eri, which was also just a short distance from Gaza.

For those unfamiliar, a Kibbutz is a small community that is a common way of living in Israel. Many of them have massive farms on-site and operate under the premise that almost everything is communal. The income generated goes into a common pool to sustain the operations of the community, and many meals are eaten together as a whole group in large halls. It can be difficult to earn the ability to live in one as the community has to first accept you, and there are a finite number of homes. You can find Kibbutzim all over Israel.[1]

Be'eri was a rather large Kibbutz compared to some of the neighboring communities, with about a thousand or so residents. But on October 7, over 100 of their people were killed. Think about that for a moment. A place of living that preaches this tight-knit communal way of life saw more than 10 percent of its population wiped out overnight. Whole family units slaughtered.

The anecdotes that came out of that community were staggering. Many hid in their bomb shelters as Hamas entered the community. One story that stood out to me, told to us by the Kibbutz leadership, was a family who barricaded themselves inside as Hamas set their home on fire. They survived by urinating on rags and holding them over their mouths and noses to avoid dying of smoke inhalation. Anything to live to see tomorrow.

When we arrived at the Kibbutz ourselves and set foot on the soil, the first thing I heard was the calls of birds in the trees and the pattering of insect wings. It was one of those moments where the sounds of nature were deafening. I looked around at the entrance to the kibbutz, and it was just so stunningly beautiful the way the sprawling tree branches arched their way over the pathway to create a tunnel of foliage. It was as if you were entering a completely different world.

Boom.

The interlude of serenity was interrupted by a blast just a few hundred feet away. Israeli artillery units were intermittently firing on Gaza, and their guns were placed directly inside the Kibbutz. This place of peace and tranquility was now very much an active combat zone.

Out of the archway of trees emerged a young IDF soldier who was set to be our guide. She had dirty blonde hair neatly tied in a ponytail. She wore her IDF uniform and a bulletproof vest—both a tan-olive color. She was part of the spokespersons' unit for the Israeli military and was tasked with taking members of the press inside these sites from October 7.

The soldier was not permitted to give her full name for the sake of security reasons, so we'll call her Anna. She walked right up to us and shook our hands, before giving us a brief safety briefing in which she explained that it was very common for rockets to fall here, even with the Iron Dome defense system in place. For that reason, helmets and bulletproof vests were a requirement. Like Sderot, we'd only have a few seconds from the moment of launch to the moment of impact, so time was of the essence.

Boom.

Another artillery blast coming from close by. Will and I gave a quick jolt, not expecting it, but Anna stood there firmly without reaction. "The symphony of war," she remarked.

Anna then led us through the archway of trees into the heart of the Kibbutz. The deeper we entered, the more lost I felt in the beauty of nature as small animals peacefully hopped around and butterflies landed on the nearby branches we brushed past.

But there was something off. Our senses were humming at full capacity. It *looked* beautiful. The *touch* of the foliage was calming. It *sounded* serene. I'm sure if you could *taste* any of the berries growing freely on the trees they would be delicious.

Yet one sense picked up how wrong everything was. The *smell.* Rancid and impossible to ignore. It was so out of place and yet so powerful. Covering enough disasters over the years, I knew exactly what it was immediately: the rotting of human remains.

The tranquility of the kibbutz evaporated in a matter of moments as we exited the pathway and came to a row of homes. The first one we saw was charred and gray. The door was gone and the windows were blasted out. Black soot was visible on the roof surrounding the holes that flames had broken through.

It was a single story ranch-style home. At one time, it had a light colored exterior meant to reflect the suns beating rays. Scattered in the front yard of this home were the remnants of the livelihood the occupants had. A small toy car that a toddler could ride in was partially melted. A washing machine and a dryer scorched to a deep orange color. Flower pots shattered with the dead plants they once contained sprawled on the ground.

But what gripped my attention the most was the spraypainted markings on the front of the buildings. Numbers, letters, tally marks. I didn't understand what they meant, but Anna intuitively began to explain.

"Do you see that circle with the dot inside of it?" She asked.

"I do," I replied curiously. It was right next to the front entrance and deep red in color.

FIGURE 21.2 What's left of a home in Kibbutz Be'eri after the October 7th attack. The circle with a dot in the middle to the right of the door indicates a body was found inside this home. Photo by Robert Sherman.

Anna turned to me. "That means the rescue crews that arrived here found a body inside."

I spun around and fixed my gaze on that circle, then looked back at all of the trinkets and family items burnt to a crisp in the yard. This place where someone built a home and a family life became their final resting place.

Then I turned to look at the house next to it. Sure enough, another circle with a dot in the middle of it. The home across from this one? Same marking. Down the line my eyes went and I kept seeing that same, chilling circle. Some had multiple.

"Houses were burned so severely it took us weeks to identify because everything was ashes," Anna explained.

I had no doubt of this. I remembered seeing photos of the recovery crews weeks after the attack bringing in archaeologists to sift through the debris in hopes of finding any indication of human remains. In some cases, all that was left was a tooth or a few bones. It was all so perturbing to think about.

Anna then motioned for us to follow her, and she led us up the pathway to this first home. I didn't even want to breathe the air here out of respect for the dead. As we arrived at the front entryway, I realized the door was not blown off the hinges but had disintegrated in the flames. There was nothing left.

The same could be said for the interior of the home. Whole walls were reduced to their frames by the fire. A few pieces of furniture were barely distinguishable. The leg of a coffee table. The grille of an air conditioner. Mere pieces of the homelife once had here.

I looked down at the ground and almost jolted back. The whole floor was covered in a thick layer of ash multiple inches deep. So thick it was like walking on a sandy beach. I felt my chest tighten as I wasn't certain if the ashes I was walking on were from the home or included any human remains. Being on the music festival grounds was one thing. It was hallowed ground to be respected. But this felt far too intimate inside of someone's home where they lost their life.

Anna explained that this house belonged to an elderly woman. She then took us to the back corner of the home where the exterior walls were now exposed cinder blocks.

"This was the bomb shelter," Anna said. I looked around and realized this was the only room that was clearly distinguishable from the rest of the house because the walls were fortified. Anna then pointed at bullet holes lodged in the cinder blocks. "People were shot through the doors because the doors are not bulletproof," Anna said. "They were holding the door handles for long hours grasping and hoping they would survive."

Standing in that bomb shelter, I tried to envision that day in my mind. An elderly woman bracing the door tightly as bullets pounded their way through. There was nothing else she could realistically do.

Anna led us back outside of the home. "There were body parts laying all over the place. Body ligaments. Bodies that were set on fire. Beheaded," Anna said, pointing down the row of homes. I kept staring at the circles with the dots inside of them. From that particular vantage point and in this specific row of homes, I didn't see one without that marking—giving the indication this particular spot was at the heart of the raid. Hamas' invasion of Southern Israel was so massive it took the IDF days to reestablish operational control.

Anna continued taking us into homes to inspect what was left for ourselves. Every home we saw on that strip was indistinguishable. The same thick layer of ashes. The same hollowed-out interior from flames. The same spray-painted markings. It just went on and on.

"A close friend of mine, both of her parents were murdered in Kfar Aza," Anna said, referencing another kibbutz that was nearby. "It took us three weeks to identify their bodies."

Another Israeli just one degree of separation from the death and destruction of October 7th. Kibbutz Be'eri was hardly the only community that was attacked like this. Kfar Aza. Nahal Oz. Nir Oz. Holit. Too many to list. The point being, what we saw was just one of many kibbutzim that was caught in the crosshairs of massacre.

Boom-boom-boom.

Another flurry of Israeli artillery blasts, and another abrupt reminder that all of this death and destruction we were seeing was by no stretch of the imagination strictly in the past tense. The war was raging on. Where we stood was the site of so much loss of life, and yet now was a staging ground for the IDF to strike targets on the other side of the border. By this point the Gazan death toll was in the tens of thousands—including both combatants and civilians.

Since the sun was going down and the Israeli artillery appeared to be ramping up its shelling, Anna told us it was time to depart. That night I sat in my room and thought about that kibbutz and the people who called it home. How many died. How many were taken hostage. The individual stories of their lives. Far too many cut short.

One year later I would return to Southern Israel for the anniversary of October 7. This time we visited Kibbutz Nir Oz where a quarter of the roughly 400 residents were killed or taken captive. For some, the one-year mark was their first time returning to the community. Others couldn't bear the thought of setting foot on that soil again.

The overwhelming sentiment that prevailed was this: October 7 may have happened a year ago, and the months on the calendar may have flipped by, but in reality, October 8 had not arrived. There were still hostages in captivity, still intense fighting in Gaza, and no sense of certainty about the future gained.

I now reflect on that day Bartley and I got the call to head to Ukraine and shake my head at the way excitement bubbled up inside of me. How disgustingly childish to think there was anything "exciting" about war. All the John Wayne films I had watched, all the toy guns I had owned, and all the hours of playing first-person shooter video games seemed like gross misuses of my time. When you start to see the consequences of conflict yourself, you quickly realize this is not a game.

What I would give to go back in time and grab younger Robert by the shoulders to tell him all of this.

22 HERE COME THE HOUTHIS

I remember very distinctly sitting down at breakfast in the first few days of the war when Adam, while glossing through his phone, shared a piece of information that would change the landscape of the Middle East.

"It looks like the Houthis have declared war on Israel," he shared.

Huh? The Houthis? What the heck is a "Houthi?" That's what I wanted to say, but to avoid sounding terribly dumb, I replied with something like "Wow, that's interesting."

I certainly wasn't alone in the world in not knowing who they were, but they would quickly become a big deal, and a big problem, for countries around the globe.

The Houthis, as of this writing, run the show in Yemen since sending the internationally recognized government into exile in 2014. Officially known as Ansar Allah (or Ansarallah), they now control Yemen's capital of Sanaa.[1] While the US State Department designated them a Specially Designated Global Terrorist group in January of 2024, few were really taking them seriously in October of 2023.[2]

"Are they a big deal?" I asked one of our in-house Middle East experts by phone.

"No," he said with a scoff. "They're a joke." And to be fair, almost everyone in military circles agreed with that sentiment. They were, however, allies with groups like Hamas, Hezbollah, and the Palestinian Islamic Jihad and had the backing of Iran.

That week, the Houthis began carrying out attacks on Israel by firing a missile or two over the Red Sea at the southeastern Israeli port city of Eilat. On average, this would happen every few days at the start.

"That's really all they're capable of," I was told by that same expert.

How wrong everyone was. The next thing we knew, the Houthis announced they would start attacking commercial ships transiting the Red Sea and Gulf of Aden that had ties to Israel. Once more, the world shrugged in an effective "good luck with that" kind of manner.

Despite the world's doubts, or perhaps because of them, the Houthis pulled off a shocking heist and hijacked a commercial cargo ship. They landed a helicopter aboard the freighter, and a group of insurgents quickly seized control of the cabin, then took the whole ship back to Yemen.[3] How do we know this? Because they filmed the whole thing. The video was practically second to none, as some of the boarders had GoPros strapped to their torsos to allow us to get a point of view perspective as the terrorists went door to door on the ship and methodically took control.

They didn't stop there, however, and started carrying out attacks on ships constantly in the region (many without ties to Israel), sinking multiple freighters and killing several sailors as well.[4] It got to the point that the situation was so treacherous in the Red Sea that some shipping companies had to start diverting their ships around South Africa, causing major delays on deliveries and increasing costs. That's a big deal considering the World Economic Forum estimates 30 percent of the globe's container traffic goes through that corridor.[5] Beyond unacceptable in the eyes of the international community.

The responsibility of securing those waterways fell upon the US Navy and allied partners in the region. One particular ship would become the effective face of the fight against maritime terror: the U.S.S. Dwight D. Eisenhower aircraft carrier. First arriving in the Red Sea in November 2023, this ship and the rest of the strike group were on the frontlines of the fight against the Houthis for the better part of a year. It became a near-daily occurrence that we would get some kind of update from Central Command (CENTCOM) that the strike group had shot down Houthi drones or intercepted missiles fired by the group.

But consider the ante raised when the Eisenhower, along with allies such as the United Kingdom, began striking the Houthi positions directly. All of a sudden, the "joke" of a terrorist group was now being put right in the crosshairs of American and British Naval aviators and bombers. Quite the turn of events in the span of a few months.

I wanted to see this for myself and was able to convince the US Navy to let us come aboard amid their operations off the coast of Yemen. The next thing I knew, Will and I were standing on the tarmac of a military base in Bahrain ready to ship off.

To get there, the Navy would pick us up in a Grumman C-2 Greyhound, which served as the Carrier Onboard Delivery plane (also known as a C.O.D.). It was a cargo plane more than forty years old that had propellers, not jets. I couldn't believe the US Navy would fly such a dinosaur in the middle of a warzone, but we quickly learned something about naval operations: if it works, is reliable, and is cheap, they're using it. The Greyhound was all of the above.

The exterior was a grayish-white metal covered in black marks from years of wear and tear. When the ramp came down and we saw the interior, it really looked like a prehistoric artifact. The windows were tiny, and the whole inside was this dark gray color with metal and machinery exposed everywhere. The seats were worn yellow and, to my surprise, arranged backward so you were facing the back of the plane. This was so when the plane landed, the force would push you into the seat, not out into your harness.

We were all required to wear helmets and goggles during takeoffs and landings. I didn't really begin to understand this until our five-hour flight was almost over and I heard one of the pilots aboard yell, "Brace yourselves!"

We were instructed to put our backs all the way into our seats to the point my shoulder blades were practically impaling the worn cushioning. My head and helmet were also glued into the headrest as I closed my eyes waiting for touchdown. I wasn't seated next to a window, which made it worse because I had no idea how close we were to the runway. Before I knew it, I felt the most force I've ever experienced in my life slamming my body into the seat. I grabbed the edge of the armrests trying to brace myself, but in two seconds (and I mean quite literally two seconds) we were at a standstill.

During the Second World War, a paratrooper named Sergeant Edward Barnes wrote, "There is no sweeter feeling than that rude jerking, letting you know your chute has opened."[6] I have no doubt that is true, but let me add my own. There is no more relieving feeling than those Gs of force that let you know your plane's

FIGURE 22.1 A weary Will Budkins waiting outside the C-2 Greyhound during a fueling stop in Saudi Arabia. Photo by Robert Sherman.

tailhook caught the cable and you landed safely on the carrier—and aren't nose first under the sea.

* * *

When the ramp came down and we could finally see daylight, I was met with the loud, never-breaking roar of jet engines. A naval sailor came aboard, dressed in a full flight jacket with helmet and goggles. I could not hear a word he said, but he was motioning rapidly with his hands, which I took to mean "come quickly."

We unharnessed ourselves from the seats and stood up, albeit a bit wobbly from the harsh landing a few minutes prior. I glided down the ramp onto the flight deck of the Eisenhower and was practically overwhelmed by the massive operation I was watching. Hundreds upon hundreds of sailors in their flight gear were moving about the deck quickly, guiding fighter jets and bombers into position for their next takeoffs. We couldn't stay up top long since we didn't have the proper protective gear, so they moved us below deck swiftly.

Nevertheless, I was still able to catch a takeoff or two atop the deck as an F-18's jet engines roared to life. A sailor dressed in a yellow flight jacket dropped his arm to signify "go," and the jet zoomed off, slightly dropping off the edge of the carrier before quickly ascending into the skies above.

We made our way down below and were heading to the Captain's cabin. The interior of an aircraft carrier is comparable to that of a city. With thousands of sailors calling it home, there were layers upon layers of floors, hallways, and doors that could lead to the weapons storage, the mess hall, or the dentist. It was, in a word, a maze that had everything you could possibly need to sustain life at sea for years.

The hallways themselves were extremely narrow, and you would have to turn your body if you crossed paths with someone heading in the other direction. Some corridors were lit in this ominous red color that made it feel as though you were in a matrix of sorts.

We arrived at the Captain's Cabin and were greeted by a tall and chubby man with a bald head, Captain Chris Hill, known by his nickname "Chowdah." His voice, accent, and diction were as Massachusetts as his nickname. He shook my hand with a firm grip as his big fingers engulfed mine with a tight squeeze.

"Welcome aboard the best damn ship in the Navy," he said proudly.

"Thank you for having us, sir," I replied.

The Captain's Cabin was the most spacious part of the ship. It had a large center table, a small kitchenette, vanilla-colored carpets and walls, as well as several couches and plush chairs. Each seat was colored green, which I would come to learn was in honor of President Dwight D. Eisenhower, who apparently stuck with that color of décor. Photos and portraits of Ike himself adorned each of the walls.

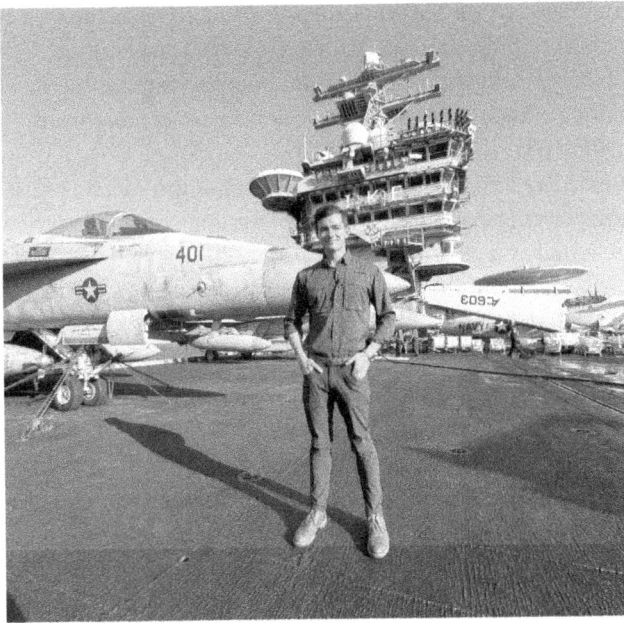

FIGURE 22.2 On the flight deck of the U.S.S. Dwight D. Eisenhower while deployed in the Red Sea near the coast of Yemen. Photo by Will Budkins

The Navy gave us a few minutes to chat with the Captain and discuss the ongoing operations in the Red Sea in the fight against the Houthis.

"Everyone has got this all wrong," he told me firmly. "They are a real terrorist organization conducting attacks out here almost daily."

The Captain went on to explain that at the time, the Houthis were firing the most advanced missiles ever fired in combat history outside of the war in Ukraine and using them against commercial ships as well as directly against the US Navy. One of the anti-ship ballistic missiles, he claimed, could go Mach 9: nine times the speed of sound, which is nearly seven thousand miles per hour.

"Our mission out here is to save lives, plain and simple," Captain Hill asserted. It was the responsibility of the Eisenhower, as well as the other ships in the strike group and allies in the region, to secure the waterways. That included shooting down Houthi attacks where possible and rescuing sailors from ships that were disabled as a result of the attacks.

By this point, the Eisenhower had been operating in the Red Sea for the better part of a year—and the fight against the Houthis was far from over. It wouldn't be until the summer of 2024 when the Eisenhower would return home, replaced by the U.S.S. Theodore Roosevelt to take up the mission.

One thing that Captain Hill explained to me is that the life of a Naval sailor in many cases has a finite amount of action. Maybe you're assigned to a ship and spend a year at sea making port calls around Europe, but it is highly unlikely you will ever shoot a missile or carry out an airstrike in combat from the time you enlist to the time you retire.

The action the sailors in this region were seeing was by comparison extreme. What I assumed was just another day of deployment for the US Navy was actually about as uncharted as it gets. There were people on that ship who had been in the Navy for thirty years, and this one particular deployment came with a new "first" on a weekly, if not daily basis.

Captain Hill had to head off to some meetings, so we thanked him for his time and proceeded on to the next person we were slated to meet: Rear Admiral Marc Miguez, who was in charge of the entire carrier strike group. We were led back through the winding labyrinth of the Eisenhower before arriving all the way atop the bridge. He was a slender man with gray hair and a strikingly warm smile, despite the fact he held such an authoritative position in the US Navy.

"First of all, you have to understand this," he said, spinning around and pointing to everything in every direction. "All of this you see here is unprecedented. In my entire career in the Navy I have never seen anything like this." He continued on. "The Houthis have decided to attack maritime shipping. And what you have to understand is it is our duty to protect the right of freedom of navigation."

That is something that gets overlooked. While in every sense of the word it sure looked like the US Navy was locked in war with the Houthis—and there are some who contended that was the case—the official purpose of the operations in the Red Sea and Gulf of Aden was to ensure freedom of navigation: something protected by international law.[7]

The US Navy is a commanding force, but with the constant threat of advanced drones and highly sophisticated modern missiles, the Rear Admiral explained that they were facing a danger in the region that most did not take seriously. Sure, the strike group had some pretty impressive firepower and defense mechanisms, but that didn't make the missiles coming their way at several thousand miles per hour any less lethal. If one thing went wrong, American service members would die. The fact that one hadn't to that point, the Rear Admiral contended, was not because of the Houthis lack of capabilities. Miguez's view is that the US Navy was effectively pitching a no-hitter.

"You have nearly 5,000 souls aboard here, what keeps you up at night?" I asked earnestly. What came next was a smirk from the Rear Admiral and the line of the trip.

"I'll tell you this. I keep the Houthis up at night. I sleep soundly," he said, making dead eye contact with me. "Because I know that these sailors onboard that are running watches 24/7. They're highly trained professionals at their job. I sleep quite well."

I was admittedly inspired by his unabashed confidence. Walking around that ship, the operations were truly like a highly choreographed symphony. Every job aboard had to be done perfectly and with the utmost efficiency. Take into account that some of these sailors hadn't even celebrated their twentieth birthday, and it was quite remarkable to see.

"I've been in a bunch of combat over my years but never at this level in the maritime," Miguez explained. "Every time I'm sitting here thinking 'I can't believe this is happening.' But every one of these sailors has mission and they know what their purpose is."

The conversations with Hill and Miguez really changed my perception of the whole operation in the Red Sea. The pundits really were wrong and the Houthis were a legitimate, well-armed threat. Having an aircraft carrier out here didn't seem like overkill after all.

It was almost time for bed but before that, the Navy said they would take us back to the flight deck as they performed nighttime drills with their aircraft. They gave us flight jackets to put on which were far too big for me. Mine was a white vest with some dirt stains on it from years of use. Then came the clunky helmet which was so tight it reminded me why I quit football in the fifth grade.

We were led back up top, and as the door opened my face was swept by scalding hot air. It was a mix of the brutal Middle Eastern heat and the exhaust of all those jet engines howling away.

Now that I had more time on the flight deck, I started to take it all in more. Each person had their own color of flight jacket. Some were yellow, others were red, green, purple, brown. What one of the airmen explained to me is that each color represents a separate job. One color group was responsible for directing the flow of traffic, another manned the "catapult" launch system which threw the planes airborne, another color was responsible for refueling. You get the idea.

The way they moved, stepping in-between treacherous spots, navigating moving jets, stopping, starting, communicating with just hand gestures. It all worked in harmonious sequence.

Each jet took off in quick succession. As soon as one was clear and airborne, a new aircraft would slide behind and follow suit moments later. Their exhaust trails and fiery engines were the only things visible as they disappeared into the Yemeni skies.

This continued on for the better part of an hour: landings, takeoffs, fueling, and clearing the flight deck. We went back inside during their last round of takeoffs when all of the planes would be airborne for some time.

Before stepping through the hatchway, I noticed something and took a moment. For the first time since I had been aboard that ship, there was near total silence.

FIGURE 22.3 Filming reports during takeoff and landing exercises aboard the U.S.S. Dwight D. Eisenhower. Photo by Will Budkins.

Save for a couple of shouting sailors barking commands and the very distant rumble of those jet engines, it was emptiness above and in every direction. At the time, the ship was a few hundred miles from the nearest inch of Yemeni soil.

We were all alone at sea, slipping away into the Middle Eastern night.

* * *

My eyes wobbled open in the pitch black. No alarm clock needed this morning; I had far too much adrenaline circulating throughout my body. I sat upright and almost hit my head on the bunk above. *Remember Robert, you're not in a hotel room anymore. You're on an aircraft carrier.*

I rolled out of the bottom bunk as my feet hit the cold floor, then proceeded to flip on the light switch. It was much smaller than my college dorm room—perhaps 5 × 10 feet. Even that may be generous. Two beds bunked on top of one another sat on one side of the room, and across there was a sink with a manila-colored countertop. Tan cabinets occupied the rest of the opposite wall.

For me, it was small, but compared to how many of the enlisted sailors aboard lived, it may as well have been the St. Regis. It was one night, and somehow we were able to fall asleep despite the loud, unmistakable sound of the catapults launching jets off of the deck above us. That racket cut through every layer of steel with ease.

We wouldn't be spending much time on the Eisenhower that day, however. Instead, we would be traveling by helicopter to the USS Laboon, one of the Destroyers in the strike group.

We arrived on the flight deck where the helicopter blades were already churning. The helicopter was gray with the US Navy logo on the side, though what I was paying the closest attention to was the two machine guns mounted on either side manned by sailors in full combat gear. Out here in the middle of the Red Sea with nothing around us except for water, you forget this is an active combat zone.

Using a chessboard as an analogy, the Eisenhower served as the effective "King" piece in the strike group as it would hang back and direct all of the other ships. In turn, the destroyers and cruisers are stationed miles away. The Laboon was the tip of the spear flowing the most south at that time. It had seen some of the most front-line action to date and was constantly in some kind of engagement with the Houthis.

We boarded the helicopter, and I threw my headset on so we could listen to the pilot. The humming of the blades was so loud I couldn't hear anything—hardly my own thoughts. After strapping into the seat, a few moments later I felt a lurch forward as we took off. I had been in a few of these over the years with the Texas Department of Public Safety down at the US–Mexico border, but this chopper moved more rapidly and wasn't afraid to dip up and down through the air.

We did a quick circle of the Eisenhower, and from this vantage point, I was able to get a better perspective of just how large the aircraft carrier was. Over three football fields in length with a dozen or so planes sitting atop the flight deck. What's more, the higher we got, the more we realized just how alone in the open water the aircraft carrier was. Even with the height advantage, there was nothing on the horizon except the crisp blue waters of the Red Sea. No land, no ships, no signs of life. Just salt water as far as the eye could see.

The helicopter ride took about thirty minutes to get to the Laboon, really illustrating just how far south toward the mouth of the Red Sea the destroyer was roaming. Finally, the ship came into our view on the horizon as it motored along all alone. Its sleek gray exterior morphed from a black dot on the water's edge into a mighty ship of war.

We approached in from a low angle and prepared to land. Down on the deck, several crew members began to get in position and scrambled to help bring us in. The helicopter slowly sank lower and lower over the pad until it hovered three or four feet above the ground. Then . . . *thump.* The Pilot slammed it to the ground, sticking the landing as I lurched forward again in my harness. Another one of those rude jerking motions that let you know you were safely on board.

The blades started to squeal as they slowed down. One of the sailors tapped us on the shoulder and gave us a thumbs up which let us know it was safe to disembark. I unbuckled the harness and slid out of the side door onto the deck. Six officers were there with hands behind their backs ready to greet us. One of them was young with a brown side part and moustache. He was a Lieutenant and would effectively be our guide while aboard. He extended his hand with a smile. "Welcome aboard the USS Laboon," he said. I took his hand firmly in mine. He motioned us forward and we followed him to the bow of the ship.

The first thing I noticed was the big gun fastened to the front of the ship with a barrel that must have been 20 feet in length. I would have called it a "cannon" had the Lieutenant not informed me it was referred to as the "five-inch gun."

The Lieutenant showed us the whole weapons layout at the bow of the boat. In addition to the five-inch gun, there were these hatches laid out behind it. Four rows of eight with large hinges that would swing open. Some of them had clear scorch marks surrounding them. This was called a Vertical Launch System (VLS) which would fire missiles used to hit or intercept targets by air. The ship also had the capability to launch torpedoes with this weaponry in case they crossed paths with an enemy submarine.

After spending a few minutes above deck, the Lieutenant led us down below to meet the Captain. We entered his quarters and were greeted by a slim man with gray hair. Commander Chris Blomberg who had a very upbeat, cheeky personality that tended to lean toward the sarcastic side. While many on these ships kept a more reserved disposition, he was very relaxed and casual. We found him leaning back in his chair with his leg crossed over his knee as he monitored the many screens sitting in his office. Some of them showed maps of the Red Sea and positions of their allied ships in the region.

"You picked a hell of a time to be out here," he said with a smile. "It is just go-go-go." Before he could even finish that thought, the phone on his desk started ringing. Still smiling, he shook his head as if to say "see what I mean?"

"Captain?" he said into the phone. His smile erasing from his face and becoming more stern. "From Yemen where?" His disposition now as serious as a gravedigger. He listened intently as he spoke into the phone. "Right at the same ship?" He asked the person on the other end of the line, now turning his full attention to his monitors. The Captain flipped through his computer monitors while giving a few orders into the phone. Satisfied with the plan put in motion, he hung up.

"So that was a call about a ship that was just hit by the Houthis today. No relation to Israel, no relation to the United States. Just transiting the Red Sea."

We had been onboard for maybe twenty minutes and already there was activity in the area. He paused for a moment as if lost for words then chuckled. "This is every day out here," he said with a sigh.

I could believe it. It was a near daily occurrence we would get an update from Central Command on some kind of activity in the Red Sea. Drones shot down, strikes on launch sites, missiles intercepted. And this was the ship that in many cases found itself right in the thick of it.

"We were the first ship to shoot down an anti-ship ballistic missile in combat history. We're constantly getting shot at by the Houthis," he said, cracking another smile in disbelief.

That sit-down with the Captain would be interrupted again and again by the ringing of his phone as he monitored the situation with this merchant vessel. The

United States would be sending support to the ship as they were disabled in order to protect the lives of the sailors. Behind the scenes, it was a constant operation. One ship would go assist, others would offer support and help defend the strike group. Decisions had to be made as to whether they would put helicopters in the air or rescue boats in the water, and we watched as the Captain worked the phones to help make all of those calls.

"Never a dull moment out here," he said, keeping the grin plastered on his face.

"Exactly how serious is the Houthi threat here?" I asked him.

He paused, selecting his words carefully. "Pretty deadly serious," he replied, the smile gone. "They have a lot of firepower that they've gotten from their buddies in Iran and they're not afraid to use it." The Captain explained the Houthis were getting new, upgraded weaponry meaning every decision had to be made more quickly to repel attacks.

"You know what, let me show you," he said, clapping his hands as he stood up and beckoned us to follow him. We obliged, and tailed him through the halls taking us down a narrow staircase before arriving at an open door with blue light pouring out of it. The lights inside the room were off so all of the emanating blue was due to the hundreds of screens covering each wall and desk. We stepped inside, and I knew exactly what this was from all the movies I had seen: it was the Combat Information Center. When you hear the Captain in Hollywood films say "battle stations" this is where the top brass went to quarterback the fight they were sailing into.

Some monitors had sonar systems on their screens to show what was around them; others had satellite images of the Red Sea or security cameras of the ship. There was one big monitor right at the front that had a more two-dimensional layout of the Red Sea, which illustrated the ship's position in these waters and gave real-time updates on distance to shore, known as Houthi hot spots, and more. I would estimate there were about thirty people in this room, glued to the screens sitting before them.

"We're going to show you a simulation now of what it's like out here," the Captain said. He gave a nod to one of the sailors to proceed.

"Missile in the air!" I heard one sailor yell as the simulation got underway. On the big screen in front of us, a little white dot appeared over Yemeni airspace as the computer started to rapidly calculate distance and speed. In that moment, the Captain's whole demeanor changed from the casual man we found in his office to now completely locked in as he issued queries and commands without hesitation in his voice.

It all moved so fast. "Vector?" "Distance?" "X nautical miles closing at Y speed." It was so rapid that the numbers being thrown out didn't even register in my mind. The Captain asked if there were any aircraft in the area to assist, to which a sailor immediately responded, "negative." Then the conversation moved to what weapons they had at their disposal ready to counter the missile strike, and another

FIGURE 22.4 Discussing the US Navy's operations with Commander Chris Blomberg inside the U.S.S. Laboon's combat information center. Photo by Will Budkins

sailor gave a list of options. The VLS, which we saw earlier, would be deployed in this situation to knock down the threat.

"Ready for fire," the Captain said calmly but firmly. "Ready," came another voice down the line. Each time the Captain said something, it was a different sailor responding. Just like aboard the flight deck of the Eisenhower, it was clear every person there had a very specific job they were required to master.

"Fire," I heard the Captain say. With that, another white dot appeared on the screen originating at the Laboon's location. The screen up front was now flickering with new calculations showing the speed of the Houthi missile versus the Laboon's countermeasure: intercept point, time to impact, and more.

The Captain remained glued to the situation, asking more questions of the sailors as they watched the two dots, moment by moment make their way toward the calculated interception, which appeared as though it would be taking place over the Red Sea. While this was going on, the Captain was working through a contingency plan in case something went wrong and the interceptor failed to knock down the threat. More missiles and weaponry were being put at the ready as an effective Plan B, C, and D.

As each second passed by, those two dots inched closer to one another on the screen. I say "inched" as that's how it appeared on the monitor, but in reality, each one was traveling thousands of miles per hour. Finally, they reached their intersect point, and I heard a sailor inform the Captain that the missile had successfully been neutralized.

Then, without missing a beat, the focus shifted to if any more missiles were coming or in the process of being readied to fire. In this simulation, the answer was "no"—a lone missile attack, although I knew that was not always the case here, as Central Command had reported numerous incidents of "barrages" or follow-up strikes that the Strike Group had to be wary of.

With a nod of approval, the Captain gave a smile and turned to me. "The men and women on my ship are pretty good, huh?" I nodded with a smile back. "The thing to remember is this is what we do out here every day. Not simulations, the real thing."

This whole episode took place over a matter of maybe a minute and a half, yet each second seemed to contain a decision or command. It was the true definition of the word "rapid-fire" as the sailors worked through how to intercept, where to intercept, how much time they had, and what weaponry was best fit for that situation.

The Captain then led us back out of the room to the fluorescent-lit hallway. It took a moment for my eyes to adjust from the dark combat room we were just in. The Lieutenant who had been with us earlier was there with his hands behind his back waiting for us. "You're in good hands with this guy," the Captain said, patting his Lieutenant on the shoulder. "If you need anything from me, just let me know." We thanked him for his time, and just like that, he departed upstairs to dive back into the *real* situation the Navy was presently dealing with regarding the commercial ship that had just been struck that day.

The Lieutenant was tasked with taking us around the ship to give us a better idea of what life was like on board. The first stop was the mess-hall which was a cafeteria-style buffet filled with trays of hot dogs, vegetables and beans. What I did not realize at the time was that the Navy worked on a set 21-day menu and it was the same no matter where you were. So, the sailors on the Laboon were eating hot dogs that day as were the sailors on the Eisenhower and those back in Bahrain and even in the United States. Quantico, San Diego, Japan, Italy, it didn't matter. If you were in the Navy, hot dogs were on the menu that day.

The tour didn't stop there as the Lieutenant took us all over the ship from the living quarters to the engine room, the gym, the doctor's office. Each layer of the floating town told the same story: not a lot of space, plenty of activity in every department, and if there was room for a "luxury" such as a treadmill, it was revered.

"There is one thing I do really want you to see," the Lieutenant said politely. He led us down a narrow corridor until we came upon a black steel door. He gave it a quick knock, and we heard a voice on the other end. A few moments later and the door swung open. A young, male sailor was standing there with a big smile and glasses. "Come on in!" he said eagerly.

I had no idea what this part of the tour was but we smiled and greeted him, then slipped inside the door and followed him up a set of black staircases to a landing that was dimly lit. There was a bed, a computer monitor, a few documents sitting out and a big narrow tube in the center of the room.

"You caught me working on my pride and joy!" He said, patting the tube with his hand. "I had heard there were journalists aboard today and hoped someone might stop by." He was an energetic young guy, maybe twenty years old with short dark hair. A bit goofy in nature, but he kept this smile on his face at all times that never seemed to break. We'll call him Jeremy.

"I have *the best* job of them all. I'm so lucky. I'm in charge of the big five-inch gun you saw up top, and this is the hardware for it," Jeremy said beaming with pride as he patted the tube once again. "You would not *believe* what we can do with that one single gun. Swear to God! We have ammunition we use for different targets, we can fire long-range, short-range, medium-range, ammunition that's best for the air, for the sea. *So much* we can do with that one gun. That's my job! I take care of it."

Already, Jeremy had to be the runaway candidate for "best attitude in the Navy" as the passion he had for this one particular job, and moreover this one particular gun, was impossible to miss.

"Most reporters don't come down here because they think they've seen it all, so it's such a treat to have you here!" He said shaking our hands rapidly once again.

I looked over at the bed sitting in the corner and realized it wasn't exactly a bed. More like sheets thrown on to a makeshift cot made from boxes. "Do you not have a bed upstairs?" I couldn't help but ask.

Jeremy gave a laugh at that. "I sure do! But I don't like staying up there very much and this way I can *always* be near my work. I've been tinkering with this thing for months and I'm proud to say I was able to bring down the reload time by about 0.3 seconds. That's huge!" Jeremy said, putting his arms out wide. "Now our best gun is more efficient than ever before."

Jeremy won me over instantly with his love for his work. Will and I sat down with him as he pulled up his computer and showed the pages of notes he had compiled detailing this one gun. I didn't understand a single bit of it, but he would point at certain things on the screen then turn to me and give exclamations like "whoa!" and "that's crazy!" And "can you believe this gun can do that?"

I turned back over to the Lieutenant. He had a big smile on his face too as he shook his head with pride. I was starting to understand why he brought us here.

"I'm trying to pitch to my commanding officer that the Navy let me go to this big conference taking place later this year," Jeremy added. "I feel there's a lot I can share about my experiences working on this type of weaponry and *so much* more I can learn! I should hear back in a few weeks. I'm so excited, I hope it works out."

That smile was still glued to his face. It no longer *seemed* unbreakable—it *was* unbreakable.

This went on for another twenty minutes or so before we ran out of time and had to get back on deck to wrap up our day aboard the Laboon. "If there's anything, *anything* I can do to help explain how this works just let the officers know and I'll help any way that I can. Safe travels home!" He said closing the door behind us.

As the door clanked shut, I felt a hand on my shoulder. It was the Lieutenant standing next to me with a very serious facial expression. "If you take one thing away from this day, I hope it's that." I nodded my head, knowing exactly what he meant before he continued. "That's what this ship is all about. That's the story of the Navy right there. A bunch of young men and women who are highly skilled and highly passionate about their jobs, no matter how big or small they might seem. There are thousands of people like Jeremy who most people don't think of yet play such a crucial role here. I hope you remember him."

I nodded my head, promising we would. He then smiled and said "come on, let's get you out of here." He led us back up top to the deck where the helicopter that was supposed to take us away was already buzzing. Many of the officers who we had spent the day with were there as well to see us off. We shook their hands and then boarded the helicopter. I threw the helmet and earmuffs back on which helped muffle the spinning blades, but considering how loud it was I was left with nothing but my thoughts.

Many of us back in the United States do a good job of thanking those who put on the uniform for their service. But that all felt so hollow now as I clearly had no idea what I was thanking them for. I thought I did, but many of my perceptions were shattered spending a day with the US Navy's 5th Fleet. The passion of people like Jeremy. The nonstop threats people like Captain Hill and Captain Blomberg had to deal with. The high caliber of discipline and efficiency I saw from every sailor. You don't understand it until you see it for yourself.

And as I watched the blue waters of the Red Sea zipping below our helicopter and glanced out over the horizon, one thing was clear: the job was not done. Somewhere over that horizon was Yemen and thousands of Houthi fighters, and they weren't stopping.

Neither was the US Navy.

23 WHERE DOES THE TRUTH LIE?

I'm extremely grateful to have had the opportunity to get out and see so much of the world during my career. Every place I've traveled to has led to a newfound appreciation of the world, a better understanding of myself, and memories.

But conversely, there are some horrendous things I have seen that I won't be able to forget and don't have the courage to tell my closest friends about. They too have molded my perception.

One of the sources we made contact with the IDF gave Will and me forty-two minutes of raw, unreleased footage from the October 7 attack. Much of it was filmed directly by Hamas. Hitting play is one of the biggest regrets of my life. In front of my eyes was a video of an Israeli woman being brutally murdered on October 7. I will not describe this in detail any further, but the video is real. It is so unimaginably gruesome that it will make you think twice about the capabilities of humanity. To this day and as of this writing, I have described the contents of that video to one and only one friend. I have chosen not to do it again. You might think I'm shortchanging you by glossing over the details. Maybe you even think I'm exaggerating. You're welcome to believe what you want. I know what I saw, and hyperbole aside, I have thought about that video almost every day since. I pray a day comes when I forget it, but unfortunately, knowing my memory, I think that's unlikely.

The concepts of death and suffering were weighing on me. If you walked down the street nearby us, you would find dozens of blood-stained teddy bears sitting on park benches—each one representing a child held in Gaza. Every lamppost, phone booth, and café had hostage posters up showing the face and giving the details of one of the people taken on October 7 who still hadn't returned home. Every casual coffee shop conversation inevitably turned to focusing on the war. The topic penetrated each level of Israeli society.

But then, there's the other side of the coin: the gut-wrenching images coming out of Gaza. As I wrote about earlier, there's a major hurdle when it comes to what's happening inside the Gaza Strip. And that is, we couldn't really get there. Unless you embedded with the IDF directly for a specific assignment, the enclave was effectively inaccessible to members of the press.

Therefore, almost every outlet was reliant upon wire services or social media. Hamas most certainly had strong influence over the photos and videos coming out of Gaza, but that doesn't make some of what we saw less disturbing.

The ribs of a starving child in the hospital dying of malnutrition. People in northern Gaza crying and pleading for food to be delivered. One that especially hit home for me was a video of a television journalist carrying his dead child through a crowd of people after a series of Israeli strikes.

Some of the interviews freelance journalists were conducting showed people attempting to make bread out of horse feed or trying to turn a single carrot into a bowl of soup. As aid was delivered, it was common to see lines of Gazans desperately holding out pots and pans begging for them to be filled with rations. The humanitarian situation in Gaza was quickly becoming the focal point of the story. Aid groups had been warning of widespread famine and even the US leadership was calling on Israel to do more in order to get aid into the hands of the people.

FIGURE 23.1 A teddy bear sitting on a bench in Tel Aviv representing one of the children taken and held hostage in Gaza. Photo by Robert Sherman.

The situation really took a turn in late February 2024 when video was released by the IDF showing dozens of hungry Gazans rushing an aid convoy in northern Gaza to try and get at the supplies on board. Many died as a result. Hamas' leadership claimed the civilians were fired upon by Israeli soldiers whereas Israel said the loss of life was due to the truck accidentally running people over in an attempt to escape the fray. The finger pointing continues as of this writing.

Either way, the sentiment from Israel's allies is that it didn't really matter who was to blame, they largely held Israel responsible for the humanitarian situation in Gaza as a whole. The chorus of calls from the West to up the aid into Gaza, already loud, grew to a feverish pitch.

This is where I give ample credit to my producer, Will Budkins. He was one of the journalists pressing the IDF for answers and explanations. Ultimately, the Israelis had no choice but to invite a select number of journalists to the Kerem Shalom crossing to see the aid delivery process firsthand to defend their efforts. There's not a doubt in my mind that Will's constant badgering played a big role in getting Israel to give access.

The Kerem Shalom crossing is a critical one. At the time, it was one of two crossings that were being used for the large-scale transit of aid into Gaza and the only one connecting Southern Israel directly to the enclave. The other access point was between Egypt and the city of Rafah in southern Gaza.

The fact that both of these entry points were geographically south is not a detail to be overlooked. This meant that the aid that did go in, which depending on the day could be over 200 trucks in a twenty-four-hour span according to Israel's numbers, was largely flowing to southern Gaza. Because of the fighting, it was more difficult to get aid to northern Gaza which is where the convoy incident took place and where the humanitarian situation was at its worst at the time, according to aid groups. Seemingly every point and detail were argued tooth and nail. Aid groups contended Israel was halting delivery trucks from going in and creating too dangerous of an environment for trucks to navigate the enclave. The Israelis hit back saying they were processing trucks at an efficient pace and the problem was the aid groups weren't working quickly enough to collect the trucks allowed into Gaza and drive them on.

Once more, when you drown out the finger pointing, what became clear is that there was a bottleneck of aid and not enough of it was getting to where it needed to go. The old adage "the truth is somewhere in the middle" is something I would come to be reminded of again and again.

Our team arrived at the Kerem Shalom crossing early in the morning which in and of itself was a massive structure. Large iron gates the size of an SUV would swing open and closed to allow diesel trucks through. We caught a glimpse of the aid trucks that were heading to Gaza. Impossible to miss as their goods on the flatbed were all wrapped in white and blue World Health Organization and United Nations packaging.

Finally, a half dozen Israeli soldiers dressed in their uniforms came around the corner and greeted us. We all gathered around to listen to what they had to say. A younger soldier came forward and tried to take center stage, but his voice had a hint of uncertainty giving the impression he was more junior. He spoke in thick military verbiage.

"Due to the ever-present danger of being in an active combat zone, the risks of attacks are not to be overlooked," he said, at times his voice skipping as if he was nervous about public speaking. "We ask that if the sirens should sound, you hastily move to one of the shelters located at the extremities of the site." As he said that, he pointed to a couple of concrete shelters located at the corners of the complex. As the crow flies, each was at least 200 yards away.

I'm no physics major, but I recall some kind of formula where velocity multiplied by time would equal distance traveled. I knew there wasn't a chance I'd be able to run fast enough to get inside of one of those bunkers in ten seconds or so. Considering we were right on the Gaza border, ten seconds might even be generous.

One of the more senior soldiers with glasses and a gray horseshoe haircut that wrapped around his balding head gave a brief smile and stepped forward to take control of the briefing. He said what we were all thinking. "If the sirens go off, you'll never make it to the shelter," he said, waving his arms as if to totally disregard what his more junior colleague said. "Just get on the ground and pray you don't die."

There it is again! I thought. The *exact* same thing Derek said while we were in Sderot. Only this time, it wasn't our fixer making do amid a vulnerable situation. It was a direct piece of guidance from the Israeli military.

The soldiers led us inside of the complex through the big iron gate that stood open. Inside was a large concrete open space. To the right was what I can describe only as a large shed that the trucks would drive through for their inspection.

"This is where all of the trucks are processed and scanned. Just like going to the doctor for an x-ray, we have equipment inside that does the exact same thing to see everything that is on these trucks and make sure no contraband goes inside," explained one of the soldiers. The scanners were looking for weapons, construction supplies, basically anything Hamas could use in some capacity to aid their war effort was a no-go.

Most trucks were just containing food, water, and medicine. In total, the Israelis said about 99 percent of trucks that went through inspections passed. The 1 percent that failed would have the contraband removed then be repackaged and sent on their way. Forty-four trucks an hour could be inspected. Getting through more than 200 trucks a day was well within the realm of possibility.

Around this same time, because the humanitarian situation in Gaza was front and center, you started seeing countries like Jordan, France, and even the United States airdropping aid from planes into the Gaza strip. The public stance was this could get aid directly into the hands of Palestinians by circumventing the inspections and the truck bottlenecks.[1]

Here's the thing. One of those typical drops would contain 35,000 or so meals. That sounds substantial until you put into context there's over two million people inside Gaza. Not nearly enough to sustain the population on their own.

There were also plans being put in motion to open up a sea corridor from Cyprus. The first ship arrived a day or two after we were at this crossing.[2] Again, every bit helps, but Secretary of State Antony Blinken made clear from the State Department podium that week a sea corridor was at best a supplement, not a substitute. The land corridors were most critical when it came to aid delivery based upon sheer volume.[3]

So here we were, face to face with one of the most critical land crossings, trying to figure out what the issue was. Colonel Elad Goren, Head of Israel's Civil Department of the Coordination of Government Activities in the Territories (COGAT), then came forward. Dressed in his full olive uniform, he had a dark side-part haircut with a neatly trimmed short beard. He was the effective boss of this operation and gave a brief statement.

He ran through some statistics about how efficient they were at processing trucks, how much manpower they had, the latest and greatest technology they were using. If you took that press briefing at face value, you'd think all was running like clockwork. No problems anywhere at all. And yet, my mind raced back to the videos of children with their ribs sticking out from malnutrition. The carrot soup. The people slumped over on Gaza beach due to a lack of energy from not eating. Something didn't add up.

As if reading our minds, he then cast the blame. "The issue is not with our inspection but with the distribution capabilities of the international organizations," he said without a hint of hesitation or a lack of confidence. They then led us through the concrete courtyard all the way to the far end. There was another large, iron gate. This one opened up to Gaza. I looked through it and the enclave seemed like a rural wasteland. The larger metro areas were several miles away outside our vision.

All I could see was some dying grass and what looked like a large, steel awning in the distance. Trucks started rolling through and made their way onto a dirt road that led off toward the structure. After a few moments, all six of the trucks that had been lined up were through the crossing and inside the Gaza strip.

"Those trucks are going to stage at that structure you see in the distance," the colonel said, pointing to the awning. "There they will wait to be picked up for delivery. There are hundreds of trucks backed up there right now as we speak."

FIGURE 23.2 Colonel Elad Goren addressing members of the press while standing in front of a truck carrying humanitarian aid for Gaza. Photo by Robert Sherman

Even with my contact lenses in, I had to squint to try and make out the whole structure. I could see a few trucks there. Hundreds of trucks? Couldn't tell you with certainty. It's not as if I could walk into Gaza and count the trucks one by one to fact check. But there were trucks there, for sure.

The colonel took questions from reporters. Most of them clarifying logistics, operational manpower, and the like. I then butted in and asked the first question that came to mind. "Do you think there's a humanitarian crisis in Gaza?" I asked.

Not the most eloquent of questions, and I anticipated the classic press conference "yes" while beating around the bush to say "but it's not our fault."

The colonel then turned and looked at me. His face was calm. His eyes were like lasers. His posture was open and casual, yet his feet were firmly planted.

"No," he said. Not a quiver of doubt in his voice.

What? I thought internally. I was taken aback by his response. *What does he mean "no"?*

The colonel continued. "I do not believe there is a humanitarian crisis looking at the numbers at other places and the assessment the United States is doing. I believe there are challenges."

I never once considered he might answer that question in such a way. Hearing what US officials were saying, the calls for more aid to come in, the images that were circulating from Gaza—I, perhaps naively, assumed *everyone* thought there was a crisis. The only place I thought there might be differing perspective would be the severity of the crisis and whether it was "acceptable" or not in the grand scheme of war. Needless to say, I was surprised by his response, but followed up to seek clarification.

"So when people in Gaza say they don't have enough to eat, you say that's not Israel's fault?" I asked. This time the colonel paused, looked at the ground, and pursed his lips. He was choosing his words carefully.

After a moment, he looked up. "I say there is a narrative they are trying to create," the colonel said. "Because this narrative is the only way that they think we will stop the war. We'll continue the war. We will engage. We will dismantle Hamas."

The colonel then moved on to other reporters and questions varying in subject matter. Frankly, I was so caught off guard by his answer, I don't know what would have bumbled out of my mouth next.

One thing that this Middle East assignment had exposed in my internal dialogue is an utter lack of confidence that I understand the world or what is going on. When it comes to campaign politics? I'm pretty good at reading between the lines. Natural disasters? Those are to an extent straightforward when it comes to messaging and discourse.

But this? A whole new animal. And in that moment the little voice inside my head that I have tried so hard to suppress piped up. *Am I an idiot?*

The images out of Gaza came flashing back. *The starving kids. Were they real? The carrot soup. Was that staged? Am I just a gullible buffoon?*

We left the Kerem Shalom crossing and shortly thereafter I started going through videos from the wire services of interviews they conducted with displaced civilians in Gaza. That anxious feeling continued to creep up my spine.

Just that day, a new interview had come in from the wire services from a civilian. It was a woman standing next to a tent in a refugee camp, holding back tears. Her face was tired. Her body slumped over as she spoke.

"We've been unstable, moving from one place to the next. There's no shelter or anything, there's no food, no water, nothing," the woman said, per the translation we were given. "Even the most basic living essentials like bread do not exist. We forage wild plants when it rains and cook them. That's our situation."[4]

I scanned through the video as carefully as I could, playing back the woman's words. *That looks legit to me*, I thought. Even further, I couldn't even begin to relate. Foraging wild plants and cooking them? Unimaginable if true.

Additionally, many of the aid groups were sounding the alarm again that day about the situation in Gaza saying large portions of the population there were on the brink of famine. Some were already dying from malnutrition, according to those agencies.[5]

And yet, I thought back to the way the colonel looked me in the eyes and said there wasn't a crisis. That a false narrative was being perpetuated.

I'm no expert on reading body language. I wish I was one of those people who could tell off the bat if someone was speaking the truth or not. But I remember thinking he was so sure of what he was saying. It wasn't the fabricated confidence of a pickup artist or a con man. It was as if he really believed it.

That whole night I kept tossing these different perspectives back and forth. I lamented about the lack of access to the enclave and how I wanted to see it for myself. I so desperately wished I had seen Gaza City or Khan Younis before the war and met the people who called that place home. To have at least *some* perspective on what was happening.

I wish I was able to see the refugee camps for myself. To see the damage up close. Based upon the situation, I felt so troublingly disconnected from the story.

Remember how I said earlier you can't cover a hurricane in Louisiana from New York? How you have to be there? Feel the wind? Smell the sewage-laden streets? Step into the environment in order to have a grasp of the matter at hand? Human to human connection is critical in journalism. Seeing, smelling, tasting, feeling, listening. All senses must be engaged to immerse yourself in that story.

This is what made covering the humanitarian situation in Gaza so difficult for me. Without being there and without fully embodying it, all you are left with is the proverbial game of "he said, she said."

The bit of solace I could take? I was far from alone. There's a photo circulating on the internet of reporters and photographers trying to climb the gates of Gaza near Rafah to try and get a glimpse, any glimpse, of what was happening inside with their own eyes. Every interaction we had inside the enclave was with the accompaniment of the IDF. The restrictions applied to almost all of the journalists covering the war.

In the Israelis' defense, it was an active war zone and a big topic of conversation at the time was evacuating civilians out of Rafah as they prepared an invasion of the southernmost city. Dozens of journalists running around would surely have caused issues. It is war, after all.

Nevertheless, this is one of the biggest struggle points I personally had covering the war in Gaza. You look at the photos and videos come out of Gaza? They're moving. You hear the words coming out of Colonel Goren's mouth? They're convincing. The only way to truly get to the heart of the truth is to, quite literally, get into the heart of Gaza. And that wasn't an option. It's reinforced this lesson in my mind: what you read and what you see will never compare to what you live and what you experience firsthand.

That day I left southern Israel feeling dejected. But it put this feeling in my heart that as I go forth in journalism, whatever assignment it may be, I must always put an emphasis on experiencing the story as deeply and personally as I can.

So, yes, when it comes to the humanitarian situation in Gaza, "the truth is somewhere in the middle" I suppose. I thought back to the promise I made to myself in the stairwell in Tel Aviv my first day that I would only report on what I knew, and there I was not having the faintest clue what was true and what wasn't. Even with a notebook of questions answered, I was somehow less sure of anything.

I still am.

24 CLEVELAND WILL NEVER BE THE SAME

Whack.

I woke up with a start, peering around my hotel room to see what had made that noise. It came from outside my window, so I tiptoed over to the curtains and pulled them open, letting the blinding light of dawn in. I gave a smile, realizing it was nothing more than a palm tree branch dancing in the wind and scratching the other side of the glass. Nothing to worry about. Palm Beach, Florida, is notorious for its breezy days once November arrives.

I glanced down at my phone to check the time. "7:30 A.M." *Geez. Three whole hours of sleep,* I thought. My head was throbbing from the exhaustion that I knew was going to stay with me throughout the day. There was no point in trying to get back into bed, as it seemed like a lost cause, but that was fine because this was a big day, and it was best not to sleep in and let it drift by me.

The date was Wednesday, November 6, 2024. One day prior, millions of Americans went to the polls to cast their ballots for president. By the early morning hours of Wednesday, the whole world knew that Donald Trump, the forty-fifth president, had bested Vice President Kamala Harris to become the president-elect.

When the dust settled, he had carried all seven battleground states and secured the popular vote. One by one, Georgia, North Carolina, Arizona, Pennsylvania, Michigan, Wisconsin, and Nevada each dropped into his column. As such, he was assured a spot in the history books as the only president other than Grover Cleveland to win two non-consecutive terms. In less than three months, he would be sworn in as the forty-seventh president of the United States.

When I wasn't overseas, I was assigned to cover the Trump campaign. What a whirlwind it had been—and a marathon at that. He officially announced his candidacy in November of 2022, making for two years of nonstop curveballs, and I was there for many of them. Four arraignments, a presidential debate, the Republican National Convention in Milwaukee. Heck, I was even in Butler, Pennsylvania, the day a would-be assassin was able to fire off a shot at him during his rally, though I wasn't inside the venue the moment it happened. As far as campaigns go, I can't imagine we'll see anything like that one again.

As it so happened, less than a month before election day, I was in Israel for the first anniversary of the October 7 attack. From there, I traveled back to the United States to ride the campaign trail all the way to the finish line. Multiple friends and loved ones remarked that I went straight from a war fought with guns and missiles to another with political arrows. It's not a completely ridiculous comparison as the political fervor in the United States truly hit its apex in the days leading up to the election. Both sides promised their supporters it was the end of America as we knew it if the opposition won, though from my vantage point in that Palm Beach hotel room it seemed Mr. Trump's victory hadn't caused hellfire or volcanic eruptions. The sun rose that morning, and America looked practically the same.

You know by now that conflict zones were never my specialty before these two wars broke out. In fact, my journalistic trade up to that point was mainly campaign politics. I had cut my teeth during the 2020 presidential election, the subsequent Georgia Senate runoffs, the 2021 Virginia Governor's race, and the 2022 Midterms. I had been all over and seen it all. There was nothing more for me to really learn.

Or at least, that's what the overly confident, arrogant voice in the back of my head was telling me. That's what I truly believed until I started to do an internal audit brought on by my coverage of Ukraine and the Middle East.

FIGURE 24.1 Reporting from the Trump campaign official election night watch party in West Palm Beach, Florida. Photo by Kimberly Anderson.

When I went to the European theater, I quickly realized I had a lot to learn about the world. The Middle East, on the other hand, taught me I really didn't know much of anything in the grand scheme of things. The more I saw, the less I was certain of.

Looking back, I'm admittedly a bit ashamed of the person I used to be. Due to my experience covering politics, and by that same token believing I knew more than my friends and family, I'd routinely go home and pound the table saying things like "this is the way the world is, this is the way it should be." What I had seen up to that point confirmed in my mind I had it all figured out. Such hubris.

Throughout 2024 I would swing back and forth between the Middle East and the Trump campaign trail. I'm very thankful for my time overseas because it made me realize that not only did I have a shallow understanding of foreign affairs, but I probably had severe blind spots elsewhere. That included what I thought was my infallible wheelhouse of political knowledge.

So, in those few months leading up to the election, I changed course. I stopped leaning on my previous sets of campaign coverage experiences, and instead started to take it all in as if this was my first round on the trail. I focused less on talking and more on listening to the candidates and, much more importantly, the voters.

At a time in which our nation is so divided, you quickly realize just from speaking with people on both sides of the political aisle that most Americans want the same things: a stable job, the ability to pay their bills, and a brighter tomorrow for themselves and their children. All of the political noise distracts from this fact and is, in the end, just that: noise.

The other thing I noticed is the average American is pretty forthcoming with their political mentalities. Over the last few years, I've heard countless people say something to the effect of "I just don't understand how someone could vote for Donald Trump/Joe Biden/Kamala Harris, etc." My response to that now is a rather blunt one: "Did you even bother to ask them?" If you did, you'd find a striking candor to their answers: the economy, immigration, abortion. Whatever motivates them, they have an explanation.

I know I sound like I'm on an ivory tower at the moment, but I only say this because I shamefully just started to piece this all together. And it took two war zones for me to do so. You don't have to go to the extremes I did to find the same conclusion.

Essentially, those two wars changed my life and, more pointedly, changed the way I see the world. There is a struggle with empathy and mutual understanding in our society today, but let me tell you: as a kid from Cleveland, it is much easier to understand the perspective of, say, a Californian than someone from a country thousands of miles away with an entirely different set of fundamental values. I've come to find that to truly begin to chip away at understanding foreign affairs, you have to get outside of your comfort zone and try and see the world through their lens. That sounds basic and cliché, I know, but to do that, you really need to throw away every shred of your upbringing to meet them on a mutual playing field.

As a result, once you start to see the world through the eyes of a Western Ukrainian, for example, it is by contrast much easier to understand the viewpoint of someone from Northeastern Pennsylvania because of the inherent shared set of values you both have. The gap to bridge is much narrower.

My new favorite expression is this: the table looks different depending on where you sit. How a Russian views the global landscape is not the same as how an Israeli does, which is certainly in stark contrast to how a Palestinian sees it. The same can be said for Floridians and New Yorkers, for example. It doesn't necessarily mean any of those points of view are inherently right or wrong, they're just different: largely built upon a set of experiences beginning from the day they were born all the way up to the present moment.

I started to see that firsthand on the campaign trail. When I spent more time listening, my picture of America started to fill out more in color. Looking back, I am not at all surprised the forty-fifth president won the election. I heard too many Americans, be they in Nevada, Wisconsin, or Georgia, say that they were hurting and wanted change. The polls indicated Kamala Harris was surging in the days leading up to the November election and she was in line for victory. The swirling narrative didn't track with what I was hearing from voters, and the ultimate outcome solidified that.

Now, the focus shifts to the future. I hope by this point you weren't expecting me to deliver some kind of solution to all of the wars and tensions plaguing the globe. I have none, and I'm not close to formulating one. There is still far too much for me to learn and understand before I begin pounding the table again.

But I'm okay with that. I'm now comfortable in knowing my place in this world. My arrogance has been squashed and my hubris extinguished. I have no idea what the coming years and decades will bring, but what I can tell you is I will be navigating them with open ears and a closed mouth: listening and learning.

And in light of these eye-opening experiences in Ukraine and the Middle East, this is one of the biggest vows I have since made to myself: I will never again so condescendingly dismiss anyone's point of view. A coal miner in West Virginia likely hasn't seen what I've seen, and conversely I haven't experienced what they have. Who am I to tell them what's right or wrong? What kind of smug reporter would I be to argue what's best for their lives and their families when I haven't sat at their kitchen tables?

I still think back on that 25-year-old Robert boarding that flight to Europe en route to Ukraine. That kid who was so convinced he was exceptionally smart and believed in his soul he didn't need to commit all his energy to learning. Consider his high horse grounded and his humble pie consumed. I'll proudly admit how incomplete my view of the world was.

But the silver lining? I now have a lifelong pursuit: to figure all of this out. To develop a firm understanding that stretches across the globe, nation to nation, and culture to culture. Will I ever get there? Probably not. It's a wide world out there, but at least now I have something to chase until I'm old and gray.

Yes, my Dad was right. A boy can't grow up in his own backyard. We've come a long way from the whipping winds of Lake Erie, and it's safe to say:

We're not in Cleveland anymore.

NOTES

Chapter 6

1 "History of the City | Travel Ivano-Frankivsk," n.d. https://iftravel.com.ua/en/city/history/.

Chapter 8

1 Emily Birnbaum, "Democratic Lawmakers Press for White Supremacist Groups to be Labeled Foreign Terrorist Organizations," *The Hill*, October 16, 2019. https://thehill.com/policy/national-security/466064-dozens-of-dem-lawmakers-press-state-department-to-designate-white/.

2 United States Department of State. "Terrorist Designations of Nordic Resistance Movement and Three Leaders – United States Department of State," June 14, 2024. https://www.state.gov/terrorist-designations-of-nordic-resistance-movement-and-three-leaders-2/.

3 Reuters. "US Clears Way for Ukrainian Military Unit to Use American Weapons," June 11, 2024. https://www.reuters.com/world/us-clears-way-ukrainian-military-unit-use-american-weapons-2024-06-11/.

4 X (Formerly Twitter), "x.com," n.d. https://x.com/azov_media/status/1800425382853615696.

5 RT, "US 'Flirting with Neo-Nazis'—Kremlin," *RT International*, June 11, 2024. https://www.rt.com/russia/599117-kremlin-azov-arms-ban-us/.

6 Giovanna Faggionato, "Zelenskyy Brings Home Azov Fighters from Turkey, Angering Moscow," *POLITICO*, July 9, 2023. https://www.politico.eu/article/russia-accused-turkey-and-ukraine-of-violating-prisoners-deal-war/.

Chapter 9

1 "Lviv Travel," February 24, 2020. Accessed November 18, 2024. https://lviv.travel/en/news/zasnuvannia-lvova.

Chapter 12

1 White House, "Remarks by President Biden in State of the Union Address," *The White House*, March 2, 2022, https://www.whitehouse.gov/briefing-room/speeches-remarks/2022/03/02/remarks-by-president-biden-in-state-of-the-union-address/.

Chapter 15

1 Peter Paret et al., "On War," in *A List of Other Center Publications*, edited by Michael Howard and Peter Paret (Princeton: Princeton University Press, 1976). http://slantchev.ucsd.edu/courses/ps143a/readings/Clausewitz%20-%20On%20War,%20Books%201%20and%208.pdf.

2 "Israel Defense Forces," October 17, 2023. Accessed November 12, 2024. https://www.idf.il/en/mini-sites/israel-at-war/all-articles/al-ahli-al-ma-amadani-hospital-initial-idf-aftermath-report-october-18-2023/.

Chapter 17

1 International Criminal Court, *Rome Statute of the International Criminal Court* (The Hague: International Criminal Court, 2021). https://asp.icc-cpi.int/en_menus/asp/RomeStatute/pages/default.aspx.

Chapter 19

1 AP Archive, "Daughter of Israeli Hostage Released by Hamas Recounts Mother's 'Horrific Story'," October 29, 2023. https://www.youtube.com/watch?v=6j0Y4FWOQyg.

2 Bring Them Home. "Medical Report on the Hostages Three Months," n.d. https://media.bringthemhomenow.net/media/Medical+Report+on+the+hostages+three+months/1_t9uk5ko0/320857172.

Chapter 20

1 "Middle East – The World Factbook," n.d. https://www.cia.gov/the-world-factbook/middle-east/.

2 Pew Research Center, "The Future of the Global Muslim Population," April 14, 2024. https://www.pewresearch.org/religion/2011/01/27/the-future-of-the-global-muslim-population/#:~:text=The%20Middle%20East%2DNorth%20Africa%20will%20continue%20to%20have%20the,reach%202.1%20million%20by%202030.

3 United States Department of State, "The Abraham Accords – United States Department of State," January 13, 2021. https://2017-2021.state.gov/the-abraham-accords/.

Chapter 21

1 The Jewish Agency for Israel–U.S., "What Exactly Is a Kibbutz | The Jewish Agency—U.S.," November 20, 2022. https://www.jewishagency.org/what-exactly-is-a-kibbutz/.

Chapter 22

1 United States Department of State, "U.S. Relations With Yemen – United States Department of State," June 8, 2022. https://www.state.gov/u-s-relations-with-yemen/.

2 United States Department of State, "Terrorist Designation of the Houthis – United States Department of State," January 30, 2024. https://www.state.gov/terrorist-designation-of-the-houthis/#:~:text=This%20designation%20seeks%20to%20promote,the%20expense%20of%20Yemeni%20civilians.

3 Isabel Debre and Jon Gambrell, "Yemen's Houthi Rebels Hijack an Israeli-linked Ship in the Red Sea and take 25 Crew Members Hostage | AP News." *AP News*, November 20, 2023. https://apnews.com/article/israel-houthi-rebels-hijacked-ship-red-sea-dc9b6448690bcf5c70a0baf7c7c34b09.

4 United States Department of State, "Houthi Sinking of Merchant Ships in the Red Sea – United States Department of State," June 20, 2024. https://www.state.gov/houthi-sinking-of-merchant-ships-in-the-red-sea/#:~:text=The%20Houthis%20previously%20killed%20three,until%20all%20detainees%20are%20released.

5 World Economic Forum, "Red Sea Attacks: What Trade Experts Have to Say about the Shipping Disruptions," September 10, 2024. https://www.weforum.org/stories/2024/02/red-sea-attacks-trade-experts-houthi-shipping-yemen/#:~:text=%E2%80%9CThe%20Suez%20Canal%2FRed%20Sea,the%20Cape%20of%20Good%20Hope.

6 Phil Nordyke, *All American, All the Way: A Combat History of the 82nd Airborne Division in World War II: From Market Garden to Berlin* (Minneapolis: Zenith Press, 2010).

7 Rüdiger Wolfrum, "Freedom of Navigation: New Challenges" (International Tribunal for the Law of the Sea, 2005). https://itlos.org/fileadmin/itlos/documents/statements_of_president/wolfrum/freedom_navigation_080108_eng.pdf.

Chapter 23

1   Devan Markham, "US, Jordan Conduct Second Humanitarian Aid Airdrop into Gaza." *NewsNation*, March 5, 2024. Accessed November 21, 2024. https://www .newsnationnow.com/world/war-in-israel/us-jordan-humanitarian-aid-airdrop -second/.

2   Wafaa Shurafa, Samy Magdy, and Menelaos Hadjicostis, "Israel-Hamas War: Aid Ship Leaves for Gaza from Cyprus | AP News." *AP News*, March 13, 2024. https://apnews .com/article/israel-hamas-war-news-03-12-2024-d2ba829df1df1092cf421fc591af9063.

3   United States Department of State, "Department Press Briefing – March 4, 2024 – United States Department of State," March 4, 2024. https://www.state.gov/briefings/ department-press-briefing-march-4-2024/.

4   Reuters Archive Licensing, "Palestinians in Northern Gaza Break Ramadan Fast, Pray among Rubble," n.d. https://reuters.screenocean.com/record/1771986.

5   UN News, "Gaza: Starvation Claims More Young Lives as UN Advocates for New Aid Routes," March 8, 2024. https://news.un.org/en/story/2024/03/1147342.